A DAY IN SEPTEMBER

A DAY IN SEPTEMBER

The Battle of
Antietam
and the World
It Left Behind

Stephen Budiansky

W. W. NORTON & COMPANY

Independent Publishers Since 1923

For information about permission to reproduce selections from this book,
write to Permissions, W. W. Norton & Company, Inc.,
500 Fifth Avenue, New York, NY 10110

For information about special discounts for bulk purchases,
please contact W. W. Norton Special Sales at
specialsales@wwnorton.com or 800-233-4830

Manufacturing by Lakeside Book Company
Book design by Lovedog Studio
Production manager: Gwen Cullen
Maps by Dave Merrill
Jacket image: *The Aftermath at Bloody Lane,* painting by Captain James Hope

ISBN 978-1-324-03575-6

W. W. Norton & Company, Inc., 500 Fifth Avenue, New York, N.Y. 10110
www.wwnorton.com

W. W. Norton & Company Ltd., 15 Carlisle Street, London W1D 3BS

1 2 3 4 5 6 7 8 9 0

CONTENTS

LIST OF ILLUSTRATIONS

A DAY IN SEPTEMBER

Prologue

DIVERGING RAYS

ITS RED VORTEX

Three days after the Battle of Antietam, Dr. Oliver Wendell Holmes, Boston physician, Harvard anatomist, renowned poet, popular lecturer, genial egotist, creator of the genially egotistical "Autocrat of the Breakfast Table" who entertained the readers of the *Atlantic Monthly* with his gratuitous opinions on everything, was making his way slowly west on the National Road from Frederick, Maryland. Accompanying him were three chance acquaintances he had met on the road, part of a stream of the distraught and curious heading for the battlefield seeking news or corpses of loved ones, bearing aid for the wounded, in a not always disinterested display of philanthropic benevolence, or just to morbidly gawk and collect relics.

Throughout the day of September 17, 1862, telegraphs and trains had carried to points hundreds of miles distant rumors of a great battle in Maryland. That night in Boston a loud knock at the door wakened Dr. Holmes from an uneasy sleep. A telegraph boy placed in his hands, in exchange for one dollar and thirteen cents due, the message he had been awaiting with dread anticipation:

HAGERSTOWN 17TH

CAPTAIN HOLMES WOUNDED SHOT THROUGH THE
NECK THOUGHT NOT MORTAL AT KEEDYSVILLE

WILLIAM LE DUC

Thought not mortal, or *not thought* mortal—which was it, Dr. Holmes immediately wondered; the first was better than the second. *Through* the neck, no bullet lodged in the wound: his anatomist's mind summoned a picture of the complex tangle of vital organs, windpipe, esophagus, jugular vein, carotid artery, a half-dozen smaller but still substantial vessels, a braid of nerves each as big as a lamp-wick, the spinal cord itself, each a thin strand of mortality. A shot in the neck ought to kill at once, if at all: a glimmer of miraculous hope.

Dr. Holmes had boarded a train the next morning to New York, then on to Philadelphia and Baltimore, then west across Maryland on the B&O Railroad to Frederick. The only conveyance he could obtain at Frederick was a farm cart pulled by two stolid bays, which he counted himself lucky to find for hire among a confused throng of carriages and wagons meeting the Baltimore train where the rail line came to an abrupt end, two miles short of the depot, at a bridge over the Monocacy River that had been blown up by the departing rebels a week earlier.

Outside of Frederick, over the gap of South Mountain, approaching the hills and woods bordering Antietam Creek, signs of the great armies that had passed through began to appear. It was beautiful country, the corn still standing, the wheat already harvested and the ground neatly plowed. But the fence rails were down and heaps of ashes showed where they had been put to use as camp fires. "The long battle had traveled," wrote Dr. Holmes, "like one of those tornadoes which tear their path through our fields and villages." Soon the road was filled with straggling and wounded soldiers, a sight which put Dr. Holmes in mind of another metaphor that would more truly capture what had taken place, and how it would not soon be forgotten. "Just as the battle-field sucks everything into its red vortex for the conflict, so does it drive everything off in long, diverging rays after the fierce centripetal forces have met and neutralized one another."

More than a century and a half later the rays are still diverging from the battlefield of Antietam, where, on that singularly brutal day of September 17 in the second year of the Civil War, more Americans died in combat than on any other day in American history. The doctor's son, Oliver Wendell Holmes Jr., would survive his wound, and several equally close brushes with death in the war, to live to ninety-three, serving three decades as a renowned justice of the United States Supreme Court. Like the 130,000 who were there that day, and the millions more touched by its events, he would be forever changed, in ways obvious and subtle, abrupt and long-delayed, by the experience. "The men who have been soaked in a sea of death and who somehow have survived," Justice Holmes remarked forty years later to a gathering of some of those fellow survivors, "have got something from it which has transfigured their world. They know the passion and irony of life." More bluntly, he told his friend Lewis Einstein, "The world never seemed quite right again."

Antietam was tactically a draw, but as a moral victory for the Union its consequences were felt literally around the world. In Washington, Abraham Lincoln seized the psychological moment to issue the Emancipation Proclamation; in London, talk of recognizing the Confederacy evaporated at once and forever; in Vienna's *Die Presse* newspaper, Karl Marx, who had been closely following events in America, began his column of October 12 with words of preternatural insight: "The short campaign in Maryland has decided the fate of the American Civil War, however much the fortune of war may still vacillate." In an exhibit that opened just a few weeks later in New York City, civilians for the first time saw photographs of soldiers lying dead on a field of battle, the start of a long and slow process by which the romanticism of war would, over the next century, and through many more horrific lessons that finally overcame mankind's stubborn habit of convenient amnesia, unravel once and for all.

"Every war is ironic because every war is worse than expected," Paul Fussell asserted in his study of meaning and memory of the First World War. The Army of the Potomac was no stranger to the realities of war by the time of Antietam, having fought major battles at Bull Run, the Peninsula, and, just three weeks before, at Bull Run again. But Antietam would be something different, the first battle where the Union army held the ground afterward and could see its effects, the first fought on Northern territory, which meant Northern civilians could, too; it was fought by men on open ground behind few fortifications with a relentless fury unlike anything up till then, and it tested the faith of more than a few. Private Roland Bowen of the 15th Massachusetts, which in twenty minutes lost 330 of its 606 men, 118 of them killed or mortally wounded, wrote his uncle wondering what it had all meant. "I want to say a word more about 'The Great Victory at Antietam.' . . . Both parties fought with a desperation. Both parties wavered at times. . . . Each side slew the other by Thousands. . . . Now both sides claim a monstrous Victory. Question. Who was victorious? Answer. Neither."

In the wake of the battle even nature herself seemed stunned by its violence. For twelve hours the big guns had fired without pause, fifty thousand rounds, one a second, the noise of the artillery "multiplied and confused by the reverberations from the rocks and hills," the Confederate general James Longstreet remembered. No one counted the number of musket balls fired, but a million is a safe guess. A young hired man on the Nicodemus farm near the center of the fighting recalled years later the unnatural, deathly silence that followed. Not a dog barked; not a bird chirped, all had been frightened off—even the circling vultures who he thought would have been irresistibly drawn to the stench—and did not return until the next spring. "When night come," he said, "I was so lonesome that I see I didn't know what lonesome was before. It was a curious silent world."

"WORDS CANNOT DESCRIBE"

No army in history wrote so many letters or kept as many diaries as the soldiers who fought the Civil War. An estimated 80 percent of Confederate and 90 percent of Union soldiers were able to read and write, and paper and stamps were as sought after as delicacies and warm clothing in the lists of items they asked for from home. But words failed nearly all who attempted to convey the sensation of the battle. The phrases "no words can describe," "words cannot describe," "impossible to describe" occur over and over in soldiers' letters. Even years later, Justice Holmes, never one usually at a loss for words, would speak only of "the incommunicable experience of war."

Army surgeons, older and more reflective men than eighteen-year-old privates, and who often played the role of mentor and camp philosopher, left some of the most vivid accounts of their sensations, physical and moral, if not of battle itself then of its more describable aftermath. The inescapable sensation was the reek of the unburied dead and of the gangrenous sores of the wounded that enveloped the entire area. A week after the battle, the surgeon of the 121st New York Infantry, Daniel M. Holt, wrote his wife from Antietam of the horrors that filled his days. "I have seen, stretched along, in one straight line, ready for interment, at least a thousand blackened, bloated corpses with blood and gas protruding from every orifice, and maggots holding high carnival all over their heads. . . . Then add the scores upon scores of dead horses—sometimes whole batteries lying along side, still adding to the commingling mass of corruption and you have a faint, very faint idea."

William Child, assistant surgeon of the 5th New Hampshire regiment, still shaken by the sight of the dead and wounded lying unattended for days, exhausted from dressing the wounds of sixty-four soldiers in a single day, wrote his wife a few weeks later.

When I think of the battle of Antietam it seems so strange. Who permits it. To see or feel that a power in existence that can and will hurl masses of men against each other in deadly conflict—slaying each other by thousands—mangling and deforming their fellow men is almost impossible. But it is so— and why we can not know. . . . Someone has written something like this, "To the feeling man life is a tragedy—to the thinking man a comedy." To the feeling man this war is truly a tragedy but to the thinking man it must appear a *madness*.

If every war is worse than expected, every war also paints the time that preceded it in a golden hue of lost innocence. Pre–Civil War America had more claim to the reality of that memory than most nations shocked by the brutality of combat. Except for the brief, triumphant interlude of the Mexican-American War in 1846, the country had gone a half century without a major conflict. Jacksonian Democrats denounced the very idea of a standing army as antithetical to American values, and unnecessary to a nation with an ocean to separate it from the perpetually warring kings of Europe. To point out America's anti-militarism and neutrality was a regular boast of national pride; even the small military academy at West Point had to fight for its existence against repeated assaults by Jacksonians who dismissed it as "an aristocratic excrescence," "contrary to the true spirit of our country," "obnoxious to all our notions of equal rights," an encouragement to military adventurism of the kind that America, showing the way to a better world, had left behind to the kings and princes of the Old World.

In the mid-nineteenth century, 85 percent of Americans still lived on farms or in towns of fewer than 2,500 people. Although the populations of Boston, New York, Philadelphia, Baltimore, and other cities had doubled in just under twenty years, more than half of gainfully employed men still worked on farms, most of them on land they owned themselves. The yeomen farmers of the North owned an average of 128 acres apiece, and despite the industrial revolution that had begun to transform the production of textiles, firearms, and other specialized goods, most manufacturing still took place in farmhouses and small handcraft shops. Less than 10 percent of the population of New York City in 1860 was employed in manufacturing; even in one-industry mill towns like Lowell, Massachusetts, the figure was no more than one-third. Technology was still more a wonder than a threat, work was plentiful, growth was good and seemingly boundless. Even as the cash economy was upending the isolation of self-sufficiency, and the railroad, telegraph, and steamboat were busily annihilating distance and time, faith in the Jeffersonian ideal of the yeoman farmer and the self-employed artisan remained strong in the hearts and minds of mid-century America.

So did an overpowering belief in American individualism, egalitarianism, and destiny that is not always easy today to fully appreciate. America's abiding secular religion of popular government was buttressed by a parallel bulwark of religion itself. New England Unitarians shared precious little theological ground with the evangelical Methodists who fired the Second Great Awakening that burned across western New York and the Midwest—there was the small matter of the divinity of Christ, for starters—but both embraced a conception of free will and individual agency that at once reflected and reinforced the anti-hierarchical zeitgeist of pre–Civil War America. Recoiling from the Calvinists' undemocratic ideas about predestination of the elect and the damned, most American Protestants of the mid-nineteenth century came to believe that salvation was open to anyone who willed it, either through the path of grace that evangelicals preached, or in the rational pursuit of goodness that Unitarians believed God had endowed in every human being. America's political experiment in self-government and egalitarianism was literally the work of Christ too, and a message for the world.

That the innocence and idealism of pre–Civil War Americans was so firmly bound to the conviction of national destiny, a belief at once naïve and grandiose, guaranteed not only that the coming war would be unremitting, terrible, and fought to the end, but that it would fervently be imbued with meaning ever after by those who "somehow survived." It *had* to be, even for those like Private Bowen and Dr. Child who entertained doubts in the stunned aftermath of a terrible battle like Antietam. Otherwise war would truly be madness, a conclusion that only the rare postwar cynic like Ambrose

Bierce dared to say out loud. He had the rejection slips to prove how unwelcome an idea that was.

WARS OF PEOPLES

Speaking at the dawn of the twentieth century, Winston Churchill warned that "the wars of peoples will be more terrible than those of kings." In Britain's imperial wars of the preceding century, total combat fatalities ranged from a few hundred (Sudan, 1898) to 22,000 (Crimea, 1854–1856), at their most a few percent of the 620,000, or possibly as many as 850,000, Americans killed in the Civil War. No peoples in the mid-nineteenth century could rival the utopianism, amateurism, individualism, political and religious self-righteousness, enthusiasm, and unpreparedness of Americans, North and South. None were ever so ill-prepared for war, none so unblinkingly accepted fighting in such a war as the price of admission of citizenship in democracy. The sense that America was a lonely beacon of self-government that *must* not be allowed to fail was a living belief to Americans just two and three generations removed from the Revolution.

"If America is lost, the world is lost," declared the Methodist minister Gilbert Haven in a sermon, "The War and the Millennium," preached on Thanksgiving Day in Boston the year following the Battle of Antietam. "The Union must be preserved," he insisted, "not alone because it was essential to our own welfare, but because through its preservation would the divine doctrine of popular government live among men."

The depiction of life under British rule as "slavery" figured prominently in the chip-on-the-shoulder pride of free Americans in their nation's first century. ("One is in a free country and has come from a country in which one has been brought up to hug one's chains—so at least the English traveller is constantly assured," reported the visiting English novelist Anthony Trollope in 1861.) It was an image powerful enough to leap the rhetorical and moral divide required for Southern slaveholders to cast even their cause as one of resisting the bonds of tyrannical "slavery," in their case, "Northern slavery." A phrase that appeared again and again in the letters of Southern volunteers underscored the belief that they, too, were the rightful heirs of a holy crusade bequeathed by forefathers who fought the Revolution. "Our cause is the sacred one of Liberty, and God is on our side." As James McPherson wrote, "Confederates professed to fight for liberty and independence from a tyrannical government. Unionists said they fought to preserve the nation conceived in liberty from dismemberment and destruction." The only thing more terrible than the wars of peoples was a war of *two* peoples each holding exactly the same conviction of national and divine destiny.

From the moment the guns fell silent, Antietam was seen as an event that had cleaved the war, if not indeed the nineteenth century. It was not only the event that gave forth the Emancipation Proclamation, fundamentally changing the moral meaning of the war; the Battle of Antietam introduced new ideas about the obligations of the living to the wounded and dead in battle, the place of women in society, the rise of pragmatism, organization, and skill over faith, improvisation, and derring-do, realism over sentimentality; it provided lessons to generations of American military leaders seeking to improve on the amateurism in leadership and training that characterized that day; it was one link in the chain of experience that forged James Longstreet's remarkably modern grasp of war at the operational level, a fundamental concept of twentieth-century military thought.

Thinking a century and a half later about the intertwined, ramifying consequences of this one September's day led me to an unconventional approach to telling the story of the Battle of Antietam, built around the experiences of nine people whose lives intersected there, each of whom emblemizes an aspect of human existence that was changed by what took place there. This is at heart still a story of war, and fighting, and dying; but military history is also human history, few corners of which are left untouched by Dr. Holmes's diverging rays, which I have tried to bring into focus by following their societal, technical, and ideological refractions in this way.

If this book had a different subtitle, it might be The Surprisingly Interesting Consequences of War, or perhaps even The Paradoxical Benefits of Military Disasters. Those are troubling ideas to many Americans these days, who probably agree with Dwight Eisenhower's famous admonition, "War settles nothing," and regard much of the traditional kinds of military history as glorification of what should be discussed only with an air of appalled condemnation. The recent trend in Civil War scholarship certainly agrees. It is now routine to express disdain for those naïve enough to cling to the "triumphalist narrative" of that war as a successful struggle for the end of slavery and the rebirth of the nation. This self-declared "dark turn" in Civil War history aims, instead, to expose it as a horror that, presumably like all wars, warped men and glorified brute destruction. To that end, historians of its dark side dwell on atrocities, disease, suicide, alcoholism, and mental illness among the men who fought its battles.

The truth is of course somewhere in between. Eisenhower's caution about wars settling nothing was the voice of dire experience speaking in the age of the atomic bomb, a time when any lingering notions of war as exalted or glorious had met its final end in the total devastation of the Second World War, with its fifty million dead, great cities obliterated, and an entire people nearly exterminated.

Americans of the nineteenth century emerged from the Civil War with a very different sense of war and its meaning. As Montaigne wrote, "The sensation of fortune and misfortune depends in large part on our attitude toward them," and, quoting Cicero's words, "Grief arises not from nature but from opinion."

For all the terribleness of the Civil War, the willingness of men to risk death for a cause greater than themselves was afterward still something openly exalted and valued by nineteenth-century Americans, which in turn became a source of solace to those who endured its ordeals. The blunders, naïveté, and incompetence that produced the appalling toll at Antietam still make for agonizing reading. But the inspiration that those who "somehow survived" took with them was no less real for the false and romantic language that they sometimes were wont to cloak it in.

The selective focus of a work like this is inevitable. No African Americans fought at Antietam; their decisive contribution to tipping the scales of Union victory came only later in the war. I have implicitly paid most attention to the Northern side, since the U.S. Army was the institution that survived to inherit the legacy of Antietam. I am sure some readers will also take issue with my seeming emphasis on the faults and flaws of many of the principal actors. But that is what war does, to lay bare failings of human nature that, under less trying circumstances, we all usually do a pretty good job of concealing. Those human flaws in turn are generally reflective of deeper yet also normally hidden flaws in society. That is one of the things that make wars worth studying, and interesting.

1

WHO WOULD BE A SOLDIER

Robert E. Lee

"UNDER OBLIGATION TO NO ONE"

Much has been written of Robert E. Lee's honor and loyalty. But his conception of both, as Henry Adams remarked of the Harvard education of 1850, stood closer to the year 1 than the year 1900. His loyalty was always to his family, and his sense of honor was mainly the personal dread of financial ruin.

In 1857, after nearly three decades in the army, he laid down the paternal law when his second son wanted to abandon his studies at Harvard for an army commission. "My experience," he admonished him, "has taught me to recommend no young man to enter the service." But Lee himself never dared give up the security that a military career almost uniquely provided. More than half of his West Point class of 1829 resigned at the first opportunity to turn their engineering education to private fortune, building the canals and railroads of a rapidly expanding nation. Lee, who outshone them all—he was an assistant mathematics professor while still a student and graduated second in his class—stuck with it, bemoaning his "want of money," disputing bills, keeping strict charge of the family checkbook even when posted thousands of miles from home, chiding his wife from afar to keep a precise record of all her expenditures in a memorandum book.

His marriage into one of the wealthiest families in Virginia, and personal investments worth $1 million in today's money, prudently accumulated from the husbanding of a modest inheritance from his mother, did little to diminish his ever-present dread of the dishonor of impoverishment. As his biographer Allen Guelzo concluded, "Lee never ceased to believe that nothing but the Army stood between him and poverty."

Duty is usually thought of as obligations owed others; to Lee, duty was the means to avoid such obligation altogether. He had done the extraordinary by graduating from West Point without a single demerit, handed out for thousands of enumerated offenses ranging from drinking, swearing, smoking, and fighting to tardiness, insolence, or laughing during drill, or not hanging up one's coat or arranging one's shoes properly for inspection. He was saved from being regarded as a prig for his insufferable "correctness" and "dignity" thanks to a charming "agreeableness" that his companions also often remarked upon, which perhaps made them miss the steely quest for self-sufficiency that lay behind it all. When his eldest son Custis was accused along with his freshman-year roommates at West Point of concealing a bottle of liquor in their room and threatened with dismissal, Lee was gratified that Custis had spurned an offer made by the entire class—the standard solution proposed in such circumstances—to take a pledge of total abstinence from alcohol for the year in return for the offense being forgiven. Independence of others, he counseled his son, should be among the foremost objectives of his life. "It is that feeling that prompts me to come up strictly to the requirements of law and regulations. I wish neither to seek or receive indulgence from anyone. I wish to feel under obligation to no one."

Lee was as little troubled by introspection and imagination as he was by fellow feeling. He instructed his wife not to let their youngest son "touch a novel, which will teach him to sigh after that which has no reality," wrote his son Custis at West Point, "Do not dream, it is too ideal, too imaginary," and told his daughter, "Do not even *wish* for what you ought not to have or do." His conventional religious piety as a member of the Episcopal Church, the established church of the Virginia establishment, was unmatched by any evidence of deeper reflection. Some of his only rare flashes of slight humor were self-mocking observations about religious devotion: engaging in a long-running, wan joke with an army friend in which he referred to the High-Church Oxford Movement of Edward Pusey as "pusseyism," or gently deflecting his wife-to-be's urgings that he read the Bible with a promise to try, but cautioning that one should "not expect miracles in my case."

Lee would later insist that he had "never been an advocate for slavery," a "moral and political evil in any country." A theoretical evil; but to attempt to do anything about it was, to Lee, always something worse. He indignantly instructed his wife in 1856 that Northerners who sought "to interfere with & change the domestic institutions of the South," even through such incremental measures as limiting the expansion of slavery into the territories, were not only acting lawlessly and unconstitutionally, but were doing more harm than good by their meddling and intolerance of "the spiritual liberty" of their fellow citizens. "If he means well to the slave, he must not create angry feelings in the master." Meanwhile, "the painful discipline" slaves were subject to "is necessary for their instruction as a race." Only "a wise & merciful Providence" knew "how long their subjugation might be necessary." But, Lee pointed out, "The doctrines & miracles of our Saviour have required nearly two thousand years to convert but a small part of the human race," which offered a hint as to God's timetable for emancipation. "We must leave the progress as well as the result in his hands, . . . who Chooses to work by slow influences; & with whom two thousand years are but a single day." God was clearly in no more of a hurry than Robert E. Lee.

Except for the time he gave way to a rare loss of self-control and had three slaves on his father-in-law's estate savagely whipped for attempting to run away, slavery was, in Guelzo's words, "an abstraction" to Lee. "Its three and a half million victims were personally invisible" to him.

The cold and inward-turning core of Lee's outward propriety was similarly invisible to the admirers who would exalt him after his death as a paragon of "manly decorum," "modest demeanor," and "humble, devout Christian" spirit. Nor did they ever quite perceive the solitary self-pity such feelings so easily fell into. Accepting the presidency of tiny Washington College in Lexington, Virginia, after the war, he lamented to his cousin Annette Carter that his "only companion" now was his horse Traveller, whom he would take on long, lonely rides over the mountains surrounding the town. But that did not stop him from sabotaging any potential romances that might take away the companionship of his daughters, now in their twenties, admonishing one to "eschew weddings and stick to her papa," the other that "notwithstanding all appearances to the contrary, you will never receive such a love as is felt for you by your mother and father."

Neither ever married.

BLOOD IS THICKER THAN REPUBLICANISM

Mary Custis Lee left a melodramatic account of the great moral dilemma of her husband's life, his decision in April 1861 to renounce his commission in the United States Army and accept command of the troops of his seceding state of Virginia. Weeping "tears of blood," falling to his knees to beg divine guidance, he wrestled with his conscience, pacing the floor all night, torn between loyalty to the Union and loyalty to his native state.

More reliable accounts suggest that the only agony he experienced that night was in composing a personal letter to his comrade and mentor Winfield Scott, the army's commanding general, thanking him for his "kindness and consideration," while wistfully assuring him, "It has always been my ardent desire to meet your approbation." The five other Virginians holding the rank of colonel in the United States Army suffered no recorded agonies: they remained loyal to their oaths, and their nation.

The loyalty that Lee expressed in explaining his actions was in any case not to Virginia or to the Confederacy as political entities, but to his own family: "my own kith & kin," he said, that he always preferred "to anyone elses." At his last interview with General Scott, during which Scott pressed him for an answer to Lincoln's offer of a principal command in the Union army, Lee pointedly noted that his children "will be ruined if they do not go with their state . . . all they possess lies in Virginia." As he explained to his staunchly Unionist sister Anne Lee Marshall in Baltimore the morning of his decision, "I have not been able to make up my mind to raise my hand against my relatives, my children, my home."

Whatever his feelings about slavery, nothing so affirmed Lee's determination to fight for the South's victory and independence as Lincoln's Emancipation Proclamation. In a letter that the Civil War historian Gary Gallagher archly refers to as "seldom quoted by historians," Lee wrote Confederate Secretary of War James A. Seddon immediately afterward calling for the total mobilization of Southern manpower and resources as the only possible response. Lincoln's "savage and brutal policy," Lee insisted, "leaves us no alternative but success or degradation worse than death, if we would save the honor of our families from pollution, our social system from destruction."

Save for his abhorrence of debt, never something to bother the arrogant cavaliers of preceding generations, Lee's conception of honor and allegiance owed more to Virginia's landed gentry of the eighteenth century—or England's feudal lords of the fourteenth— than the new values of the American republic. The world Robert E. Lee was born into, among the antebellum aristocracy of tidewater

STRATFORD HOUSE. — Birth-place of Gen. R. E. Lee.

Robert E. Lee's boyhood home, Stratford Hall

Virginia, was one that still worked on networks of kinship and personal patronage rather than modern abstractions like the rule of law or the democratic institutions of government. Lee's father, a hero of the Revolution, "Light Horse Harry" Lee, was the model of the type. Commanding his troops like a feudal baron, dispensing personal punishment and favor, he once had a deserter's head displayed on a pike as a warning to others until George Washington told him it might make a bad impression; on another occasion he rallied a detachment of horsemen under his command caught in a British ambush by promising that, if they refused to surrender, he would "consider their future establishment in life as his particular care." They carried through.

Like the charming blackguards of a Trollope novel, Light Horse Harry constantly looked to wills and advantageous alliances for financial salvation. Marriage to a cousin brought him Stratford Hall, one of the grand houses erected by Virginia gentlemen seeking to imitate the life and style of England's landed gentry. Like many of its type, it was more show than substance, built with tall windows and a raised basement to make its single story look more imposing than it was. He then swiftly burned through his wife's inheritance, inducing her to pledge or sell off piece after piece of property to finance speculations he was convinced would make him a fortune; at one time he controlled a million acres in Ohio and western Pennsylvania and elsewhere on the frontier, never realizing a penny while continuing to throw good money after bad. Expecting to inherit a thousand-acre plantation in Virginia from a childless widower uncle, he was thwarted when his aged relation suddenly remarried and produced five heirs of his own.

Harry Lee's second marriage in 1793 to Ann Carter, the daughter of a wealthy tidewater family that owned Shirley Plantation on the James River, brought five children who survived infancy—Robert the second-to-last child, and the last son, born in 1807—and no relief from financial woe; sponging on his new wife's relations to the limit, he still could not pay off his previous debts and ended with a stint in debtor's prison. After that, Ann moved the family to Alexandria, living ever afterward on the indulgence and assistance of her relations and a small trust fund her father had prudently settled directly on her to keep the money out of the hand of her spendthrift husband.

At the commencement of the War of 1812, Harry was severely beaten in Baltimore by a mob that attacked the offices of a Federalist newspaper which had imprudently editorialized against the war, and spent the remaining six years of his life wandering the Caribbean, hoping to recover his health and evade his creditors. Robert never saw him and only rarely mentioned him again.

Stratford fell into the hands of another family ne'er-do-well, Robert's half-brother Henry Lee IV, who after the tragic death of his young daughter in a fall down Stratford's stone front stairs and his wife's ensuing mental collapse, proceeded to impregnate his wife's nineteen-year- old sister, and then, as her guardian, embezzle her trust account. To escape scandal and prosecution he fled to France, "persecuted unrelentingly by my enemies," he moaned, "and still more unrelentingly neglected by my friends." Stratford was sold in the ensuing legal proceedings. Robert E. Lee forever after dreamed of buying back his boyhood home, even inquiring in the midst of the war if it was for sale (it was not), as he also made it his unstated but manifest life's intention to redeem the family honor by retracing his father's footsteps, this time without the shame of debt and dependence. Education at the Alexandria Academy was free, as it was at the United States Military Academy, and there Lee determined to go, his mother's heartbreak in bidding farewell to her last son ("both son and daughter to me") notwithstanding.

But to a man who forever equated duty with independence, sentiment was never high on his list of considerations. "I thought & intended always," he later said to his wife-to-be, "to be one & alone in the World."

OFFICERS FOR A DEMOCRACY

The West Point which Robert E. Lee arrived at in 1825 excelled at producing engineers. If none of them knew how to fight a war, that was as much by design as neglect. The same widely shared sentiment in the young republic that regarded a standing army as an invitation to adventurism abroad and oppression at home cast a beady eye on the national military academy, with the extra animus Jeffersonian and Jacksonian republicanism reserved for anything that smacked of elitism or social superiority. Populists derided cadets as dandies, fops, arrogant and pretentious "lily fingered" aristocrats, the privileged products of a "closed corporation," and regularly called for the academy's abolition. "Confident that the common man could master any profession in a short period," noted Stephen Ambrose, Americans insisted that the militia was up to any military task the nation might legitimately require.

Thomas Jefferson, fully sharing the populist aversion to a standing army or navy and the wars of conquest they might tempt America into, nonetheless saw a national military academy as the means for advancing one of his many Enlightenment hobbyhorses, a sweeping and democratizing reform of university education that would eliminate the classics and emphasize scientific subjects in their place. His proposal to establish the academy at West Point as part of the 1802 Military Peace Establishment Act almost foundered, however, when he injudiciously added that it could supply professionally trained officers to the state militias: politicians weren't about to give up their patronage in doling out militia commissions.

The more successful argument in favor of education for army officers was the one Secretary of War Henry Knox had made a decade earlier in a cabinet debate over how best to protect America's neutrality when war broke out between England and France. When Jefferson objected to a proposal to construct a series of coastal forts, arguing that the job should be left to the states, Knox interrupted to say that Jefferson was obviously wrong, but the point was moot anyway since no one in America knew how to build a fort. Teaching officers to design and construct defensive fortifications fit well with the spirit of American republicanism and nonbelligerency, while neither threatening to usurp the place of the militia nor incur the ongoing cost of a large standing army. Once built, forts protecting America's harbors would "require but little expenditure for their support," the army reported to Congress, and "can never exert an influence dangerous to public liberty."

More generally, the army saw its Corps of Engineers, established by the same 1802 act, as its best public relations tool to justify what Secretary of the Treasury Albert Gallatin termed "that perhaps necessary evil" of a peacetime army to a public that remained deeply skeptical. ("The distribution of our little army to distant garrisons where hardly any other inhabitant is to be found" would be the best solution, Gallatin wrote his wife, "but I never want to see the face of one in our cities and intermixed with the people.") In a memorandum for the chief engineer, an officer of the newly established corps advised that they should "take pains to render ourselves useful in various ways" and show how they can "serve the public." Over the next two decades the corps relentlessly pushed to expand its role to include highly visible civil engineering projects such as roads, bridges, and harbor and river improvements. The 1824 General Survey Act permitted the corps to loan its technical expertise to private endeavors, such as the Chesapeake & Ohio canal that would connect Washington, D.C., to the West; even after that authority was later rescinded, the restriction was usually artfully evaded with the ready justification that surveying for roads and riverways was historically a military responsibility, and that such transportation links were vital to the national defense.

From 1802 to 1861 the superintendent of the academy was always an officer from the Corps of Engineers, and the chief engineer was its inspector, with overall supervision. Training the thousands of the engineers needed for the corps' projects in the decades before the Civil War gave West Point a piece of the public goodwill the work generated, while catapulting the academy to the forefront of the engineering profession in America. Until Rensselaer opened its doors in 1824, West Point was the only engineering school in the country, and it was not until 1840 that the former began to rival its output of graduates.

Every engineering program in America subsequently copied West Point's. Its graduates provided the first faculty for the engineering schools Yale and Harvard established in the 1840s and 1850s. Textbooks by West Point professors—in civil engineering, mechanics, mathematics, chemistry, and many other technical and scientific subjects—dominated their fields. The demand for civil engineers, surveyors, map makers, and architects in the private sector generated widespread public support for West Point and its curriculum entirely apart from any justification for its role in training military officers or supporting the work of the Corps of Engineers.

The program at West Point was the creation largely of one man whose presence in the lives of the cadets for his two and a half decades as superintendent was strict, seemingly omniscient, and unrelenting. Dynamic, humorless, punctilious, Sylvanus Thayer took charge in 1817 and at once upended the small and floundering institution with a new curriculum, directly modeled on the one that had impressed him on a tour of France's École Polytechnique two years earlier. Unlike France's military academy at Saint-Cyr, which prepared infantry and cavalry officers with a traditional education in the classics and liberal arts alongside the study of military tactics, the Polytechnique's program was a sharp break from the classical model of higher education. With the motto *Pour la Patrie, les Sciences et la Gloire*—for country, science, and glory—the school offered a rigorously technical education to turn out engineers, civilian and military, who would serve the nation: precisely Thayer's vision for West Point.

The four-year program at West Point when Lee arrived in 1825 began with two years of intensive study in mathematics—algebra, geometry, trigonometry, plus calculus for more advanced students—along with French (the language in which the leading texts in military fortification and related subjects were written), followed by two years of topographic drawing, physics, engineering, chemistry, metallurgy. The engineering instruction by Lee's time covered roads, tunnels, inland navigation, artificial harbors, and railroad construction.

In a bow to Jeffersonian egalitarianism, Thayer made a point of keeping entrance requirements low and forbade students to receive spending money or to return for visits home during their first two years, to break down any "false pride" and "aristocratic pretensions" among those from more privileged backgrounds. To prevent favoritism in postgraduation assignments, he instituted the scheme of numerically ranking the class with a comprehensive system in which performance in every class session was graded, and cadets' behavior mercilessly tracked with merits and demerits.

Military instruction was limited to summer encampments where cadets learned to march in formation, fire artillery, and lead small detachments. Those who might have wished there had been some time devoted to the command of troops in battle got the message clearly enough about what talents and knowledge were valued in the peacetime army when they received their first postings. The top graduates were always assigned to the engineers, those next in line to the other technical branches, artillery and ordnance, while those at the bottom of the class were relegated to the cavalry, and last of all, to that place where ambition and intellect went to die, the infantry.

OLD SOLDIERS NEVER DIE

Drawing a plum assignment that befitted his place as No. 2 in his class, it did not take long for Lee to discover that even for those so favored, the army was no place for a man of even modest brains or ambition. As assistant to the engineer tasked with constructing one of the great new "Third System" forts being planned for the mouth of the Savannah River, Lee found himself loaded down with duty as supply clerk and acting commissary assistant while his engineering decisions were ignored or overruled by his incompetent superior. Even after he was swiftly promoted to management of a project of his own, at Fort Calhoun in Virginia, the work remained both demanding and dull, his long days an endless series of administrative burdens he personally had to attend to: hunting up supplies of curbstones and iron pipe, negotiating contracts for hay and pork, hiring stonemasons, overseeing workmen.

For most officers, life in the army did not even offer those diversions. "I have absolutely nothing to do at all," reported one West Point graduate in the mid-1840s. "Monotony" was the word that frequently appeared in officers' letters home. A young company commander during his third year at Camp Floyd in Utah wrote despairingly, "I am suffocating, physically, morally and intellectually—in every way." He said he felt like "begging to be taken out and hung for the sake of variety."

At frontier outposts the chief tasks were maintenance, plus staying alive. "We lived more like pioneers than soldiers," said one recruit during the 1850s, growing food, spending three months of the year cutting 1,200 cords of firewood for the winter, receiving no military training other than guard duty for three years.

The lack of a mandatory retirement age and stagnation in the size of the army meant promotion was extraordinarily slow—half of the regimental commanders in 1823 were still in their positions twenty years later. Top positions turned over at an even more glacial pace. Two of the bureau chiefs appointed in 1818, the quartermaster general and commissary general, held their posts in the 1860s. In 1836 the adjutant general calculated that an officer graduating from West Point that year could expect to reach first lieutenant in eight years, followed by ten years to captain, twenty years to major, ten years to lieutenant colonel, finally reaching the rank of full colonel in 1894, after fifty-eight years of service. A West Point graduate assigned to the Fourth Artillery Regiment in 1836 explained to his sister that it was known as "The Immortal Regiment" for the stubborn refusal of its officers to die and make way for those below. "There are lieuts in it with grey heads," he wistfully reported, "fine prospects for me!"

In retrospect, it probably did not bode well for the fostering of an intellectual culture in the army that the first attempt at classroom instruction for officers, a few years before the founding of the academy, terminated before it began when the incensed officers burned down the instruction room the night before. Thayer's science-heavy reforms of the curriculum notwithstanding, a good many cadets regarded their West Point education as a gauntlet to be run rather than a stimulant to mental curiosity. The mind-numbing tedium of garrison duty following graduation did little to counter the deep anti-intellectual streak in the army, even if it offered time that might be put to better use. A few officers applied themselves to study but the more typical experience was that reported by the young officer who, joining the Fourth Infantry in California in 1852, discovered that the principal daily pastime of the regiment's officers was to get drunk, the exception being the major whose innovative variation was to get drunk, "pitch furniture in the center of the room, and set fire to it."

The other activity that recommended itself to many was filing charges and countercharges against fellow officers, which was so much an occupation to members of the old army that it reached to the top, the most famous instance being the long-running feud in the 1850s between General-in-Chief Winfield Scott and Secretary of War Jefferson Davis, which had begun with a dispute over reimbursement of Scott's travel expenses during the Mexican War. When all the cross-accusations were published in a Senate document, it ran to 354 pages of insult and venom.

Incentives for self-improvement, especially the study of the art of war or the skills of higher command required in wartime, were by comparison nil. "The study of generalship," observed a much more recent West Point history professor, J. P. Clark, "was so far removed from the realities of daily life—even for senior officers in the field ranks—that it was more of a hobby than a duty." In 1835, only two of the army's fifty-three posts had garrisons of more than 500 men. Most had fewer than 200, consisting of one to three companies, and the duties of field officers who ran these posts, majors, lieutenant colonels, and colonels, were chiefly administrative. According to regulations, every officer within two years of receiving his commission was to know all administrative and tactical duties of a company commander; but since it took twenty-five to thirty years to reach the rank of major, with higher responsibility for the first time, everything an officer learned as a cadet plus two years of on-the-job training would serve for over half his career, well into his forties or even fifties. Little or no advanced professional training was provided by the army, and equally little pursued by serving officers.

What the mastery of official duties did encompass was perfectly reflected in General Scott's 1825 *General Regulations for the Army,* which devoted three of its 425 pages to the topic of how to fight a battle. The remaining pages were filled with precise directions for how many mathematical instruments an engineer should carry, how many corporals are to be detailed to prepare a field cantonment, the permissible dimensions of ledger books for recording descriptions of horses and mules (12 x 17 1/2 inches, or, alternatively, 8 1/2 x 13 inches), and countless other specified tasks that occupied the days of company and regimental officers, plus a blizzard of forms to be employed when requisitioning straw, paying washerwomen, certifying the receipt of wheelbarrows, inventorying the supply of hospital eating utensils, and scores of other much-loathed paperwork assignments. As a twenty-seven-year-old second lieutenant Lee confessed, "I abhor the sight of pen and paper and to put one to the other requires as great a moral effort as for a cat to walk on live coals."

Jacob D. Cox, one of the abler civilian-soldier generals of the Civil War, expressed his surprise to a regular officer in 1861 at how little most officers of the army had seemed to have added to their knowledge of military science after leaving West Point. "What would you expect," the officer replied, "of men who have had to spend their lives at a two-company post, where there was nothing to do when off duty but play draw-poker and drink whiskey at the sutler's shop?" An instructor at the academy was less colorful but more categorical in his reply to an inquiry from a War Department commission investigating officer training. "I have never known of a single instance of an officer studying theoretically his profession (when away from West Point) after graduating," he said.

By 1838, more than one hundred West Point graduates had left the army for far better, more interesting, and more lucrative positions. In 1835 and 1836 alone, 120 officers resigned their commissions, prompting Congress to increase from one to four years the required service commitment of academy graduates. Still, by 1860 almost a quarter of all academy graduates were in private practice as civil engineers.

The flight of the best only reinforced the reputation of the army as "a safe harbor for indolence and imbecility," as the sister of future Confederate general Edward Kirby Smith, unsuccessfully attempting to dissuade him from a military career, scornfully told him in the 1840s. A dozen years later, as superintendent of West Point, Robert E. Lee offered the same blunt advice, writing a friend, "I can advise no young man to enter the Army. The same application, the same self-denial, the same endurance, in any other profession will advance him farther and faster."

But as for himself, Lee admitted, "The more comfortably I am fixed in the Army, the less likely I shall be to leave it." He was, in short, stuck on his own contradictions. Had he been a more reflective man, he might have perceived the paradox in seeking to avoid the mistakes of his father's life through allegiance to the aristocratic code that had produced those mistakes. The new democratic ethos of America valued self-reliance, but the very notion of democratic egalitarianism implied individual social responsibility: as the historian Richard Hofstadter noted, this flowed from the Yankee Protestant tradition in which "everyone was somehow responsible for everything." The self-reliance of the Lees and Custises that had caused so much trouble was something else again, the aristocratic license of privilege, irresponsibility, and unaccountability to anyone who might presume to judge their actions.

Like his father, Lee had sought financial and social independence through marriage. Mary Custis was charming but shallow, one of the many Lee cousins whose curiosity and admiration had been aroused by reports of the "beauty and fine manners" of the young cadet when he returned home to Alexandria on his first furlough. A painted portrait from a few years later is the image of a dashing officer, resplendent in dress uniform, Lee's strikingly handsome and manly face set off by curly black locks and stylish long sideburns. By all evidence theirs was a mutually devoted marriage. But Lee learned quickly enough the nature of the bargain he had contracted. The heiress-expectant to two of the largest estates in Virginia, Mary carried all the baggage of Virginia wealth and class. An early warning was evident in Lee's confiding comment in a letter to a friend not long after their marriage, "Mrs. L is somewhat addicted to laziness and forgetfulness in her housekeeping."

Marriage also brought a father-in-law who was a constant reminder of all of the worst traits of his own father. George Washington Parke Custis, was, much like Light Horse Harry Lee, full of undisciplined enthusiasms and the self-assurance of unaccountable privilege. The proprietor of Arlington House and its 11,000 acres overlooking the new capital across the Potomac, G. W. P. Custis— who took every opportunity to let it be known that he was the step-grandson of his namesake—was a failed politician, a failed painter of historical scenes from the Revolution, a failed playwright (his drama set in thirteenth-century Scotland closed after four nights), a failed breeder of Merino sheep, and a failed real estate developer. Arlington was even more an artificial showplace than Stratford, its massive Doric columns actually concrete-covered wood painted to look like marble, the surprisingly small interior behind its massive Greek-temple front slowly going to decay. G.W.P. had great ideas about farming, but could never get his cornfields fenced or plowed on time.

Ironically, the alliance left Lee more firmly "fixed"—comfortably or not—in the army. Mary's expectations of inheritance, and their on-again off-again home at Arlington for the next thirty years that marriage to her brought, was additional security to stay where he was, and avoid putting self-reliance to any real test in the world of private enterprise. The apprehension of being sucked into a role as Arlington's glorified overseer, however, as G.W.P. always seemed to expect, devoting his days to rescuing his father-in-law from his endless aristocratic follies, was much more incentive to stick with his army career. Only drawing a paycheck allowed Lee to preserve the illusion that he was beholden to no one, a knight-errant of old.

SCIENTIFIC WARFARE

However much a throwback in his notions of personal honor, Lee was very much a man of his age in his views on military tactics, and arguably ahead of his time on strategy.

Those who tried to shape American thinking about war amid the indifference and neglect of the pre–Civil War army were strongly influenced by Enlightenment ideals, which viewed reason, progress, and mathematics as the basis of all scientific endeavor—and, by extension, that war, like any human endeavor, could be reduced to a system of logical scientific precepts. "Our officers are to be men of science," the academy's first superintendent, perhaps not coincidentally a nephew of Benjamin Franklin, optimistically declared. While continuing to emphasize the broader usefulness to the nation of a trained cadre of officers versed in the technical skills of surveying, road building, and construction, the early leaders of the Corps of Engineers and West Point had more quietly advanced the idea that those same skills were the basis of systematic thinking about war. The mastery of mathematics worked to "exercise and discipline the reasoning faculties, and to introduce a system and habit of thought" that would serve leaders of any profession, the chief engineer noted in 1844. But more than that, as a series of influential treatises by French military theorists of the early nineteenth century argued, the movement of formations in battle was itself the kind of mathematical problem that could be solved through geometric and algebraic analysis scarcely different from that employed in laying out the walls of a fort or calculating the optimal emplacement of an artillery gun.

Several of these works, translated by American officers in the first decades of the century, introduced the geometrical concepts of interior lines, lines of advance, bases of operation, and decisive points that feature prominently in subsequent American writing in what was now termed "the science of war." A fundamental concept was the concentration of forces advancing along converging lines meeting at a sufficiently wide angle to permit freedom of maneuver while avoiding exposing one's flanks and risk being enveloped in turn by the enemy; ideally the angle would be more than 90 degrees, the theorists decreed, but key was maintaining a convex area of operation that forced the enemy to move on longer, exterior lines, exposing his lines of supply while preserving to the advancing force the ability to respond by shifting his own forces on shorter, interior lines.

The more down-to-earth lesson that American military writers distilled from French authorities, beyond the dozens of abstract diagrams of triangles and quadrilaterals they reproduced in their books to illustrate the science of movement, was the primacy of attack over defense. Dennis Hart Mahan, who taught the senior-year engineering course at West Point, underscored the point in the six three-hour lectures on the science of war he incorporated into the class after returning to the academy in 1830 from a long tour of French fortifications and military academies. During his four years abroad he had been particularly impressed by the courses he attended at France's renowned School of Application for Engineers and Artillery at Metz, on whose faculty were many officers who had served under Napoleon.

The legendary general was, forever after, Mahan's model. Napoleon, he wrote, "confessedly stands unrivaled. . . . To him we owe those grand features of the art, by which an enemy is broken and utterly dispersed by one and the same blow." A decade later Mahan organized a "Napoleon Club" open to all commissioned officers at West Point, devoted to the study of the great Corsican's campaigns. An 18- x 11-foot map painted on the walls of the club's meeting room, depicting his battles and victories, caught the eye of a visiting Abraham Lincoln in the summer of 1862 when he came to confer with Winfield Scott on war strategy, and the President requested a copy be made for him and sent to the White House.

Personally an unlikely apostle of the offensive-minded attack, Mahan weighed scarcely 100 pounds, never rose beyond the rank of second lieutenant or heard a hostile shot fired. He suffered from a sinus condition that earned him the nickname "Old Cobbon Sense" for the way his favorite maxim—"common sense, gentlemen, common sense"—emerged through his chronically stuffed nose. But he instilled a generation of army officers with principles of war derived largely from the writings of French theorists, notably Antoine-

Henri Jomini, a member of Napoleon's staff who became the foremost explicator of his campaigns.

In his textbooks and printed lecture notes, Mahan recognized the value of defensive measures like field fortifications as a way for an army like America's, which relied mainly on untrained militia volunteers, to bolster its assurance against professional troops and to spare the lives of valuable members of a democratic society. He also allowed that in some situations, bypassing, or "turning," an enemy's position could force to him to fall back to secure his lines of communication, thereby avoiding the need for a direct assault.

But Mahan's key maxim was that an advantageous outcome in war can be achieved only through "decisive strokes," and to maneuver, delay, or waver in resolution was as a rule to court disaster. Turning the flank of a defender risked exposing one's own flank, while a vigorous and audacious frontal assault, preferably with the bayonet, could always overcome any defensive position. Field fortifications were in Mahan's view but a means to that end; their only value was as a springboard to take the offensive at the opportune moment. Ultimately, the only real defense was attack.

Mahan's best-known textbook that presented these ideas bore the unwieldy title *An Elementary Treatise on Advanced Guard, Out-Post, and Detachment Service of Troops in Presence of an Enemy*. The name it was known to cadets by was *Out-Post*, which well reflected its emphasis on small-unit operations. Some principles like the characteristics of a good defensive position were as applicable to a corps as to a company, to be sure, but it was chiefly a manual for junior officers on the kind of small, detached service they were likely to encounter at small posts in the West. The four hundred or so West Point graduates who would serve as generals on both sides in the Civil War would come to their jobs with remarkably similar stores of knowledge— and voids of ignorance—about how to fight a war.

Although Lee would be one of the few Civil War field officers to have graduated from West Point before Mahan began teaching, the principles set forth in his textbooks and lectures permeated even the unstudious culture of the United States Army through the generation exposed to them at West Point. (On his return to the academy as its superintendent in 1852, Lee would participate in the Napoleon Club's meetings, at which papers were presented and discussed.)

In 1846, the year the army would be put to the test in a real war with Mexico, one of Mahan's ablest students, Captain Henry W. Halleck, published a widely disseminated book that reiterated these lessons to a broader audience. *Elements of Military Art and Science,* based on a series of twelve well-attended lectures he delivered at the Lowell Institute in Boston, closely follows Jomini in stressing the "moral superiority" that adheres to the attacker. Halleck, who would serve as general-in-chief during the Civil War, defined military strategy as "the art of directing masses on decisive points." Wars were determined by battle, and battle by attack.

The Mexican War was rapturously welcomed by officers eager for glory, and relief from dredging harbors. About to graduate from West Point when the news arrived, nineteen-year-old George McClellan wrote home with ingenuous glee, "Hip! Hip! Hurrah! War at last sure enough! Aint it glorious! . . . Well it appears that our wishes have at last been gratified & we shall soon have the intense satisfaction of fighting the crows—musquitoes & Mexicans &c. . . . You have no idea in what a state of excitement we have been here." Lee, eighteen years his senior, expressed his enthusiasm in more restrained language, but with the added anxiety of missing out on his great chance. From New York, where he was overseeing the expansion of Fort Hamilton at the western tip of Long Island, Lee wrote, "I am the last man ordered, every one is ahead of me & I am hurrying on to endeavour to reach San Antonio. I have but little hope of accomplishing anything, or having anything to accomplish."

But the bold amphibious landing of 10,000 troops under General Winfield Scott at Veracruz on March 9, 1847, bypassing Mexican forces that had stalemated General Zachary Taylor's army pressing down from the north, found Lee right in the midst of it. Assigned to Scott's personal staff, Lee took personal charge of scouting and pre-

Battle of Contreras, August 19–20, 1847

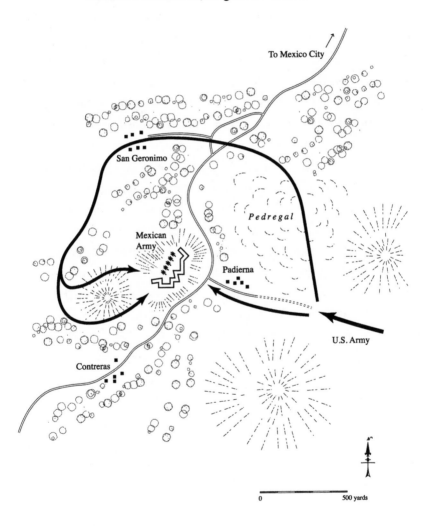

paring the sites for a battery of six large naval guns brought ashore to take part in the siege of the forts ringing the fifteen-foot-high walls of the bastion-like city. Three weeks later, cut off by siege lines and helpless against Scott's batteries, the city surrendered, saving an estimated 2,000 American lives it would have taken to carry out an infantry assault. Five months later, at the Battle of Contreras, Lee scouted a route through what the Mexicans had safely assumed was an impassable ancient lava field, a *pedregal*, barred by huge blocks of basalt. Returning with a party to clear a path wide enough for artillery and wagons, Lee then recrossed the hazardous route to lead a small force that completely turned the flank of a powerful Mexican position guarding the way to Mexico City from a commanding height over the San Angel Road. Facing simultaneous attack front and rear, the Mexicans abandoned their position with a loss of 37 artillery pieces and 2,700 prisoners including eight generals. The next month American forces entered the enemy capital as the Mexican junta leader Santa Anna fled, and the war was effectively over.

The brief war more than proved the competence and courage of junior officers and the capability of the regular U.S. Army when operating at the level of companies and regiments. But any larger implications for what constituted effective tactics and strategy in modern warfare were far more ambiguous. Fighting a military dictator, the strategy was straightforward: defeat his army and seize his capital. Each battle fought by Scott's army, as it pressed down the road to Mexico City, worked directly to advance that strategic objective. That a far more comprehensive approach would be required in a war of democracies and ideas was a difficult conclusion that Civil War leaders would only learn through much subsequent failure.

The other obstacle to American officers' learning useful lessons from the experience was that the United States won. In his *Elements of Military Art and Science*, Halleck approvingly quoted a critical observer who noted that there are three kinds of generals: martinets, who know "only the mechanical part of their trade"; self-proclaimed "practical men," who have "no other or better guide than their own experience"; and theorists, who by "study and reflection" have mastered the principles that can be adapted to new circumstances. But winning does not tend to stimulate "study and reflection." Jefferson Davis was far from the only officer who came away convinced that his service in Mexico—all of five days in his case—had conferred upon him ever after a mastery of tactics and strategy superior to any insights offered up by theorists like "Old Brains" Halleck.

And then there was the fact that just about *every* tactic used against the Mexican army had worked. Americans won every battle, and when they attacked always inflicted more casualties than they received. Scott ordered frontal assaults against enemy positions protected by stone walls, trenches, earthworks, and cannon at Churubusco and Chapultepec; used turning maneuvers to outflank Mexican forces at Cerro Gordo and Contreras; employed siege tactics with heavy artillery methodically emplaced at Veracruz; and even deployed cavalry, in the classic Napoleonic manner, against fleeing infantry in a saber charge led by Captain Phillip Kearney's 1st Dragoons.

From the war with Mexico, America's future Civil War commanders would draw the lessons they wanted to. Unsurprisingly, they were often flatly contradictory ones, many of which would not survive the realities of a much larger and different conflict.

INVASION AND AGGRESSION

The lesson Lee drew proved much more resilient. Characteristically it was a personal one: He loved war. No one could ever forget, an English journalist later said while observing Lee in command during the Civil War, "the light of battle . . . flaming in his eyes" as he prepared to meet his enemy. John Mosby called Lee "the most aggressive man I met in the war . . . always ready for any enterprise."

The "incongruity between Lee's private character as a humane, courteous, reserved, kindly man, the very model of a Christian gentleman, and his daring, aggressive, but costly tactics as a general," wrote the historian James McPherson, "is one of the most striking contrasts in the history of the war." The fusion of these two competing images in a single, Homeric hero became a staple trope of Lee's later idolators, epitomized in the words he may or may not have uttered while taking in the slaughter of waves of advancing Union troops at Fredericksburg: "It is well that war is so terrible—we should grow too fond of it!" Frederick Douglass acerbically remarked upon the "nauseating flatteries" of Lee that filled the newspapers on his death in 1870, from which "it would seem . . . that the soldier who kills the most men in battle, even in a bad cause, is the greatest Christian, and entitled to the highest place in heaven."

But the incongruity was in any case on the outside only. Though Lee would come to criticize the purpose of the war with Mexico, saying he was "ashamed" of America for having "bullied" a weaker nation in pursuit of territorial gain, it had shown him a soldier to the core. Winfield Scott praised Lee for his "skill, valor, and undaunted energy," called his repeated crossing of the *pedregal* "the greatest feat of physical and moral courage performed by any individual, in my knowledge." He was "the very best soldier I ever saw in the field," said Scott, indeed "the greatest soldier now living." War gave Lee the purpose, emotional release, and independence that had always eluded him before.

Appointed as Jefferson Davis's chief military adviser at the start of the Civil War with the more nominal than actual title of "commander in chief of the whole army," Lee found his instinct for aggressive action stymied at once by Davis's confidence in the wisdom of the South's remaining on the defensive. To secure independence, after all, the Confederacy had only not to lose; the North faced the infinitely greater task of defeating an enemy's army and occupying its territory. The conventional wisdom of military experts abroad agreed. Just as George Washington in the Revolution had forced the British to abandon the war by making it too costly to continue, so the South could succeed against a better equipped and more powerful foe. As the military correspondent for the London *Times* observed early in the war, "It is one thing to drive the rebels from the south bank of the Potomac, or even to occupy Richmond, but another to reduce and hold in permanent subjection a tract of country nearly as large as Russia in Europe." Davis was confident that a show of military resolve would be sufficient to convince the North of the impossibility of the task. By the first winter of the war, in the wake of the Union defeats at the battles of Bull Run and Ball's Bluff, the *Times* reported that every foreign diplomat but one in Washington agreed that "the Union is broken forever, and the independence of the South virtually established."

One of the few observers who saw that time was not on the South's side, given the inexorable mobilization of the North's far greater resources in manpower, economy, and industry, was Karl Marx. "For the South," he wrote in March 1862, "everything depended on a swift, bold, almost foolhardy offensive." Without such a bold stroke, "their position must become worse day by day, while the North gained strength." Lee decisively agreed. Despairing of what he felt was an absence among the Southern populace of the urgency and total commitment required to withstand the grinding power of the North, Lee was convinced, as he subsequently put it, that the "true policy" for "gaining our independence was to concentrate all of our troops & fight a great battle with everything at stake—or if possible to have made it a war of invasion & aggression."

Taking command in the field in June 1862 in place of the wounded Joe Johnston, Lee put action to words. McClellan's Peninsula Campaign, a plodding but steady advance of a force of 100,000 inching forward, digging in at every step of the way, supported by gunboats and huge siege guns hauled by rail and capable of firing 200-pound shells, epitomized what Lee saw the South was up against. "McClellan will make a battle of posts," Lee reported. "He will take position after position under cover of his heavy guns." Lee's response was to prepare a fortified defensive line he could hold with a part of his force in the enemy's front while sending the rest of his army in a sweeping flanking movement to force McClellan into an open fight. The Confederate attacks during the Seven Days Battles were a shambles of miscarried orders and poor coordination that showed the limits of organization and command of large forces at this stage of the war, but were enough to shake McClellan's nerve and send him into retreat. Lee, though, was disappointed he had not achieved the decisive Napoleonic victory he imagined had been in his grasp: "Under ordinary circumstances the Federal Army should have been destroyed," he reported following the Battle of Gaines Mill on June 27.

With the defeat of Union forces outside of Washington at the Second Battle of Bull Run at the end of August, Lee saw the opportunity he had been hoping for all summer to transfer the war "from the banks of the James to those of the Susquehanna." A "proposal of peace" combined with the shock of invasion might suffice to bring about an end to the war. As he subsequently explained to his son Custis, nothing could "arrest" the enemy's continuation of the war "except a revolution among their people." A formal proposal that the United States recognize Southern independence at this juncture would not in any sense be regarded as "suing for peace," Lee reassured Davis. Rather, "being made when it is in our power to inflict injury upon our adversary," it would "show conclusively to the world" the South's limited and honorable intentions in the war, and where the blame would lie for its prolongation. It would be well timed, too, to influence the upcoming congressional elections in the North, in which a heavy vote against the administration could prove decisive. In recognizing that his target was as much Northern opinion as Northern armies, Lee was strikingly ahead of his time in appreciating the strategic dimensions of modern warfare.

On September 4, a signal corpsman stationed atop Sugar Loaf Mountain, an anomalous peak that juts an abrupt 800 feet over the farmland of the surrounding Maryland countryside thirty miles up the Potomac River from Washington, spotted clouds of dust of a long wagon train moving out of Leesburg, Virginia, just across the river, heading for the crossing at Edwards Ferry. Lee's great chance for his war "of invasion & aggression" was at last at hand.

2

A PROBLEM
OF
ENGINEERING

George B. McClellan

GOD'S CHOSEN INSTRUMENT

George B. McClellan's fatal combination of hubris and insecurity was at least honestly come by, since they were characteristics of his place and time.

As the visiting Anthony Trollope with the gentlest of sarcasm pointed out, a country that is confident about the superior virtues of its social and political institutions does not constantly seek reassurance in the form of buttonholing foreign visitors and demanding their agreement on the point. Alongside the rising spirit of egalitarianism, optimism, and enterprise that marked the emerging American national identity in the years following the Revolution, reflected no more clearly than in the constant celebration in newspapers and books of "self-made men," there remained, as the historian Gordon S. Wood wrote in *Empire of Liberty*, a bristling touchiness and uneasiness about being looked down upon by those who retained more traditional notions of aristocratic rank. Another English traveler a few decades before Trollope noted that "every man is conscious of his own political importance, and will suffer none to treat him with disrespect." The leveling of the old marks of distinction of education, cultivation, and manners produced an odd and uneasy mix of emulation and resentment. As one contemporary remarked, "A most uncommon union of qualities not easily kept together— simplicity and refinement."

The members of the social elite that led the Revolution had imagined, Wood wrote, of "raising ordinary people to their level of gentility and enlightenment" as the path to greater social homogeneity in the new republic. Instead, "ordinary folk were collapsing traditional social differences and were bringing aristocracy down to their level." Those who had once assumed a natural deference was owed them by virtue of ancestry, profession, education, and position were not quite sure where they stood anymore in a world where "common sense" and a smattering of self-acquired knowledge was now brashly asserted to be just as good as a fancy college education or professional qualification, and where common good manners and moral conduct rather than rank, sophistication, and the leisure to cultivate higher things (and serve as the natural leaders of their community) defined a "gentleman." The "vernacular gentility" that was the new coin of respectability left everyone a bit uncertain. But what arguably united Americans of all classes of the era in a true national characteristic was touchy pride—plus a craving for the public approval that was now the universal mark of democratic distinction.

George McClellan had enjoyed all the benefits and pretensions of a privileged upbringing. His father was a prominent Philadelphia physician, founder of the Jefferson Medical College; George, educated by private tutors, could converse in French and Latin at age eleven and entered the University of Pennsylvania at thirteen, transferring two years later to West Point. With the arrogant laziness of a gifted student, he studied little: "He was well educated," recalled an academic rival, "and, when he chose to be, brilliant." He wrote his mother that he preferred to associate with the Southerners among his fellow students; as "gentlemen," their "manners, feelings & opinions" were more to his taste.

In Mahan's class he found he was "passionately fond of Military Engineering, & Military Tactics," and subsequently amassed a library of several hundred volumes of military science and history, including Jomini's treatises and all the leading studies of the Napoleonic wars. In Mexico, he had two horses shot out from under him at the Battle of Contreras and served as Lee's assistant placing four batteries of siege guns at Chapultepec, receiving a mention in Scott's dispatches for his "bold" undertaking of difficult tasks. Quitting the army in 1857 at age thirty to take the position of chief engineer of the Illinois Central Railroad, he immediately doubled his salary, then a few years later tripled it again to $10,000 a year, which was 100 times the average laborer's wage of the time, the equivalent of some $5 million in modern terms.

His contempt for superiors and subordinates alike never wavered. In his time in the army after the Mexican War he picked a series of petty fights with anyone who differed with his judgment. He scorned the chief engineer of the army and the superintendent of West Point ("I don't care much for anybody's opinion, as long as I am in the right," he told his brother), rebelled at taking orders from the official directing a survey of rail routes in Washington Territory ("I will not consent to serve any longer . . . unless he promises in no way to interfere," McClellan huffed), and, not humbled in the least by the enormous honor of being selected at the age of twenty-eight to join a delegation sent to observe the Crimean War, mercilessly mocked his two far more senior colleagues on the mission ("these d——d old fogies!! I hope I may never be tied to two corpses again").

Later, as general-in-chief of the army and commander of the Army of the Potomac, his abuse of colleagues and administration officials, even the President himself, never let up. He actually knew Lincoln before the war when Lincoln had represented the Illinois Central in several legal cases, and McClellan recalled with amused condescension listening away the night sitting in front of a stove at out-of-the-way county seats to the future president's "unceasing flow" of "seldom refined" anecdotes, wondering how many Lincoln had actually heard before and how many he "invented on the spur

McClellan as Napoleon, on a carte de visite by the political caricaturist H. L. Stephens

of the moment." But now there was not even amusement in McClellan's furious condescension. Lincoln was "a well-meaning baboon," "an idiot," "the original gorilla." The rest of the cabinet was no better. Secretary of War Edwin Stanton was "the most unmitigated scoundrel I ever knew," Secretary of State William Seward "a meddling, officious, incompetent little puppy," Secretary of the Navy Gideon Welles "a garrulous old woman," General-in-Chief Winfield Scott "a dotard or a traitor." McClellan concluded, "I do not believe there is one honest man among them."

Meanwhile, even the smallest detail could never be trusted to anyone but himself. "Everything here needs the hand of the master," he wrote his wife while preparing his first campaign of the Civil War, an advance of 12,000 men against a ragtag band of 4,500 Virginia militiamen guarding the western mountains of the state.

Jacob Cox, one of McClellan's brigade commanders, recalled him on their first acquaintance. "Muscularly formed, with broad shoulders and a well-poised head, active and graceful in motion. His whole appearance was quiet and modest, but when drawn out he showed no lack of confidence in himself." It would take Cox, like most of McClellan's early admirers, almost no time at all to discover that lurking just one layer deeper than "no lack of confidence" was a paralyzing terror of failure.

He masked it with a bluster that was saved from ridicule only by the North's eagerness at the moment for a hero, and for victories. "Soldiers!" he declared upon taking the field in western Virginia, in his soon-to-be habitual parody of Napoleonic oratory, "I have heard there was danger here. I have come to place myself at your head and share it with you. I fear but one thing—that you will not find foemen worthy of your steel."

Explaining that he hoped to "repeat the maneuver of Cerro Gordo" by turning the enemy's entrenched position at Rich Mountain and avoiding a frontal assault, he informed Scott that "no prospect of a brilliant victory shall induce me to depart from my intention of gaining success by maneuvering rather than by fighting." The plan was to draw off the defending Confederates with a flanking attack and then follow up by striking on their front with two brigades that McClellan remained behind to command. Overestimating the enemy force by a factor of four, and hearing sounds of battle not quite where he expected, McClellan decided the flank attack had failed, and did nothing. The action dislodged the rebels but allowed most to escape. Cox wrote, "The Rich Mountain affair, when analyzed, shows the same characteristics which became well known later. There was the same over estimate of the enemy, the same tendency to interpret unfavorably the sights and sounds in front, the same hesitancy to throw in his whole force when he knew that his subordinate was engaged."

McClellan's chronic exaggeration of the size of the enemy was his most well-known failing. "No amount of experience seemed to cure it," Cox said, his inflated figures surviving even into his postwar memoir, "in which he unconsciously showed that the illusions which had misguided him in his campaigns were still realities to him," though by that time they had been definitively refuted by Confederate as well as Union official records that had since become available. Cox's crushing epitaph on McClellan's years after the war said it all: "He had forgotten much, but he had learned nothing."

That "tendency to see his enemy doubled" was but a symptom of a deeper pathology, however—which, since it might accurately be termed an extreme form of bourgeois anxiety, was appropriately first called attention to by Karl Marx. He "wages war not to defeat the foe," wrote Marx, "but rather not to be defeated by the foe and thus forfeit his own usurped greatness." As Gerald Linderman observed in his Civil War study of character in battle, *Embattled Courage*, successful later generals like Grant and Sherman, who had experienced failure and humiliation in their private lives, knew "how little men control their destiny." Conversant with the ironic disjunction between aspiration and results, endeavor and reward— old hat to anyone on intimate terms with the routine outrages of fate—they were able to approach battle with a fatalism and a willingness to take risks that was simply alien to a man like McClellan, who had known only the successes of a charmed life, and who looked upon war as but another showcase to display his accomplishments before an always admiring audience.

McClellan's never-to-be-shaken belief was that war was at heart an engineering problem. Solved in the planning stage, the outcome would follow ineluctably. At the start of the war he had submitted to Scott a grandiose, and wholly impractical, proposal to advance an army of 273,000 men with 600 guns to seize vital objectives throughout the South—Richmond, Charleston, New Orleans among them—in one grand campaign, a massing of force on decisive points straight out of Jomini. Key was meticulous preparation— men, training, equipment, logistics—that would make victory all but certain and prove (one is tempted to add "mathematically") "the utter impossibility of resistance."

But even in the more realistic operations he subsequently com-

manded, McClellan's notion of how long it took to be perfectly prepared was usually a synonym for "never." He told Scott that he had
learned from him in Mexico the one great lesson of war: "Not to
move until I know that everything is ready," an ideal attained by no
army that ever existed outside the mind of George B. McClellan.

Fatal hesitation and belief in one's own God-given destiny are
an odd combination, but McClellan's extreme manifestation of the
two together speaks to the tragic void within him where in other
men character is found. Halleck had noted McClellan's selfishness,
and Dennis Mahan what he termed his former pupil's "deficiency
of certain moral traits," but McClellan's messianic convictions were
something else again, at once sniveling and megalomaniacal, "the
ultimate escape from responsibility," his biographer Stephen W.
Sears wrote.

A man like Lincoln saw the will of God in America's ordeal, but
the lesson was nearly always a humbling one. In a private "Medita-
tion on the Divine Will" that Lincoln wrote in September 1862, he
wryly reminded himself, "Each party claims to act in accordance
with the will of God. Both *may* be, but one *must* be wrong." He
continued: "In the present civil war it is quite possible that God's
purpose is something different from the purpose of either party."

McClellan suffered no such doubts as to the purpose for which
God intended him. "Who would have thought when we were married," he wrote his wife the day he was given the command of the
Army of the Potomac, "that I should so soon be called upon to save
my country?" Ellen was always his surest audience: he was never too
busy to telegraph her with reports of his latest triumphs of "the military art," the praise showered upon him by his legion of admirers,
or the scurrilous machinations of his rivals within the army who
would deny him his due. They had met when she was eighteen, he
twenty-seven; she was the daughter of the officer who commanded
a surveying expedition McClellan was assigned to, later his chief
of staff in the Army of the Potomac. She had been engaged to the
future Confederate general A. P. Hill, a match her mother had bro-

ken up in part because of reports reaching her that Hill had contracted a venereal disease while a cadet at West Point. Whether Hill nursed a grudge or not, he would have his cosmic revenge at Antietam, arriving with his division at the end of the day just in time to thwart a clear-cut Union victory.

McClellan asked Ellen to remind him ("should I ever become vainglorious and ambitious") of the pathetic sight of his ousted predecessor General Scott departing on a train for New York, an ouster McClellan himself engineered in November 1861: "a feeble old man scarcely able to walk; hardly anyone there to see him off but his successor." She tactfully refrained from ever so doing, and McClellan forgot all about that uncharacteristic moment of humility. His messianic delusions only grew from there. "When I see the hand of God guarding one so weak as myself," he remarked to his colleague Ambrose Burnside a few months later, "I can almost think myself a chosen instrument to carry out his schemes." To McClellan, the role of savior was another image to burnish, one he dared not put to the test lest it tarnish. His inclination to act as if the actual outcome of a battle lay in the lap of the gods once his painstaking work of preparation was done, and his odd passivity at moments of crisis, showed as much.

WITHOUT A STAFF TO LEAN ON

"All quiet on the Potomac," the bulletin McClellan's headquarters issued day after day to reassure the jittery capital in the months following the Battle of Bull Run, quickly became a source of mockery as the autumn of 1861 slipped away with no sign of movement by the Army of the Potomac beyond the parade ground drills and grand reviews its commander regularly staged. Lincoln's doubts about the military and even technical acumen of his new commander were not eased when, as spring approached, McClellan finally did stir into action with two preliminary moves to restore important Union transportation links. Aiming to reopen the lower Potomac, he advanced cautiously toward Confederate earthworks bristling with cannon at Manassas, twenty miles southwest of Washington, only to discover that their defenders had slipped away undetected twenty-four hours earlier to a new defensive line behind the Rappahannock River. Much of the imposing artillery turned out to be decoys made of logs.

An elaborate plan to retake Harper's Ferry and restore the destroyed B&O Railroad bridge linking the Ohio Valley to the East and secure the Shenandoah Valley had even more humiliatingly fizzled. The centerpiece was a feat of engineering prowess. Specially constructed pontoon boats were hauled up the C&O Canal to form the base of a permanent bridge across the Potomac. But when they reached Harper's Ferry it was discovered that the lock connecting the canal to the Potomac there was six inches too narrow for them to pass through: the river lock had been built to permit the transit of the smaller boats used on the nearby Shenandoah Canal.

Lincoln was simply incredulous at the failure. "Couldn't the General have known whether a boat would go through that lock, before spending a million dollars getting them there?" he asked in despairing bewilderment. "I am no engineer, but it seems to me that if I wished to know whether a boat would go through a hole, or a lock, common sense would teach me to go and measure it. . . . Everything seems to fail."

Visiting Washington that winter of 1861–1862 Anthony Trollope judged the still half-built capital city "the saddest place on earth," its "ragged, unfinished" broad avenues at once dreary and pretentious, the stones for the one-third completed Washington Monument heaped in a "useless, shapeless, graceless pile" on an ugly mud-covered field within sight of the White House, and a feeling in the air "that nobody seemed to have any faith in anybody." At the camps of the Army of the Potomac he was struck by the insubordinate slovenliness of the volunteer soldiers; their equally manifest intelligence, zeal for their cause, proficiency in arms, and personal bravery; and the "absurdly useless" review of the army by their commander that he witnessed. At one of McClellan's grand reviews he had inspected the entire Army of the Potomac, ninety infantry regiments, nine cavalry regiments, twenty artillery batteries, 100,000 men assembled altogether. "If before his review he did not know whether his men were good as soldiers," Trollope concluded, "he did not possess any such knowledge after the review. If the matter may be regarded as a review of the general; if the object was to show him off to the men, that they might know how well he rode, and how grand he looked with his staff of forty or fifty officers at his heels, then this review must be considered as satisfactory. General Maclellan does ride very well. So much I learned, and no more."

Yet morale is an elusive quantity, and McClellan's reviewing and drilling had restored confidence to an army shaken after Bull Run, even if he had made himself the characteristic centerpiece of its newfound spirit. He knew how to be loved by his men. Extending his hat at arm's length as he galloped past the ranks always elicited a rapturous cheer from men electrified by his charismatic presence. As Lincoln would explain his later decision to retain McClellan even after his worst failings were manifest, "We must use the tools we have."

He had had to force McClellan's hand with a direct order to move by Washington's Birthday to get him even to reveal his overall plan. Clearly thinking of Veracruz, McClellan conceived a great strategic turning movement to bypass the Confederate defenses between Washington and Richmond. At the beginning of January Lincoln had requested from the Library of Congress Halleck's *Elements of Military Art and Science* and had evidently absorbed its lessons about simultaneous lines of advance and interior lines when he expressed his doubts about the plan to McClellan. Operating on shorter lines, the Confederates could shift troops to meet any single movement by Union forces, Lincoln pointed out. He would "find the same enemy, and the same, or equal intrenchments" on the Peninsula.

But with Lincoln's reluctant assent, McClellan pressed ahead. His all but exclusive attention to logistical preparations seemed to regard fighting a war as a mere footnote to the main business, which was to supply and safeguard a base to feed 121,000 men and 25,000 horses while they hauled 5,000 wagons and 300 artillery pieces over the roads to Richmond. The movement and landing of troops and supplies at Fort Monroe at the tip of the Virginia Peninsula went well. Nothing after that did, revealing a gaping void in the Army of the Potomac command structure. It would take nearly two more years for the army to learn the simple truth that the difference between leading a company and leading an army was more than just a matter of scale, and that entirely new systems of organization and command would be required to make *anything* work as planned in a large war.

The basic organizational and tactical unit of the army was the regiment, about 1,000 men composed of ten companies and commanded by a colonel. Larger formations, such as brigades of two or more regiments, were wartime commands that few American officers had had experience with. When the Civil War began there was, besides General Scott, only one other officer in the entire army who had ever commanded a brigade. Both were in their mid-seventies. No officer in America had *ever* commanded a force even approaching the size of the Army of the Potomac. At the start of the Peninsula Campaign it consisted of twenty-four brigades containing four to six regiments each, further organized into eight divisions of three brigades each, and three corps of two to three divisions each.

Logistics and training were one thing, but maneuvering large forces over unfamiliar and hostile terrain, not to mention fighting battles, was something else again. Scott's infantry manual covered drill and training from "the school of the soldier" to "the school of the brigade," and the skills required to move a brigade in formation and perform maneuvers such as shifting from columns to lines were indeed mostly just a matter of doing the same things on a larger scale. Likewise preparing supply rosters, calculating ammunition and forage requirements, organizing wagon trains to haul them was just more of the same no matter how large the army.

But the moment McClellan's force went ashore the woeful inadequacy of existing systems for everything else began to tell with a vengeance. Uncoordinated attacks fell apart, wagons clogged roads for days, units went astray for lack of basic topographic information or cavalry guides to lead the way or post directional signs at crossroads. No systems were in place to anticipate or even coordinate supply needs with ordered movements. Not a single division in the entire army had the supplies or transport immediately on hand to move when the Confederates slipped away overnight from their defensive positions at Yorktown which McClellan had been laboriously laying siege to for a month (and which on inspection were revealed to be almost as much of a paper tiger as the wooden "Quaker guns" at Manassas). Whenever the army did advance, quartermasters in charge of each regiment's baggage wagons, without an order of march or knowledge of the roads, simply picked their own routes and hoped for the best.

Nothing is more astonishing to anyone familiar with modern armies than McClellan's lack of a general staff to coordinate operations in the field. It astonished a knowledgeable French observer who was on the scene, too. McClellan must have encountered the French and Prussian general staff systems, by then the most advanced and logically organized of the world's armies, during his tour of Crimea and subsequent visits to European military headquarters. But organizational matters seem to have made little impression on him. The voluminous reports from his European trip deal almost exclusively with technology, logistics, and materiel, from field fortifications to the construction of cavalry saddles. (What seemed to impress him as much as anything, however, was the technique of the French general in galloping past the Imperial Guard during an inspection, accompanied by a band playing martial music.)

By the nineteenth century the French and Prussian general staffs were a corps of experienced officers, fully informed of the commander-in-chief's operational plans ahead of every movement and battle, placed at lower echelons of corps and divisions with the authority to see that instructions were followed, deal with problems as they arose, even alter plans on the fly to changing circumstances. McClellan's idea of the commander's role remained firmly in the eighteenth century, with everything in his sole hand, his orders delivered personally or by his small personal staff of aides on horseback. The French observer, the Prince de Joinville, described the predictable chaos that ensued on the Peninsula.

> We should have seen the General Staff Officers of a French army taking care that nothing should impede the advance of the troops, stopping a file of wagons here and ordering it out of the road to clear the way, sending on a detail of men there to repair the roadway or to draw a cannon out of the mire, in order to communicate to every corps commander the orders of the General-in-Chief.
>
> Here nothing of the sort is done. The functions of the adjutant-general are limited to the transmission of the orders of the general. He has nothing to do with seeing that they are executed. The general has no one to bear his orders but aides-de-camp who have the best intentions in the world, and are excellent at repeating mechanically a verbal order, but to whom nobody pays much attention if they undertake to exercise any initiative whatever.

The want of a general staff was particularly evident in the failure to coordinate operations when in actual contact with the enemy. It was a particular challenge in country broken by numerous woods and swamps, but as the British military writer G. F. R. Henderson observed in his assessment of the Peninsula Campaign, a proficient staff is organized to overcome even those difficulties by maintaining constant communication between units, by thorough reconnaissance in advance to discover weaknesses in the enemy's position and topographic features to choose the best line of attack, and through clear written orders that anticipate and provide for numerous contingencies. None of this was done: McClellan's staff was simply too small, inexperienced, and untrained in the functions of a general staff. "It was a defect in the organization," Joinville observed, "and with the best elements in the world an army which is not organized cannot expect great success. It is fortunate if it escape great disaster."

The lack of organization was exacerbated by McClellan's insistence on personally intervening to take charge of details—posting troops, placing guns, arranging supplies. At the crucial moment following the Battle of Malvern Hill, when many of his generals wanted to halt the Union army's retreat and launch a counterattack against the badly mauled Confederates, McClellan, his attention on logistics as always, was steaming down the James on a gunboat to attend to "what I did not wish to trust to anyone else—i.e. examine the final position to which the Army was to fall back."

McClellan ever after insisted that his masterful handling of the intricacies of pulling an army back to a new base of supply deserved to rank with the greatest victories on the battlefield. He genuinely expected to be applauded for the skill he had shown in retreat, just as he boasted to his friend Burnside that his empty victories at Manassas and Yorktown "will be my brightest chaplets in history. . . . I accomplished everything in both places by pure military skill. I am very proud, and very grateful to God that he allowed me to purchase such great success at so trifling a loss of life."

His retreat down the Peninsula, he told his wife, was likewise "one of the grandest operations in Military History," and he assured Lincoln that when all the circumstances were known, "It will be acknowledged by all competent judges that the movement just completed by this Army is unparalleled in the annals of war." Marx had already pegged McClellan as a "maneuvering general." A disgusted Gideon Welles wrote in his diary following the collapse of the Peninsula Campaign, "McClellan is an intelligent engineer but not a commander. . . . He likes shows, parade and power. Wishes to outgeneral the Rebels, but not to kill and destroy them."

A WANT OF INTELLIGENCE

Lee's invasion of Maryland would from the start expose another gaping hole in the embryonic staff organization of the Army of the Potomac. McClellan would not be the last commander to experience the inevitably disastrous consequences of attempting to act as his own intelligence officer. But unlike those who would repeat the folly in the conviction that knowledge is power, it simply never seems to have occurred to General McClellan that gathering and interpreting information about the enemy was a job for anyone else, or that the other generals who reported to him might benefit from knowing the reasons behind the movement orders he issued them.

The modern general staff system assigns an entire section ("G-2" in modern terminology) the responsibility of issuing orders for the collection of intelligence, bringing together the information from disparate sources for central sifting and analysis ("intelligence fusion"), and then making sure that the results are conveyed to everyone who needs to be informed about enemy intentions, movements, locations, and threats. McClellan in part was just paying the inevitable price of being the first to confront the momentous problems of commanding a force the size of the Army of the Potomac, but his own worst instincts as always compounded the problem.

Historians who defend McClellan have placed the blame for his inflated estimates of the size of Lee's forces on the numbers supplied him by Allan Pinkerton, the head of the nationally known private detective agency whose services McClellan employed, having personally known him from his days as a railroad executive. But that merely begs the question, since Pinkerton only performed the tasks McClellan assigned him, chiefly trying to penetrate government circles in the Confederate capital (rather than their armies in the field), hunting down enemy spies in Washington, and interrogating prisoners, deserters, and refugees passing through enemy lines. McClellan himself directly received reports from all other sources.

Moreover, Pinkerton, a man with no particular military knowl-

Lee's invasion of Maryland
September 3–13, 1862

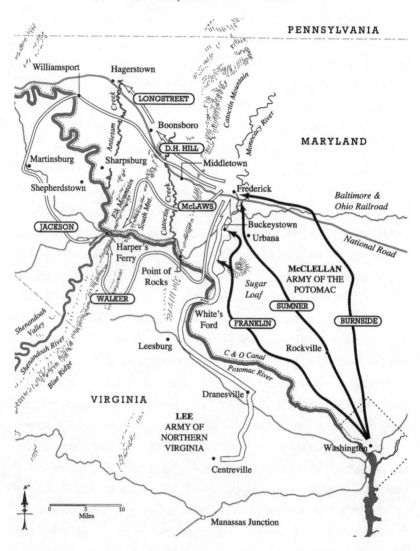

edge or experience, clearly had fallen victim at once to the universal failing of all intelligence systems under the personal control of the commander-in-chief, namely the tendency to tell the boss what he wants to hear. "It is almost incredible that he should be deceived" by Pinkerton's inflated numbers, wrote Jacob Cox of McClellan, "except willingly." McClellan's habitual practice of justifying "additions to be made for the sake of safety" to reports of known enemy numbers, arguing that there must be others unreported and unknown, in any case undercuts the excuse that he was simply misled by a trusted subordinate.

In fact, more reliable estimates were readily available, and as readily ignored. In July 1862, in the midst of the Peninsula Campaign when McClellan was frantically informing Washington that he faced a force of 200,000, double his own numbers, the army's quartermaster general Montgomery Meigs from his desk in Washington provided an object lesson in the superiority of arithmetic and a cool head to overwrought guesswork by one private detective and a panicked commander. Working from nothing but dispatches in Southern newspapers that reported the names of regiments involved in the fight, Meigs performed the now routine intelligence exercise known as order-of-battle analysis, and came up with a figure of 60,000 for the total Confederate force. When the official Confederate records became available after the war, they showed the actual figure to be surprisingly close, 70,000–80,000.

Forty-eight hours after Lee's men began crossing the Potomac into Maryland on September 4, McClellan began his cautious pursuit. For the next week he moved his four corps in short steps, an average of no more than six miles a day, always keeping them within mutually supporting distance in case Lee made a move toward Baltimore or Washington. On September 8, from Rockville, Maryland, fifteen miles from Washington, McClellan reported to General-in-Chief Halleck, "Our information is still entirely too indefinite to justify definite action. . . . As soon as I find out where to strike, I will be after them without an hour's delay."

McClellan had made one significant improvement in staff organization and procedure since the Peninsula; characteristically it addressed shortcomings in logistics, the matter that still consumed his attention, rather than operations or intelligence. In place of the former free-for-all in which wagon teams chose their own routes, there was now something like a modern staff system in which regimental and brigade quartermasters throughout the army followed precise written orders issued from the chief quartermaster assigning routes of march and schedules. Instituting strict limits on the baggage officers could transport, forbidding army wagons from transporting the goods of camp-following peddlers (as they routinely had done before), and having soldiers carry their own shelter tents and blankets, he was able to cut down the number of wagons from the 45 per 1,000 men on the Peninsula to 30 per 1,000. That was still double the standard Meigs was pushing for, in emulation of the French army's "flying columns" which were able to slash their cumbersome logistics trail by having soldiers carry eight instead of the usual three days' marching rations and divide up heavier items like picks, shovels, and cooking kettles among squads of eight men. But the good roads in Maryland helped, too, and between its wagon trains and what could be foraged from farms along the way, McClellan's army was fully capable of marching for ten days at two or even three times the rate it was going, before needing to be resupplied. McClellan's slow advance, in four columns spread over a thirty-mile front, stemmed entirely from his fear of surprise, and ignorance over where Lee was.

The dearth of information was compounded by the anemic performance of McClellan's cavalry, under the command of General Alfred Pleasonton. In the Peninsula, Lee had undertaken a revolutionary reorganization of the cavalry in his Army of Northern Virginia, abandoning the orthodox Napoleonic system of combined arms in which infantry, artillery, and cavalry are distributed throughout the army, instead concentrating his cavalry into a single corps directly available to him for strategic purposes of reconnaissance, intelligence, attacking supply lines, and screening his own movements from observation. McClellan continued to use his cavalry piecemeal, in some cases parceled out to individual brigades.

Pleasonton's cavalry never succeeded in getting far ahead of the infantry, leaving his troopers to pick up secondhand information from stragglers or credulous citizens fed false reports by Confederate general James E. B. "Jeb" Stuart's cavalrymen on their wide-ranging patrols. "We should at least have known where the enemy was by being in contact with him," fumed Cox, who now commanded a division in Burnside's corps, "instead of being the sport of all sorts of vague rumors and wild reports." Pleasonton passed on directly to McClellan without comment the stories his men had been told: Lee's target was Washington, it was Baltimore, it was Pennsylvania; he had 110,000 men, or 190,000, or 440,000. By September 10, McClellan had "conclusively" determined that Lee's force numbered 120,000 and was concentrated "in the vicinity of Frederick City," the source of this intelligence apparently being a church elder from the city who had passed through the rebel lines.

In fact, Lee's men were already marching out of town by then, west on the National Road, a fact that could easily have been verified had Pleasonton acted promptly to retake Sugar Loaf, which had been in the hands of rebel cavalry since September 5. Neither McClellan nor Pleasonton seems to have fully appreciated the importance of the observation post atop the mountain, which commands a clear view for dozens of miles in all directions, including Frederick and the road over the Catoctin Mountains to Middletown. After three half-hearted attempts by Pleasonton failed, McClellan on September 10 ordered an infantry corps to support the cavalry in driving the Confederates off the mountain the following day— "if possible," he added. The embarrassing overkill required to brush aside two small cavalry regiments was evident in the denouement, a brief skirmish in which a few shells were fired off and the rebels fled, eluding capture and leaving three casualties behind. From atop the mountain late in the afternoon a Union signal party reported no sign of the enemy, except for two cavalry regiments near Frederick and a large force across the Potomac at Point of Rocks.

Taking no chances, McClellan nevertheless sent Burnside a dozen miles *east* of Frederick, to New Market (a false report had placed Thomas J. "Stonewall" Jackson's command there in force), ordering him to "move with great care, feeling your way cautiously." He followed up immediately with a second order cautioning Burnside to do so only if he could avoid provoking "a general engagement." Only by the twelfth, when Cox's division, at the head of Burnside's column, briskly pressed down the National Road from New Market nearly all the way to Frederick encountering no opposition, was McClellan confident that Lee's main body had moved on. A brief skirmish at the bridge over the Monocacy at the outskirts of town drove off a rear guard of Stuart's cavalry, and McClellan arrived in the city the next day, a full seventy-two hours behind the Confederate army. He was met with a tumultuous reception, young girls running out and hugging his horse by the neck and showering him with flowers. "I was seldom more affected than by the scenes I saw yesterday and the reception I met with; it would have gratified you very much," McClellan wrote Ellen.

A day earlier he had already concluded about his foe, "From all I can gather secesh is skedaddling. . . . He evidently don't want to fight me—for some reason or other."

UNDELIVERED ORDERS

Lee, to be sure, had had his own troubles. His officers were squabbling; his men poorly fed and ill-clothed, many lacking even shoes. In an odd ill omen, all three of his army's top commanders were left hobbled by accidents that left them unable to ride, reduced to traveling ignominiously in ambulances. Lee's horse Traveller had shied as Lee stood by his side holding the reins, pulling him to the ground and breaking one arm and spraining the other; Jackson had been thrown by a horse, a gift from a pro-Southern Maryland admirer, which had reared the instant he tried to spur it forward into a walk, leaving him stunned and bruised; Longstreet had a painful blister on his heel that left him shuffling in carpet slippers. Two of his division commanders, A. P. Hill and John Bell Hood, were technically under* arrest for insubordination, having volubly resented orders addressed to them by superior officers as an affront to their honor.

But nothing compared to the appearance his unkempt troops presented. "How the rebels manage to get along no one can tell," said one Frederick resident who watched their very unmilitary entrance. People said they could smell the approaching army before they saw it. The *Baltimore American* quoted one man their reporter had interviewed, "I have never seen a mass of such filthy, strong-smelling men. . . . They were the roughest set of creatures I ever saw, their features, hair, and clothing matted with dirt and filth; and the scratching they kept up gave warrant of vermin in abundance." Their uniforms—"multiforms," onlookers described them with greater accuracy—were begrimed with sweat, and worse; subsisting on green corn and apples picked from roadside fields, many of the men had suffered diarrhea for days.

Even so, said one young Marylander, "there was a dash about them." That was an apt description of those able to endure the hardship; many were not. Lee's force, probably 75,000 on the eve of the campaign, melted away into the Maryland countryside at a frightful rate. Some were too ill to go on, some deserted outright, many practiced the time-honored soldier's art of straggling, dropping out of the march to rest by the side of the road, to fall farther and farther behind their regiments.

Both sides were chronically beset with the problem. At the start of the Maryland campaign, Cox was shocked at the sight of this "roadside brigade," which often seemed as numerous as his own division marching in the middle of the road. They sat huddled in groups "from two to fifty—indeed enough to make themselves, if consolidated, a large army," wrote one New York private describing his march from Rockville to Frederick. "It is quite common to see two or three dozen groups, within the space of half a mile, boiling their food in their tin cups over fires made with fence rails. . . . They are thoroughly disgusted with the life they led and swear that if they ever get out of the army they will commit suicide before entering it again." He added that most, however, were sick or "miserably worn," and the rest were "skulkers." But the Confederate army had it far worse, "our one great embarrassment," Lee confessed to Davis. His Army of Northern Virginia would arrive on the battlefield of Antietam two weeks later with nearly half of its force having vanished, leaving 38,000 men.

The reception Lee's army found in Maryland was a disappointment, too. Many Southerners were sure that Maryland, a border state with a significant number of Confederate-sympathizing slaveholders, was eager to join the South and was being held in the Union only by coercion and force. On September 8, Lee issued a proclamation in Frederick "To the People of Maryland" calling upon them to throw off the "foreign yoke" to "enjoy the inalienable rights of freeman" in the Confederacy. Privately, he wrote Davis the day before, acknowledging, "I do not anticipate any general rising." Although sympathies were divided in western Maryland, and a few Confederate supporters in Frederick cheered Lee's men while the local Southern belles immediately arranged a ball to entertain their officers, the overall atmosphere was distinctly frosty, the town filled with "a death-like silence— some houses closed, tight, as if some public calamity had taken place," one Southern soldier recorded. To maintain goodwill, Lee had ordered his officers and men to pay for anything they requisitioned from shops and farms. But the Confederate money they offered in exchange was regarded by most locals as merely making the transaction a slightly more elaborate form of theft. The old line about not being worth the paper they were printed on did not even meet the case, a Frederick resident mockingly observed: Confederate notes "depreciated the paper on which they were printed." On leaving, "Rebel officers were unanimous in declaring that 'Frederick was a d—d Union hole,'" reported a resident.

Lee was keeping his strategic options open as he marched west. As he had explained to Davis, the chief objective was to galvanize Northern opposition to the war before the fall elections and seize the moment "when it is within our power to inflict injury" to issue a proposal for an end of the war and recognition of Southern independence. His observation that doing so would "show conclusively to the world" the South's honorable intentions was not merely a figure of speech: "the world" was a pointed reference to England and France, which already were edging toward formal recognition of the South, a move that would have lent powerful and perhaps irresistible weight to a negotiated peace.

One dramatic blow Lee had in mind to demonstrate the power of his army "to inflict injury" was a raid into Pennsylvania to destroy the long arched bridge that carried the Pennsylvania Railroad over the Susquehanna at Harrisburg, the Union's vital connection to Ohio and the West. But Lee had logistics preoccupations, too. Like a cork in a bottle, a Union garrison of 10,000 at Harper's Ferry blocked the line of supply from Winchester up the Shenandoah Valley he was counting on to support the operation. From a military standpoint it seemed inconceivable that the Union forces would try to hold on to Harper's Ferry once his invasion of Maryland left the position cut off and strategically flanked. But instead of the expected withdrawal, General-in-Chief Halleck had ordered the garrison's commander to hold Harper's Ferry "at all costs." With three days' head start over McClellan's pursuing army, and determined to carry on with his plan to invade Pennsylvania, Lee was prepared to take an audacious gamble to reduce the Union garrison in his rear.

No one knows to this day exactly how a copy of Lee's orders miscarried and landed in a field of clover a mile outside of Frederick, where troops of the Union Twelfth Corps stopped to rest around 9 a.m. on September 13 as they approached the city from the south. What is certain is that by early afternoon the document was in

McClellan's hands. Dated September 9, Lee's Special Orders No. 191 split his army into four parts. Longstreet's command, one half of the army, plus all its baggage wagons, was ordered to follow the National Road over South Mountain to Boonsboro, with D. H. Hill following as a rear guard. Jackson was to take the same route, but continue on and recross the Potomac, then turn south to advance on Harper's Ferry from the northwest. To complete the envelopment of the isolated Union garrison, John G. Walker was sent to occupy Loudoun Heights to the south and Lafayette McLaws to Maryland Heights to the east, two commanding positions from which artillery fire could be unloosed with impunity on the town below.

"Now I know what to do!" McClellan reportedly exclaimed on reading the document. McClellan had 61,000 men, four full corps plus George Sykes's unattached division, in the vicinity of Frederick to catch Longstreet's and Hill's force left waiting near Boonsboro with one-fourth as many men. South of Frederick was William B. Franklin's corps near Buckeystown plus Darius N. Couch's unattached division at Licksville, each twelve miles from Crampton's Gap—the pass over South Mountain at Burkittsville, six miles south of the National Road—that would allow them to fall on McLaws's isolated and scattered detachment at Maryland Heights from the rear.

At least three days earlier a series of unusually reliable reports from a Pennsylvania militia cavalry patrol had been sent to McClellan, not only confirming Longstreet's and Jackson's movements, but strongly indicating that Lee had decided to further split his army into five parts, sending Longstreet with nine brigades and the army's baggage trains ahead to Hagerstown close to the Pennsylvania line. Equipped with a portable telegraph that could be attached to the wires along railroad tracks, the patrol proved far more effective than any of McClellan's own cavalry and scouts. On September 11 the captain of the Pennsylvania cavalry unit, slipping into civilian clothes and remaining behind in Hagerstown, reported that he had personally observed the arrival of Longstreet's forces. That meant

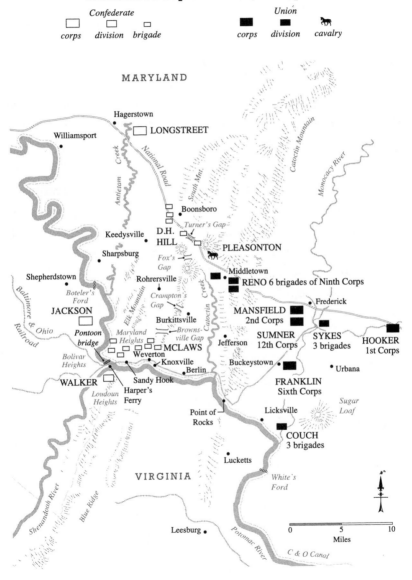

Situation on September 13, 1862, p.m.

D. H. Hill's five brigades, twelve miles behind at Boonsboro, were for the moment on their own and outnumbered 8 to 1 by a Union force that could be over the mountain early the next day.

The absence of anyone on McClellan's staff to sift and make sense of reports about the enemy left the signals swamped in a sea of noise. It would fall to one of McClellan's successors as commander of the Army of the Potomac, Joseph Hooker, to benefit by the example of his failure and, in January 1863, create its first professional intelligence staff. Headed by a New York lawyer, Colonel George Sharpe, Hooker's Bureau of Military Intelligence would have the distinction, as a CIA historical report noted a century and a half later, of being "the first 'all-source intelligence' organization in U.S. history." (Sharpe "obtained, collated, analyzed, and provided reports based on scouting, spying behind enemy lines, interrogations, cavalry reconnaissance, balloon observation, . . . flag signal and telegraph intercepts, captured Confederate documents and mail, Southern newspapers, and intelligence reporting from subordinate military units.")

With no one's counsel but his own to rely on, McClellan heeded the inner voice that, as always, counseled hesitation. At 3 p.m. on the thirteenth he sent Pleasonton an anemic request to "ascertain whether the order of march" directed by Lee's order "has thus far been followed by the enemy," but warning that because the pass where the National Road crosses South Mountain at Turner's Gap "may be disputed by two columns"—i.e., Longstreet and D. H. Hill—he should "approach it with great caution."

He needn't have worried: his cavalry commander had no intention of taking any risks, either. Three hours later, having learned nothing yet from his scouts or cavalry patrols, Pleasonton sent a waffling reply. "As near as I can judge," he reported, Lee's army had adhered to his plans "as closely as circumstances would permit."

It was not until 6:20 p.m. that McClellan issued orders to Franklin to move—not now, but in the morning—to Crampton's Gap by Burkittsville and advance from there to relieve Harper's Ferry.

"My general idea is to cut the enemy in two and beat him in detail," McClellan explained in his lengthy instructions to Franklin. But orders to the rest of the army sent later that night betrayed no sense of the urgency required to put action to those words. Neither Pleasonton's cavalry, which had already cleared the National Road to the foot of Turner's Gap, nor Cox's lead division of the Ninth Corps, in the vanguard five miles behind at Middletown, received new orders at all, much less any warning of a general advance for the next day. Cox was left with no instructions beyond his earlier orders to support a cavalry reconnaissance of Turner's Gap in the morning with a single infantry brigade from his division. Two other divisions of the Ninth Corps, likewise following plans almost certainly in train before the discovery of Lee's order, made a short march from Frederick that afternoon, halting a few miles behind Cox east of Middletown; they too received no orders for a further advance.

The next closest corps, Edwin V. Sumner's Second and Joseph Mansfield's Twelfth plus Sykes's division, were just west of Frederick. But the orders McClellan sent them between 8:45 p.m. and 1 a.m. directed them to stand aside in the morning and let Hooker's First Corps, encamped on the far side of Frederick, take the road first. That may have been favoritism on McClellan's part toward Hooker or a desire to keep the two corps under Burnside's overall command, the First and the Ninth, together, but for whatever reason it added an incomprehensible delay in getting the entire army in motion. Hooker's troops would not arrive at Turner's Gap until mid-afternoon on the fourteenth; Sumner and Sykes would not arrive at all in time to make a difference. Mansfield's corps did not receive orders to move until the next morning, and found the road ahead clogged with artillery, ordnance, and baggage wagons, forcing them to take to fields and side roads and get hopelessly lost, at one point heading back toward Frederick. ("If there is a point of the compass toward which the head of the column did not march," wrote Ezra Carman, whose New Jersey regiment was part of the

confused march, "it is unknown to us.") The lead of the Twelfth
Corps did not arrive at the foot of Turner's Gap until midnight, half
of the men asleep in cornfields and fencerows strung out along the
route of march.

McClellan considered but quickly rejected the idea of trying to force the narrow passage at Weverton where the C&O
Canal, B&O Railroad, and a road from Jefferson to Harper's
Ferry all squeeze between the edge of the Potomac River and
the southernmost ridge of South Mountain, which was the most
direct route to the besieged Union garrison: he had received
information—incorrect as it turned out—that Confederate artillery commanded the pass from the opposite river bank. But even
a diversion there could have drawn off McLaws's forces to aid
Franklin's advance.

Agony over the missed opportunity that McClellan let slip
through his hands was still alive in the words written decades later
by some of his officers. Ezra Carman would spend the rest of his
life meticulously compiling the history of the Maryland Campaign
in a manuscript still regarded by historians as one of the most objective and thorough records of the events, and in it he minced no
words about McClellan's failure to seize "possibilities that come to
a commander but seldom, and not to one man more than once in
a lifetime."

There was nothing to prevent a rapid advance of the entire
army. Nothing was wanting but the order to march. The afternoon had been practically lost; the loss should have been
retrieved by an order to march at sunset. The roads were good,
the nights were cool, and the evening dews, which fell early,
partially laid the dust. A night march would have been welcomed by the soldier, and the twelve miles between Frederick
and the foot of Turner's Gap were over a broad road as smooth
as the floor.

Except for the cavalry and one brigade of infantry, none of the Union army had come in contact with the enemy that day. Two-thirds had marched less than seven miles and, Carman noted, "all save the cavalry, the First Corps, and a part of the Ninth Corps" were in bivouac by early afternoon, and "consequently, well rested by sunset."

McClellan's hesitation gave Lee an extra eighteen hours to reassemble his scattered forces to mount a determined defense of the passes. In his memoir of the war, Cox quoted with barely concealed contempt the triumphant messages McClellan had telegraphed to Halleck and Lincoln late on the night of the thirteenth. With "all the plans of the rebels" in his hands, McClellan promised, he "would catch them in their own trap" ("will send trophies," he boasted)— before adding the weaselly proviso, "if my men are equal to the emergency." Cox articulated what all of McClellan's men must have thought when they later read those words. "The failure to be 'equal to the emergency,'" wrote Cox, "was not in his men."

In his telegram to Halleck at 11 p.m., McClellan engaged in another piece of preemptive posterior covering, referring to the copy of Lee's order that he had received at least eight hours earlier as having "come into my hands this evening," aware no doubt that he had left himself open to well-deserved censure for his dilatoriness in not acting at once. In his memoirs McClellan later insisted, "I immediately gave orders for a rapid and vigorous forward movement," the only accurate adverb or adjective in that statement being the word "forward."

Had McClellan indeed moved at once, Franklin would have encountered nothing to hinder his march but a few Confederate cavalry scouts thrown out in front of Burkittsville, as known from Union scouting earlier in the day; Pleasonton's cavalry along with the entire Ninth Corps could have been at the top of South Mountain before dark, the way cleared for the rest of the army to follow close behind. Even had McClellan waited until nightfall to set the army in motion, the Ninth, Second, and Twelfth Corps could have been at the foot of Turner's Gap by midnight, rested and ready to attack at dawn, opposed by nothing but a single Confederate cavalry regiment, two small infantry brigades, and eight artillery pieces.

Instead, Cox found himself the next morning on his own, and in the fight of his life.

3

THE
ASSAULT
HEROIC

Jacob Cox

FOX'S GAP

"No one who campaigned with Generals McClellan or Lee in September 1862," wrote Ezra Carman, "can ever forget the incomparable beauty of the valleys of western Maryland."

To men from the rough-hewn West or even settled New England, the large farms scattered among gently rolling hills seemed an idyll of rural prosperity, the unadorned elegance of their ample stone, brick, or clapboard-sided farmhouses and solid bank barns framed by the mountain ridges that cut the country west of Frederick into valleys six to twelve miles wide. The wheat stood in neat shocks, the corn ripening in bronzing rows for gathering, the cows sleek and fat, the woodlots so neat one could drive a wagon through them in any direction, the grass and clover meadows watered by creeks and streams that ran year-round. "Here is the best farming land in the country," an army surgeon from New Hampshire marveled: he had never seen finer beef, potatoes, or draft horses. Jacob Cox, admitting he may have been affected partly by the contrast with the forest-shrouded gloom of West Virginia he had earlier passed through, nonetheless found himself overwhelmed by the pastoral beauty of the Maryland countryside. "An evening march, under a brilliant moon, over a park-like landscape with alternations of groves and meadows which could not have been more beautifully composed by a master artist, remains in my memory as a page out of a lovely romance," he wrote years later.

Passing over the Catoctin ridge a few miles west of Frederick, the National Road, smooth and well drained by its macadam surface of rolled and compacted gravel, dropped sharply into Middletown, then across Catoctin Creek on one of the many stone arch bridges that marked its progress, naturalistic forms that seemed less technological intrusions than organic forms growing from the landscape. Ahead, two sharp notches cutting into the silhouetted curtain of South Mountain, the last gasp of the north-south–running Blue Ridge before it dwindled away north of Gettysburg, marked the passes where roads cut across its 1,300-foot summit. These "wind gaps," remnants of ancient rivers, were 200 to 300 feet below the surrounding peaks: Turner's Gap, through which the National Road passed, on the right; Fox's Gap, a mile to the south, where the smaller and rougher Old Sharpsburg Road wound its way through.

The morning of September 14, a Sunday, dawned bright and Cox was in the saddle early, ready to accompany the one brigade from his division ordered to support Pleasonton's reconnaissance of South Mountain. He was an unlikely warrior. As a young man he had been an apprentice to a lawyer, a bookkeeper to a broker, a student for the ministry, a school superintendent, and, after finally being admitted to the bar in 1853, an organizer of the Republican Party in Ohio, and a state senator. At Oberlin, where he received his degree in theology, he had married the college president's daughter, a nineteen-year-old widow who already had a child; when the war began Cox was thirty-three, of indifferent health, with six children to support.

But he had taken to soldiering, mentally and physically. He recalled the "weight at the heart," the "half-choking sense of grief" that for months had dragged him down in helpless despair as secession and disunion loomed, an oppression which abruptly lifted when he found relief in action upon entering military service. The vigorous outdoor life agreed with him; his health blossomed; he added weight to his spindly six-foot frame, and the standard Civil War general's bristling full beard to his features.

The Civil War's many "political generals" who owed their appointments at the start of the war more to connections than skill would come in for scathing assessment, but if anyone made the case for entrusting high command to volunteer amateurs it was Jacob Cox. Though he would always hold fast to the American democratic belief in the leveling force of personal virtue—that "patriotic zeal and devotion" were more important than professional qualifications and that when it came to the essential qualities of a commanding officer, "a bold heart, a cool head, and practical common-sense were of much more importance than anything taught at school"—he himself had studied war more seriously than most West Point graduates.

State militias before the war had more in common with fraternal orders than military organizations, and Cox's prewar appointment as a brigadier of the Ohio militia had been equally nominal as far as giving him any actual experience in military command. But seeing war on the horizon, he had immersed himself in works on military strategy and tactics, and especially military history. Even in the field he had a rule always to be reading a work of military history, sending home one volume and receiving another. He read all of Jomini's works in the original French, British histories of the Crimean War, and "in this way I gradually went through all the leading books I could find." Seeing where even the renowned commanders of the past had blundered was a "most useful means of military education," he concluded, both instruction on how to think through a military problem and reassurance that "our capacity to learn was at least as quick as theirs." Cox had quickly proved himself leading a brigade in the West Virginia campaign at the start of the war, and would end it as a major general in command of the Twenty-third Corps during Sherman's march through Georgia and the Carolinas.

Approaching the foot of Turner's Gap, Cox found two of the Ninth Corps' batteries already exchanging long-range shots with

Battle of South Mountain
September 14, 1862

▭ *Confederate* ▬ *Union*

Turner's Gap

Longstreet

Mountain House

Wise farm

Fox's Gap

D. H. Hill

woods road

farm lane

Hooker
4 p.m.

McClellan's
observation post

Cox
9:00 a.m.

Old Sharpsburg Road

National Road

Ninth Corps
reinforcements
2 p.m.

South Mountain

Crampton's Gap

McLaws

Burkittsville

Franklin
4 p.m.

Sharpsburg
South Mountain   M D
Washington
VA

0   1/2   1
Miles

N

the Confederates out of sight at the top of the gap. Standing by the side of the road, to Cox's astonishment, was Colonel Augustus Moor, one of his brigade commanders who had been captured two days earlier at the outskirts of Frederick, when he had galloped around a turn in the road directly into the rear guard of the Confederate cavalry. Moor explained he had been paroled, released on his pledge not to take up arms until he was duly exchanged for a Confederate prisoner, and was making his way back on foot from the other side of the mountain.

"But where are *you* going?" asked Moor. Cox replied he was supporting a reconnaissance of the gap. Moor gave an "involuntary start" and blurted out, "My God, be careful!" before checking himself and hastily adding, "But I am paroled!" and turning away.

It would have taken a considerably more obtuse man than Cox not to take the hint, and he galloped off at once back toward Middletown to order his other brigade to come up at once. Returning again to the foot of the gap near where the Old Sharpsburg Road branched off to the left from the National Road, he found Pleasonton, who advised against a frontal assault and suggested that Cox's brigade attempt to flank the rebel force by advancing on Fox's Gap on the old road.

It was a long two-mile climb, the last half mile up a farm lane through woods that ran along a steep gully to the left of the road up to the ridge. The summits flanking the gaps rose in scattered hills thickly covered in mature forest and dense tangles of mountain laurel, but on the eastern slopes the mountainside was broken with patches of open fields where smallholders, far less prosperous than the owners of the large acreages in the valleys below, had built rough log cabins and eked out a living on stony ground. Nearing the top of the ridge, Cox's men came in range of a rebel battery along the edge of the timber line, firing spherical case shot and canister— exploding shells with a timed fuse that burst in the air with a rain of jagged fragments and musket balls, and, even more lethal at short range, large tin cans packed with balls that sprayed out of the barrel of a cannon like a huge shotgun blast, along with an incongruous gentle falling shower of sawdust which the balls were packed with, covering its victims in a soft yellow blanket of dust that prompted the sardonic gunner in one of Ambrose Bierce's tales to grimly observe, "We bury our dead."

Advancing through the woods, the three regiments of Cox's first brigade found themselves in a skirmish action amid thickets and a confusion of ravines. It was standard practice to send one or two companies of each regiment ahead in small groups of skirmishers who would fire from cover to probe the enemy and push back his outposts, then fall back to the line of battle for the main attack. But throughout the morning's fight the terrain played havoc with textbook tactics, as parts of units became lost or separated and entire regiments became skirmishers or grappled with the enemy at close quarters. The 23rd Ohio regiment, moving through thick woods on the left, had the heaviest going, as the rebels picked off officers, wounding in short order two captains, five lieutenants, and the regiment's commander—and future President of the United States—Lieutenant Colonel Rutherford B. Hayes, the bone of his left arm shattered just above the elbow by a musket ball. Another prime target were the artillerymen manning a gun at the right end of the Union position, its commander killed and three of his five men wounded.

But at mid-morning the Ohio regiments were able to re-form along a stone fence, a more or less continuous line of battle a half mile end to end. The two regiments in the center were separated by 100 yards from a stone wall and woods road along the crest of the mountain where North Carolina regiments awaited them, across open pasture and stubble fields that sloped gently uphill. On the command to charge, Cox's men gave a furious yell and advanced with fixed bayonets. The 12th Ohio, in the center of the line, was within 40 yards of the woods road when the North Carolina men opened fire. But most had hit the dirt on a shouted warning from an officer to lie down ("never did men lie quicker even when shot," said one of the Ohioans), then rose up to resume the charge. The North Carolinians broke and scrambled down the steep drop behind them on the western slopes of the mountain. Turning to the right, a further charge by the 12th Ohio drove off a rebel battery at the Wise farm near the Old Sharpsburg Road.

Cox's second brigade had joined the fight by this time, and the entire division fought back several desperate attempts by the Confederates to retake the crest. When the fighting lulled around noon Union troops had 200 Confederate prisoners in their hands. Cox decided to wait for the remaining divisions of the Ninth Corps that a messenger had brought word hours earlier were on the way, rather than risk his gains by pressing at once toward Turner's Gap along a small road that ran along the ridge between the two gaps, whose southern end he now controlled.

The success of the morning's by-the-book bayonet charges across open ground had come at brutal cost. The 12th Ohio lost 35 killed and 100 wounded of its 500 men; the 23rd had 32 killed and 95 wounded. Pulling back from the hollow of the gap to the more defensible higher ground to the south overlooking the woods road, they now waited for the promised reinforcements while the Confederate guns, which now perfectly had the range of the slopes around and behind Cox's position, kept up a steady fire, shells bursting in the tree tops and canister shot gouging long furrows in the sod "with a noise," Cox recounted, "like the cutting of a melon rind."

THE PHYSICS OF BATTLE

Men advancing elbow to elbow in a steady lockstep cadence across an open field directly into a line of enemy rifles is the enduring image of the Civil War, and to modern eyes it remains utterly incredible that men could be ordered to do such a thing, or that they would do it. Dwight D. Eisenhower once took British field marshal Bernard Montgomery to visit the Gettysburg battlefield, and the two Second World War commanders stood baffled on the

Infantry regiment in line of battle

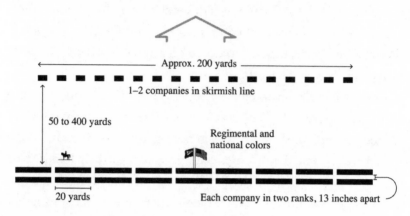

Approx. 200 yards

1–2 companies in skirmish line

50 to 400 yards

Regimental and national colors

20 yards

Each company in two ranks, 13 inches apart

site of Pickett's famous charge. Montgomery asked, "What would you have done if I gave the order to Pickett to charge?" Eisenhower replied: "Fired you."

Influenced in part by the example offered by the obdurate folly of First World War generals who sent wave after wave of men over the top to their slaughter by enemy machine-gun fire, many historians similarly attributed the horrific casualty rates of the Civil War to an almost incomprehensible mismatch between traditional tactics and modern technology. In the long-accepted conventional view, the linear tactics inherited from an era of martial splendor and inaccurate and short-range smoothbore muskets had become suicidal in the age of the far deadlier rifle, adopted by the U.S. Army only in 1854.

More recent studies, however, have suggested that the effect of the rifle on the Civil War battlefield was considerably less than has been assumed, and the compact line of battle far more practical than the hopeless anachronism it has often been made out to be. As the military historian Brent Nosworthy noted, "When compact formations ceased to be practical, soon almost everyone forgot that they had ever been functional at all" (what Nosworthy termed the "They wouldn't have fought that way if they knew what we know" view). The reasons for the deadliness of Civil War combat in fact were more subtle, and tragic.

Scott's regulations directed that to form a line of battle, a regiment would deploy in two ranks, separated by just 13 inches, the men in each rank touching elbow to elbow. A regiment of 1,000 men would occupy a front of about 200 yards, and at a normal rate of advance would step forward at a walking pace of 90 steps per minute, about 2 1/2 miles per hour. The compact formation and the drill required to maintain it as a regiment moved across ground had several purposes. It kept men within hearing distance of their commander amid the noise and confusion of battle. It ensured that everyone kept moving forward toward the enemy, by having each man in literal touch with those on either side and by the visual reference point of the regimental and national flags carried by color bearers at the center of the line that would remain visible through the smoke of gunfire. The habit of automatic obedience that drilling in formation instilled was at least as important as anything else. One soldier recalled the sight of a whole brigade going through a complex drill of forming into columns and lines as "like an enormous machine." That was the point.

The formation in two closely spaced ranks allowed one rank to reload, a process that took at least thirty seconds, while the other fired, the rear rank extending the barrels of their weapons over the shoulders of the men in front. A second line could help maintain constant pressure on defenders, staying out of small-arms range as it moved forward, ready to fill gaps or relieve the first line if it broke apart or faltered.

Most of all, the line of battle allowed for massed fire that would make up for inaccurately aimed shots. When armed with smoothbore muskets, this was a necessity. Muskets had an effective range of only about 80 yards, and the actual direction the bullet took was determined by the last unpredictable bounce it took against the side of the barrel as it exited the muzzle. In theory, an advancing line would fire a series of volleys while advancing to 80 yards from the enemy. After the defenders fired their last volley, the attacking force would charge the remaining ground with bayonets fixed, a distance that could be covered at a run in the time it took the defenders to reload.

The idea of improving the accuracy of a musket by "rifling" the inside of the barrel with a continuous spiral groove, thereby imparting a gyroscopically stabilizing spin to the projectile, was not new. Hunters and specially equipped sharpshooter units in armies had used rifles to advantage since the eighteenth century or earlier. The problem was the tight fit required between the bullet and the barrel for this to work, which necessitated hammering the bullet down the barrel with a ramrod, not a convenient task in the heat of battle. Rifling also quickly fouled with burned powder, requiring frequent cleaning.

The French military instructor and inventor Claude-Étienne Minié solved the problem in 1847 with his eponymous Minié ball, a soft lead rifle bullet with a conical hollow in its base. It could be loaded down a barrel as easily as a loose-fitting musket ball, but when fired the base would instantly flare out under the pressure of the expanding gases, making firm contact with the rifling.

Besides its inherent inaccuracy, a randomly tumbling musket ball creates substantial aerodynamic drag that causes it to lose speed rapidly, limiting its range to a few hundred yards. The axially spinning and conically shaped Minié ball, by contrast, cuts through the air with far less wind resistance, increasing its maximum range to 1,000 yards or even more. In tests the army conducted before the war, a proficient marksman was able to hit a large target at 200 yards 74 percent of the time with the new rifle version of the standard army musket, versus 36 percent using the older smoothbore; at 300 yards the corresponding figures were 46 percent and 14 percent.

That was the theory. In practice, most Civil War engagements were fought at scarcely greater distance than earlier battles between armies equipped with smoothbore weapons. One reason for this was inherent in the limitations of the technology itself. The greater friction between bullet and barrel in the rifle musket actually caused the muzzle velocity—the bullet's speed on leaving the barrel—to drop by as much as 40 percent compared to its smoothbore predecessors. When aiming at a target 100 yards away the ballistics of the two weapons were essentially the same. But to reach a target at the rifle musket's longer range, it was necessary to compensate for its lower muzzle velocity by raising the barrel enough that the bullet described a measurably parabolic arc: so much so that the bullet would actually soar over the head of a man standing in the interval between two effective lethal zones at the start and end of the trajectory. When aiming at a target 300 yards away, the kill zones stretch from roughly 0 to 75 yards and 240 to 350 yards from the shooter. At longer distances the depth of the distant kill zone contracts even more; when aiming at 1,000 yards, it is only about 12 yards deep.

Other limitations were practical. Almost no time was devoted to target practice in either the Northern or Southern armies. Although built-in gunsights were calibrated for aiming at different distances, their use required an accurate estimation of range, which likewise took considerable practice to master. Smoke from black powder weapons quickly obscured the battlefield in any case, making aiming difficult if not impossible, and in many places vegetation limited visibility to 20 yards or less. Officers sometimes had to get down on hands and knees to peer under the smoke haze to observe the enemy. And then there was the simple truth that most men in battle are too panicked or excited to bother with such niceties as aiming: they just level their weapons and fire somewhere in the general direction ahead.

The bayonet charge accordingly remained the most effective means of attack for a regiment advancing in tight linear formation, even against a rifle-equipped defender. When carried all the way to the enemy's lines, the defender almost invariably broke and ran: bayonets accounted for only 0.37 percent of the wounds treated by Union surgeons during the war, but their psychological effect was many times greater.

Human nature interposed here too. Part of why Civil War battles were so protracted and deadly was the almost inalterable inclination of men under fire to halt and return fire. Countless Civil War battles became hours-long stalemates in which each side exchanged fire at deadly range from static positions.

Notwithstanding the recent revision in understanding of the rifle's effects, the new weapons did exacerbate this deadlock in a few significant ways that tipped the balance to the defender, ensuring that fights would be bloody, protracted, and often inconclusive. Skirmishers, who operated in small units, usually teams of four, taking cover behind natural obstacles, could take time to carefully pick their targets and make the increased range and accuracy of the new weapons tell, often concentrating their attention on officers and artillerymen and horses. The death rate of generals shows this: 1 in 10 were killed in action during the war, twice the fatality rate suffered by men in the ranks.

Rifle-equipped skirmishers also put an end to the Napoleonic tactic of moving cannon ahead of advancing infantry with the aim of blowing a hole in the defenders' lines. Increasingly, artillery was employed defensively, placed at the flanks or rear of the infantry. From a protected position, artillery firing canister at close range could wreak havoc on infantry advancing across open ground. Although artillery accounted for only 10 percent of the projectile wounds treated by Union surgeons, that relatively low figure is likely an artifact of the high lethality of injuries from exploding shells and canister shot. Soldiers with half of their skulls taken off by large chunks of flying metal did not survive long enough to be attended by a surgeon.

The innovation of rifled artillery greatly improved the accuracy and range of the solid shot and shells fired by cannons; the 20-pound Parrot Gun could strike targets almost two miles away. But its effective use required much more training and usually some means of spotting targets not in direct line of sight, often impossible in heavily wooded terrain. McClellan during the Peninsula Campaign had requested that two-thirds of his field guns be smoothbores, which could fire a larger load of canister than an equivalent rifled gun, and concentrated his artillery at the division level, enabling their defensive firepower to be shifted where needed most and unleashed with maximum effect, rather than dispersed among smaller units where many would sit idle as the battle raged elsewhere.

Likewise, men in defensive positions protected by trenches, earthworks, or other field fortifications had much more chance to exploit the capabilities of their rifles, with a steady rest to lean their barrels on and the security to take aim with a cool head. During some engagements men on the firing line were handed loaded weapons in relays by men in the rear, and were thus able to keep up a rapid fire that an attacker could not possibly match. Cox, after the war, summarized this new truth the war had taught: "One rifle in the trench was worth five in front of it." But it would take much bloody experience, and the courage to break free of some of the oldest military shibboleths regarding the valor of attack and the cravenness of defense, before American commanders learned to adapt to war as it was.

NATURAL FIGHTERS

The fact was, too, that for many commanders of new regiments it was all they could do to get their men to follow *any* directions: staying together and going where they were told was enough of a challenge for volunteer soldiers without trying to introduce innovations. Tales abounded of officers barely managing to keep one step ahead of their men in learning the rudiments of drill and marching. The surgeon of a Wisconsin regiment derisively recounted watching the colonel of another newly organized unit appear on the drill ground holding in his hand a copy of *Hardee's Tactics* and proceeding to read out orders "in a commanding voice," straight from the manual. That was arguably an improvement over the colonel of an Indiana regiment who had memorized phrases from the book literally, and would bark out commands of the form, "Battalion, right or left face, as the case may be, march!"

American schoolboys brought up on tales of Bunker Hill, New Orleans, and Buena Vista had a hard time being dissuaded of the idea that Americans were natural fighters who required no direction or training at all. Despairing over one Kentucky regiment under his command, James A. Garfield described it as "little better than a well-disposed, Union-loving mob." Northerners imbued with rural and small-town democratic egalitarianism, and Southerners with touchy feelings of personal honor, equally refused to see themselves as cogs in a machine or to recognize the right of officers to order them around. Northern citizen-soldiers, the colonel of an Iowa regiment found, simply refused to be "bossed." A member of a genteel Virginia family who had enlisted as a private in the Confederate army noted the insistence of Southern soldiers on "the right of private judgment" to fight in whatever way each thought best. Even after Gettysburg, a full two years into the war, Lee would complain, "Our people are so little liable to control that it is difficult to get them to follow any course not in accordance with their inclination."

The practices of enlisting companies from a single town and allowing members to elect their own officers further undermined the ability of officers to impose discipline on men who had known them since boyhood. "Most common soldiers," wrote Gerald Linderman, "simply refused to equate worth with rank."

The situation was hardly conducive to innovations in training or tactics, and officers who tried found themselves swatted down from above even more thoroughly than they were frustrated by indiscipline below. "The conservatism of the old army," Jacob Cox found, was immovable in its reverence for the military methods "sanctioned by European authority, especially that of the second French Empire."

The initial resistance to defensive tactics and field fortifications owed as much to civilian attitudes as military tradition. Being ordered to dig ditches was nobody's idea of the life of a soldier, and at least until they knew better, volunteers resented it even more than they did drill. Both Lee and McClellan had employed trenches and field fortifications during the Peninsula Campaign, but that was mostly in the context of formal siege warfare, and even so Lee had been mocked in the Southern press as the "King of Spades" and the "Great Entrencher" for his "dilly-dally, dirt digging, scientific warfare." Southerners in particular tended to equate even tactical defense with unmanliness, and denounced the "timid" use of field fortifications for leaving men unfit for battle. "Troops once sheltered from fire behind works never feel comfortable unless in them," complained one Confederate officer. "To attack entrenchments, give me troops who have never served behind them."

In the North, criticism of commanders who ordered their men behind fieldworks often blended with the familiar populist attacks on West Point and its effete officer graduates, "whose caution is educated until it is hardly distinguishable from cowardice." The staunchly abolitionist Republican senator from Illinois, Lyman Trumbull, declared in the third year of the war, "Take off your engineering restraints; dismiss . . . from the Army every man who knows how to build a fortification, and let the men of the North, with their strong arms and indomitable spirit, move down upon the rebels, and I tell you they will grind them to powder in their power." Edwin Stanton for his part in early 1862 fulminated about scientific ideas of warfare that owed their origin to "infidel France." Patriotism, resolute courage, and "the spirit of the Lord," he insisted, were the "military combination that never failed. . . . Battles are to be won now and by us in the same and only manner they were ever won by any people, or in any age, since the days of Joshua, by boldly pursuing and striking the foe."

By the summer of 1864 no one needed to order men to start digging trenches the moment they stopped. In the words of a New York soldier, it became "almost second nature, one duty that no one shirked." Nor was it hard to convince anyone on the front lines of the suicidal futility of assaulting fortifications in conventional line of battle. "Lie down, you damn fools, you can't take them forts!" shouted the members of a veteran regiment at the siege of Petersburg as a group of newly arrived troops gamely went forward. "You hear people say, 'Oh everyone is brave enough, it is the head that is needed,'" a Union staff officer reported.

The 1855 revision of Scott's tactical regulations by Major William Hardee had incorporated a few changes to take into account new realities. Scott's manual had specified a "quick time" of 110 steps per minute as the fastest normal movement. Hardee added a new "double quick time" of 160 steps per minute, a pace of 5 miles per hour, or twice the "common time." At double quick time a unit could cover 75 yards in half a minute.

As the war progressed, there was a slow but noticeable evolution toward increasing use of skirmish tactics, until by the end of the war entire regiments often advanced in loose order, with soldiers individually or in small groups rushing forward from tree to tree or under other natural cover while trying to keep in general alignment through visual contact. A few prewar militia units that had adopted the fanciful uniforms of the French Zouave units in North Africa—fez, blue jacket, baggy red trousers—had also attempted to emulate their athletic tactics that relied upon speed, agility, and taking advantage of terrain to advance by crawling and rushing. But the training required was far too demanding for general use, and none of these innovations was accompanied by the organizational and doctrinal changes needed to fundamentally solve the problem of the offensive. Only small units could be deployed in loose order without losing contact and control, leaving gaps an enemy could readily counterattack through. Halleck in his 1846 manual had specifically warned that a thin formation of troops during rapid movement "breaks and exhibits great and dangerous undulations." The infiltration tactics pioneered by the Prussian army toward the end of the First World War to restore mobility against entrenched defenses, with small units each probing for weak spots to exploit, would indeed only be fully realized when radio communications made it possible to maintain constant contact while rapidly pressing forward.

As with the growing reliance on fortifications, even the small changes came mostly from bloody experience and improvisation unaccompanied by any changes in the official tactics manuals. After the 12th New Hampshire lost half of its 800 men killed or wounded in a single attack into heavy musket fire at Chancellorsville, one of the survivors noted that "the terrible lesson of the last hour and a half has taught them a lesson that each one is now practicing; for every man has his tree behind which he is fighting." At the Battle of the Wilderness a Union soldier reported, "We could seldom see the enemy, and learned more and more to protect ourselves as we advanced, keeping behind trees and displaying ourselves as little as possible." And when Union forces began the Battle of Missionary Ridge in a series of probing attacks to seek a weak spot in the enemy position, it was such a striking departure from the usual heroic norm of unthinking frontal assault that John Beatty, a brigade commander, noted, "I thought I detected in the management what I had never discovered before on the battlefield—a little common sense."

Even so, it was not until the winter of 1863–64 that realistic training in attacking fortified positions was even thought of. Emory Upton, a born reformer and iconoclast who graduated at the bottom of his West Point class of 1861 and ended the war a twenty-five-year-old major general in command of a division, was the first to try. He had his troops practice assaulting mock fortifications, and at the Battle of Spotsylvania nearly succeeded in successfully storming Confederate trench lines with a variation on an attack by column. That was a method the French army had sometimes used to advantage, advancing with men packed into a narrow front to maintain tight control and relentless forward movement and concentrate their blow at a single point on the enemy's line. The problem was that most of the men in a column were unable to fire without hitting the men in front, and the formation was extremely vulnerable during its approach: a rifle shot or cannonball sent into "so large a living target" was sure to find its mark.

Upton tried a hybrid approach, a formation three regiments wide and four deep. The first line, with bayonets only, was to turn left and right upon reaching the enemy's works; the next, with weapons loaded, would press ahead to assault a second line of trenches; the third and fourth lines were to provide support, reinforcement, and defense against a possible counterattack. His plan was noteworthy for the thoroughness of preparation, the assignment of specific tasks to each subordinate commander, and his repetition of the instructions to all assembled officers—as obvious as these all seem today. The attackers reached their objectives, taking 1,200 prisoners, but Upton was forced to fall back when the division to his left failed to move in support as planned. But he proved his point, that tactics were more than drill, and all the men and weapons in the world no use without an effective organizational system to put them in action where they were needed.

"THE DAY HAS GONE AGAINST US"

The chief organizational woes afflicting the Army of the Potomac were still its staff and communications. With his usual attention to technical detail, McClellan during the Peninsula Campaign had introduced the use of both the electric telegraph and a new alphabetic system of semaphore flag signals for visual transmission of messages. But wagons frequently ran over and cut the telegraph wires strung along the ground, a lack of trained operators was a constant problem, and a rivalry between the Signal Corps and the new Military Telegraph organization led to confused lines of authority and then a disastrous organizational decision by McClellan to simply divide responsibility on technological rather than functional lines, giving the Signal Corps the flag system for field use, the Military Telegraph electrical signals for strategic communications, notably between McClellan's headquarters and Washington.

But signal flags were slow and readily obscured by smoke on the battlefield. To communicate during an actual battle with his commanders, McClellan was generally left with the traditional method of sending an aide on horseback. Gettysburg would be the first battle in which a Union commander was able to communicate directly by electric telegraph with all of his corps and division headquarters.

As he waited at Fox's Gap under the rays of the noonday sun and a steady rain of Confederate shells, failures of communication were no doubt much on Jacob Cox's mind. Although the message that had reached him at 8:30 a.m. from his corps commander, Jesse Reno, promised that the other three divisions of the Ninth Corps were on their way to reinforce him, it was 2 p.m. before even the first arrived, having been mistakenly sent up the National Road past the turnoff to Fox's Gap through a series of miscarried instructions. Hooker appeared at the base of Turner's Gap at 3 p.m., spent an hour assessing the situation, and did not have his First Corps in position to move until 4. By then four of Longstreet's brigades, having covered the thirteen miles from Hagerstown at a blistering march of four miles per hour, were atop the mountain and engaging the Union forces on two sides.

McClellan by this time had appeared on the scene, too, and from the knoll near the intersection of the National Road and Old Sharpsburg Road where Pleasonton's artillery had been firing since morning, he watched the battle from a distance. The war correspondent for the *New York Tribune,* George Smalley, stood nearby observing the commanding general's strange detachment. Occasionally a staff officer would ride up, "only to be sent off again at once." Although it was, Smalley wrote, "from a military point of view a very critical moment," McClellan's manner was "almost that of a disinterested spectator; or of a general watching maneuvers." His one action, late in the day, was to issue a pompous and thoroughly redundant order for a "general advance."

Fighting their way up the even more arduous climb to the north of Turner's Gap along winding old roads and crossing rocky woods and fields, Hooker's men managed to take the crest by nightfall, though not the gap itself. The Ninth Corps held Fox's Gap, though its commander had been killed just before sunset when he had gone to survey the scene. (D. H. Hill gloatingly reported that Reno, "a renegade Virginian," had been dispatched "by a happy shot from the Twenty-third North Carolina.") Cox assumed command.

Expecting the battle for Turner's Gap to resume at first light, the Union soldiers instead awoke to an eerie scene of empty devastation. The Confederates had slipped down the mountain during the moonless night, leaving their dead scattered grotesquely behind stone walls and lodged in crevices between boulders. Trees were splintered into bizarre twisted forms.

McClellan's army spent the morning burying the dead; McClellan spent the morning dispatching self-congratulatory letters and telegrams to Washington and to his wife. "Just sent you a telegram informing you that we yesterday gained a glorious and complete victory," he wrote Ellen at 9:30 a.m. "Every moment adds to its importance. . . . How glad I am for my country that it is delivered from immediate peril! . . . If I can believe one-tenth of what is reported, God has seldom given an army a greater victory." He wired Halleck that Lee was "making for Shepherdstown" across the Potomac "in a perfect panic & Genl Lee last night stated publicly that he must admit they had been shockingly whipped." At 10 a.m. he sent a second lengthy telegram to Washington, "Information this moment rec'd completely confirms the rout & demoralization of the rebel Army . . . It is stated that Lee gives his loss as fifteen thousand."

There was plenty of evidence that McClellan considered his work done by chasing Lee out of Maryland. Lincoln wired that afternoon: "Destroy the rebel army, if possible." But that was not the message his commanders perceived in McClellan's actions that day. McClellan would later say as much himself, insisting that only "sheer necessity" had justified sending his "thoroughly exhausted and depleted" army into action before it had had time to reorganize and resupply in Washington. Therefore its only proper course in pursuing Lee was to "put a stop to the invasion, save Baltimore and Washington, and throw him back across the Potomac," so that the important work of refitting could continue.

At noon he and his staff rode over to Fox's Gap to see the spot where Reno had been killed, then continued to Turner's Gap and passed over Joseph Hooker's battlefield of the previous day. He stopped there at a farmhouse which had been pressed into service as a hospital, around which some of the wounded men for whom there was no accommodation in the house were lying on the grass. Entering the house for a few minutes, McClellan emerged with tears running down his otherwise impassive face, mounted his horse, and headed down the road toward Boonsboro, following in the wake of Lee's army that had already been on the move for most of the last twenty-four hours.

Victory had done little to conciliate growing ill will among his corps commanders, nor had McClellan's own actions on September 15. It had been at Lincoln's suggestion that McClellan appointed Burnside and Sumner overall wing commanders in charge of two corps each, but he delayed the official order placing Hooker's First Corps under Burnside's direction until the fourteenth. Hooker, whose self-confidence, self-assertion, and good looks—six feet tall, strong blue-gray eyes, a full head of curling bronze hair with side-burns to match—were exceeded only by his naked ambition, played off McClellan's already apparent coolness toward his old friend by simply acting as if Burnside did not exist when he arrived at the foot of Turner's Gap. Burnside sent him orders four times directing his corps into action, and finally had to send an order directly to his lead division to move before Hooker complied. Hooker subsequently tried to take all the credit for the victory in his official report, even falsely claiming that Cox had been retreating when he arrived, and he had saved the day singlehandedly.

A year apart at West Point, Burnside and McClellan were "Burn" and "Mac" to one another, their friendship cemented when Burnside, failed in business and politics in his native Rhode Island, had gone west seeking employment and was hired as treasurer of the Illinois Central when McClellan was its vice-president. A genuinely humble man who acknowledged his own limitations, Burnside had twice turned down Lincoln's offer to replace McClellan as commander of the Army of the Potomac, an act of loyalty lost on a man as deeply insecure as McClellan, who apparently drew from the information—which came from Burnside himself—only the fact that his old friend was now a threat to him.

The arrival from Washington of Fitz John Porter with a division of regular army troops from his Fifth Corps on the fifteenth did nothing to ease matters. Porter, a favorite and confidant of McClellan's, had indiscreetly sent Burnside a series of increasingly sarcastic and insubordinate messages aiming to undermine General John Pope when he had briefly replaced McClellan as commander of Union forces during the debacle of Second Bull Run. Worse, there was no doubt that Porter was parroting McClellan's borderline treasonous views on the matter. Having convinced himself of the fantasy that his enemies in Washington were deliberately engineering battlefield defeats to discredit him, McClellan actually sought to do the same to Pope, writing Ellen just before the battle, "I have a strong idea that Pope will be thrashed during the coming week—& very badly whipped he will be & ought to be—such a villain as he is ought to bring defeat upon any cause that employs him."

Porter's messages, which Burnside felt obliged to report to higher authority, would become the principal evidence in Porter's subsequent court martial and cashiering from the army two months after Antietam. Burnside's act was already a source of seething resentment to Porter, and by extension to McClellan.

Orders from McClellan on the morning of the fifteenth poured fuel on smoldering enmities. Apparently acting at Hooker's behest, McClellan suspended his order of the day before placing the First Corps under Burnside. At midday, he sent Burnside a chiding note demanding to know why his Ninth Corps had not yet begun to move from Fox's Gap, and ordered Porter's division to "push by them" and take the lead in the advance to Boonsboro. Porter added a supercilious endorsement stating that Burnside's troops had "obstructed my movements" by failing to move "three hours after the hour designated for him." The resulting tangle of commands on the road that inevitably ensued from this abrupt change of responsibilities and marching orders was a warning of more trouble to come.

So was the camp scuttlebutt that Porter was all show and no fight and that he was already doing his best to encourage McClellan's view that the Army of the Potomac need not take any more risks now that Lee was running off. As Porter's Fifth Corps—which McClellan was keeping as his reserve—pushed past Cox's men at Fox's Gap, a Massachusetts soldier loudly observed that he didn't see any particular difference between regulars and volunteers. A swaggering sergeant in Porter's corps held up his perfectly burnished musket to show its regulation spotlessness and retorted, "*Here's* where the difference comes in." The Massachusetts volunteer shot back, "Yes, we use ours to fight with."

At the battle for Crampton's Gap on the fourteenth, the story had been much the same as at Fox's and Turner's gaps: the same dilatory start, with Franklin's corps not ready to attack until late afternoon; the same successful delaying tactics by outnumbered Confederate forces hastily moved up to the mountain ridge; the same furious uphill fight with bayonet charges of incredible bravery by Union regiments against rebels lodged on high ground behind stone-walled roads; the same desultory denouement, as Franklin waited to the next day to cautiously advance. When he looked down the mountain the morning after his victory, he saw that McLaws had sealed off the entire width of Pleasant Valley between South Mountain and Elk Ridge, with "a large force . . . in two lines of battle," which—a true disciple of his commander—Franklin reported outnumbered him "two to one." In fact he outnumbered them 3 to 1, but that was enough to make him halt.

McClellan had ordered Franklin to fire a gun every few minutes on his march to Burkittsville to alert the garrison at Harper's Ferry that help was on the way. Now Franklin's men could hear artillery firing from Harper's Ferry, as the encircling siege by the rebels began. Late on the evening of the fourteenth Lee had sent McLaws and Jackson orders to abandon the attempt on Harper's Ferry now that they had lost the South Mountain gaps, and to head back to the ford at Shepherdstown to cover his retreat across the Potomac. "The day has gone against us and this army will go by Sharpsburg and cross the river," he wrote McLaws, who was to make his way as he could to reunite with the rest of the army.

That decision changed abruptly as dawn broke. At about 8:30 a.m. on the fifteenth, Franklin's men suddenly heard the guns go silent, replaced by wild yells from the Confederates in front of them stretching across Pleasant Valley. "What the hell are you fellows cheering for?" one of Franklin's skirmishers shouted. "Because Harper's Ferry is gone up, God damn you," a rebel replied.

TIME'S ARROW

The news of Harper's Ferry imminent surrender reached Lee at daybreak on the fifteenth. At noon a second message from Jackson caught up with him at Sharpsburg, announcing his success and advising that all his forces but A. P. Hill's, which had borne the brunt of the engagement, would be ready to march that evening. "To what place shall they move?" he asked.

Lee sent messages to his scattered forces ordering them to rejoin him at Sharpsburg as fast as they could. "We will make our stand on those hills," he said, indicating the high ground that separated the town of Sharpsburg from Antietam Creek a few miles to the east. As he later explained simply, "I went into Maryland to give battle." To return to Virginia having forgone even a long-shot chance to "crush" McClellan would be looked on in both North and South as a failure of his entire campaign.

The one bright spot for the Union forces in the loss of Harper's Ferry was a daring overnight cavalry breakout just hours before the surrender. Seeing their chances of holding out against the encircling artillery and Jackson's large detachment of approaching infantry dwindling, and with cavalry unable to contribute directly to the fight in any case, the commander of the Union cavalry force at Harper's Ferry declared his intention to try to make a run for it and at least save what he could of his horses and men. The hapless commander of the garrison, Dixon Miles, objected vehemently, again citing his orders to defend Harper's Ferry "to the last extremity," but finally gave his reluctant assent. On the evening of the fourteenth the horsemen quietly assembled at 8 p.m. near the pontoon bridge crossing the Potomac, under strict orders to maintain silence lest their departure set off a stampede among the infantry. An officer gamely assured his men that "next morning they would either be in Pennsylvania, or in Hell, or on the way to Richmond" to the Confederate prison there. Their baggage wagons, ambulances, extra horses, and tents were ordered left behind, along with the instruments of the 12th Illinois's regimental brass band. ("We missed the tents afterward," one of its officers acknowledged, "but managed to get along without the band.")

Forming single file, they set out across the bridge at a walk, each company breaking into a gallop as it turned left onto the road that ran next to the canal on the far bank, the horses catching the pace from those in front. It was a pitch-black night, and the road that ran between Elk Mountain and the river was over wild country, nothing like the rolling farmland of the wide valleys to the east. The road itself was rough and rocky, plunging up and down steep climbs and drops. Passing unnoticed by the artillerymen atop Maryland Heights, they were challenged by a Confederate picket at the base of the mountain who fired a few ineffectual shots and galloped on.

It was a killing pace, the men clinging to their horses' manes to stay in their saddles on hills and bends unseen in the darkness. A sharp turn and a drop to the left, and then they were racing along a straight but narrow path that again followed the river and canal, hugging the edge of a looming cliff that closed in tightly from the right. At the stone bridge where the road crossed the Antietam near its mouth at the Antietam Iron Works, another Confederate sentry fired without effect, but making it clear the town ahead was likely already in rebel hands. At the road to Hagerstown in the center of Sharpsburg they were again fired on, this time from a volley of musketry that illuminated the night in a "sheet of flame," followed by a few shells fired after them as the cavalrymen pressed past. They then slowed to a walk as they picked their way around enemy bivouacs lit by campfires, moving on north toward Pennsylvania over fields, creeks, and fences.

Daylight found them near Williamsport, where the road from Hagerstown ran, when they heard the distinctive low rumbling sound of heavy wagon wheels approaching. Acting quickly, the Union cavalrymen blocked the road, and when the lead wagon came up quietly surrounded the driver with leveled weapons and ordered him to turn right on a road heading north to Greencastle, across the Pennsylvania line. Each of the following wagons was waylaid in turn as it came up, before their drivers knew what was happening. "A change of governments was probably never more quietly or speedily effected," commented an Illinois horseman. The wagons proved to be the reserve ammunition and supply trains of Longstreet's command, heading down to rejoin Lee's army. In all some 100 wagons were captured and carried off to Union lines.

The escape of 1,500 Union horsemen from under the noses of their besiegers was of no major strategic consequence, except for depriving Jackson of some fine horses the Confederates could have used. But the "Harper's Ferry Skedaddlers," as they were ever after known, offered a vivid object lesson that in war, as in life, methodical preparation is sometimes no substitute for dash and risk-taking—the lesson that McClellan's action, or rather inaction, on the fifteenth showed he still had not learned.

Having forced the South Mountain gaps, McClellan again had an enormous advantage over Lee's splintered force in front of him, thirty-five brigades to the fourteen of Longstreet and D. H. Hill. Jackson was sixteen miles away at Harper's Ferry, with a difficult ford to cross at Shepherdstown; Walker twenty miles away at Loudoun Heights on the far side of the Shenandoah; McLaws and R. H. Anderson bottled up at the bottom of Pleasant Valley by Franklin, with no way to reach Sharpsburg now but the long way around on the Virginia side, crossing the pontoon bridge to Harper's Ferry and then following Jackson's path north, a march of at least twenty-five miles. Lee would be without reinforcement for at least twenty-four hours, more likely forty-eight or more.

From Turner's Gap to Sharpsburg was but seven miles. If McClellan had decided to fight Lee that day, nothing stood in the way. For a second time he let opportunity to slip through his fingers. The afternoon of Monday the fifteenth found him standing on a rise to the east of Antietam Creek, which would become his headquarters for the coming battle, observing the enemy artillery aiming their rifled guns in their direction. "As his firing was good," McClellan later wrote to the indignant fury of his other commanders who were there, "the hill was soon cleared of all save Fitz John Porter and myself." Contrary to the implied slight of their courage, McClellan had in fact ordered them off, remaining to confer with Porter alone. "The discarded officers did not hear what passed between McClellan and Porter," Carman reported, but Hooker for one concluded that "there would be no aggressive action that night or next day should McClellan listen to the advice of Fitz John Porter."

It was obvious to his more aggressive commanders like Cox and Hooker that every delay from that point on only accrued to Lee's relative advantage. "Instead of making his reconnaissance at three in the afternoon of Monday," Cox pointedly observed, "it might have been made at ten in the morning, and the battle could have been fought before night." Or had McClellan pushed forward at once to the bridge at the mouth of Antietam and the Shepherdstown ford above, "nothing . . . could have prevented the interposition of the whole National army between the separated wings of the Confederates."

After a tough night march over terrible roads which zigzagged like a sawtooth along the edges of steep ravines that fall into the Virginia side of the Potomac, the lead elements of Jackson's two divisions from Harper's Ferry were within nine miles of Sharpsburg by dawn on September 16, Walker's division close behind. The divisions of McLaws and R. H. Anderson were another twenty-four hours behind, their departure delayed by a stream of paroled Union prisoners crossing the other way on the pontoon bridge over the Potomac at Harper's Ferry.

Another day, another opportunity lost. McClellan telegraphed Washington that morning, "Heavy fog has thus far prevented us doing more than to ascertain that some of the enemy are still there. Will attack as soon as situation of enemy is developed." But no orders came as the day wore on. "To see how they love me even now," McClellan had said of his men upon resuming command of the Army of the Potomac two weeks earlier, and, like all who crave love, he knew how to elicit love. Passing a New York artillery battery taking up its position later on the sixteenth, he stopped and saluted each driver and cannoneer individually as they went by. Which "of our other great generals ever did this?" asked an admiring soldier. "They love him, they trust him, they will follow him wherever he leads."

But with his talent for never seeing failures as his fault, or even as failures, his eagerness for success never equaled his anxiety for approval, and the day slipped by. McClellan would explain afterward that more time was needed for "examining the ground, finding fords, clearing approaches, and hurrying up the ammunition and supply trains." In a well-regarded military history published thirty years after the battle, the lieutenant colonel of Holmes's regiment, Francis W. Palfrey, who would be severely wounded and taken prisoner at Antietam, offered a succinct eulogy to what might have been. "If he had used the priceless hours of the 15th September, and the still precious, though less precious hours of the 16th as he might have, his name would have stood high in the roll of great commanders; but he let those hours go by."

"The value of time," lamented Cox, "was one of the things McClellan never understood."

4

ORGANIZING
FOR CARNAGE

Jonathan Letterman, MD

BURDENS OF REFORM

If ever a man showed the weight of the world in the expression in his eyes, it was the man in striped shirtsleeves seated on the ground with a group of casually posed Union officers and men in a photograph taken toward the end of the Maryland Campaign. When he died in California after the war at age forty-seven, heartbroken by the sudden death of his young wife and chronically ill from dysentery, twin legacies of war and personal tragedy, Dr. Jonathan Letterman left no private letters or other intimate record of what he had personally endured as medical director of the Army of the Potomac beyond the glimpse captured in the lens of Alexander Gardner's camera that day. The nine other soldiers in the photograph, wearing uniform coats, look directly at the camera. Worn but relaxed, a couple of them puff cigars. Letterman alone stares off to the side, his eyes heavy with vacant preoccupation.

He had spent the days before the Battle of South Mountain scouting out churches, hotels, schoolhouses, homes, barns, and fields for tent camps that could serve as hospitals in Frederick and Middletown, distributing among the army corps the 200 improved ambulances he had hastily ordered and which had

*Dr. Jonathan Letterman, fifth from left, with
members of the headquarters staff of the Army of the
Potomac a few weeks after the Battle of Antietam*

miraculously arrived in Frederick in time to meet the advancing army, and untangling shipments of medical supplies he had arranged to have forwarded by rail from Baltimore but now caught in the chaos at the ruined Monocacy bridge outside of Frederick. When the firing stopped at nightfall on the fourteenth, he hastened back to Middletown to oversee the reception of the thousands of wounded at the first stage of the evacuation system he had devised. The next morning he was off again with McClellan's headquarters staff to see to preparations for hospitals in Boonsboro and Keedysville, and the organization of scores of field hospitals near the ground where an even larger battle now seemed imminent.

Letterman was young, energetic, an experienced career officer and surgeon. Born in western Pennsylvania, he had followed his father's footsteps to Jefferson Medical College, then entered the army as an assistant surgeon, serving a dozen years in small outposts during the Indian wars against the Seminoles, Apaches, and Utes, and rising to the rank of major.

He carried the special burden of a man whose burning drive is to make things work, but who lacked the compensating inner resources—Hooker's ambition, McClellan's self-regard, Lincoln's humor—of other great organizers. He took everything seriously, and though he did not show it by word or deed, he took everything hard. Of his appointment as medical director in July 1862, he later said, "I knew nothing of it until it was done. It was a position I did not seek; it was one I could not decline."

The first crisis he faced was 20,000 sick and wounded men, a quarter of the entire army, left by the retreat on the Peninsula at Harrison's Landing; in two weeks he had them all evacuated by ship, as many as 5,000 in one day.

His second crisis was to somehow institute, on the fly, nothing short of a revolution in "the frightful state of disorder existing in the arrangements for removing the wounded from the field of battle," that Surgeon General William A. Hammond pointed to in the shambles of Second Bull Run. "The Medical Department of the entire army," wrote Letterman of the hectic two weeks that followed, "had to be reorganized and resupplied while upon a rapid march . . . and almost in the face of the enemy."

His great and lasting innovations all came from a willingness to confront a truth others shied away from: that thousands of men were going to be maimed and wounded in every battle, and the only way to deal with that was to be thoroughly prepared for it. More than a few Civil War generals at first hadn't believed that was a particularly good idea. From the start of the war, all regiments were required to have a surgeon and assistant surgeon to tend to the sick and wounded, but any more pointed readying of plans for reception of the injured, they feared, would be bad for morale. Even as intelligent a man as General-in-Chief Halleck thought that the presence of medical personnel on the battlefield might sow panic among soldiers, whose minds, as they marched into enemy fire, needed to be kept from straying to such unwholesome directions as the contemplation of their personal fate.

And as far as many regimental commanders were concerned, hospitals, ambulances, medical supplies, and the necessity of detailing men to help with all such things were an intrusion on military affairs, to be jettisoned at the first opportunity. Surgeons had responsibility for medical matters but no control over the resources required to carry out those duties, a situation ripe for the sadistic exercise of petty, by-the-book abuse by commanders so inclined, the practice upon which soldiers of later wars would confer the aptly descriptive title "chickenshit."

The only man permanently assigned to the regimental surgeon was his hospital steward, a warrant officer whose duties included minor surgery and charge of the dispensary. Regulations called for the commander to detail two cooks and ten nurses from the ranks for each regimental hospital, but some simply refused to do so, or assigned the jobs to sick or convalescent men already in the hospital and barely able to carry out such duties. Alfred Castleman, surgeon of a Wisconsin volunteer regiment in the Army of the Potomac, resisted his colonel's attempts to "cut down" his staff of three nurses and two cooks, and promptly discovered the power of a commanding officer to make his subordinate's life miserable through both literal and imaginative reading of army regulations. He was constantly berated for supposed irregularities in his uniform. The quartermaster refused to allow him to draw from the regiment's hospital fund, intended to provide special food for the sick and wounded based on the money they were saving by not consuming their normal army rations of coffee, hardtack, and salt meat. "I find vast trouble in doing justice to the sick, in consequence of the unwarrantable interference of military officers in matters of which they are about as well qualified to judge as would be so many of their mules," he fumed in his diary a few weeks later.

The culmination of the campaign of petty tyranny came when his hospital attendants and patients presented Castleman a dress sword as a testimonial of his selfless devotion to their care. He was immediately reprimanded by his brigade commander for a supposed violation of regulations in accepting the gift, and ordered to return to the regular ranks all of his hospital nurses who had participated in the presentation. The replacements he was sent were mostly men awaiting discharge for disabilities, a set of incompetent brutes; one who was placed in charge of dispensing medicines immediately made a blunder that poisoned three men, one fatally. And so it went.

Letterman's predecessor, Charles Tripler, a regular-army by-the-book officer, had allocated only three hospital tents per regiment, enough to shelter 3 percent of its men. When the reality of war demonstrated that waves of dysentery or single battles could leave half a regiment as casualties, some regimental hospitals were overwhelmed while those of nearby regiments sat idle, turning away any wounded soldiers who showed up at the wrong tent seeking aid. Tripler made things worse by refusing to remove the sick to general hospitals in the rear, dismissing such facilities as "nuisances, to be tolerated only because there are occasions when they are absolutely necessary—as, for instance, when the army is put in motion." He was equally dismissive of criticisms that hospitals in the field lacked the most basic necessities for caring for the sick and wounded, from food to eating utensils to bedpans. In his official report he offered a sarcastic apology. "The army was, perhaps, unfortunate," he wrote, "in having a medical director who supposed it was assembled to make war, and that cartridges were more indispensable than bed quilts."

In the retreat from the Peninsula huge stocks of equipment were abandoned, with medical supplies usually the first to go. "It would appear that many officers consider medical supplies to be the least important in an army," Letterman complained in an official report. "Medical officers have been frequently censured . . . for want of articles required in time of action, when these have been left behind, or thrown upon the roadside by orders they were powerless to resist."

The situation with regard to evacuating the wounded from the battlefield was, if anything, worse. The standard army ambulances were buggies notorious for the excruciating shaking they subjected wounded men to ("the two wheeled ambulances which were then in vogue as one form of torture," Oliver Wendell Holmes termed them after his experience when he was shot through the chest at Ball's Bluff early in the war), earning them the nickname "gut busters" or "avalanches."

That was when ambulances were available at all. Letterman noted that they were frequently waylaid by commanders for use as personal taxis or delivery wagons and "no system had anywhere been devised for their management." The members of the regimental band were supposed to serve as ambulance attendants and stretcher bearers, with predictable results. The hired teamsters who drove the ambulances were often incompetent, frequently drunk, and ran away under fire; nearly all deserted at Second Bull Run, abetted by government clerks and other civilians who had responded to a call for volunteers to help the wounded, but, having dosed themselves liberally with the whiskey in the medical supplies on the way out, bribed the drivers with the remaining stocks to take them back to Washington when they recoiled at the terrors they found waiting for them at the scene of the battle.

A week later 600 wounded men remained on the battlefield. "Many have died of starvation," Surgeon General Hammond angrily informed the secretary of war; "many more will die in consequence of exhaustion, and all have endured torments which might have been avoided. . . . consequences which will inevitably ensue on the next important engagement if nothing is done to obviate them."

Dr. Henry Bowditch, a Boston physician and member of the U.S. Sanitary Commission, came face to face with the "abominable system, or rather no system of ambulances now in use in our army." He literally had to take the reins from the drunken driver of an ambulance he had joined to travel to the Bull Run battlefield. Hammond

afterward told the shocked doctor that he "could not tell him anything new" about the "atrocities" of the current situation.

Letterman and Hammond were brought in to shake things up,
and did. Hammond owed his appointment to the energetic efforts
of the Sanitary Commission, a quasi-public corporation modeled
on successful efforts by British civilians to raise funds to alleviate
unsanitary conditions and improve the health of soldiers in the
Crimean War. Tripler, voicing the view of many in the old army,
scorned such outside meddlers as "sensation seekers, village doctors, and strong-minded women." But with its influential connections among New York business and civic leaders, the commission
promptly got the ear of important senators, and of Lincoln. Lob-
bying for a change in the army's ossified seniority system, which
had left its medical department at the start of the war in the hands
of an eighty-two-year-old surgeon general, the head of the Sanitary
Commission told Lincoln the story about the man who each day
picked from a barrel the most spoiled apple to eat, with the result he
never tasted a good one. Lincoln liked the joke, and agreed to ignore
seniority altogether in selecting the next surgeon general.

Hammond was thirty-three years old and held the lowest rank
in the Medical Bureau, but he was a renowned academic physician
who had conducted important research on scurvy and was probably the leading expert on hospital design in America, having studied European hospitals for a year during his earlier service in the
army. His immediate predecessor as surgeon general had proudly
reported that he had underspent the department's budget of $2.4
million for the fiscal year covering the first year of the war. Hammond demanded and got five times that, then promptly overspent
another 10 percent: this was no time for fiscal virtue. He had met
Letterman while working on construction of a new army hospital in
Parkersburg in western Virginia, and had been impressed. The new
surgeon general used his influence with McClellan—Hammond
was a professional acquaintance of the general's brother, a prominent Philadelphia physician—to secure Letterman's appointment

FIG. 458.—The "TRIPLER" ambulance wagon—side view.   FIG. 459.—The same—rear view.

The improved four-wheel ambulance

on McClellan's staff. One of Hammond's other first official acts was to "unwind the red tape" and authorize Letterman to hire contract surgeons and purchase necessary medical supplies "on the spot," without waiting for the usual approval from Washington.

One of Letterman's first official acts was to issue new regulations establishing the army's first dedicated ambulance corps. He had obviously been thinking about the details well in advance of his appointment as McClellan's medical director on July 4, 1862. Key was to have a group of trained and permanently assigned men, with their own officers, all under the direct orders of the medical director of each corps, to carry the wounded from the battlefield and tend the ambulances. When on the march, the ambulances would take their place at the front of all wagon trains, to be available for immediate use. Their horses, wagons, and equipment were to remain at all times under their sole control. Ambulance corpsmen were to be given a distinctive green band to wear on their caps.

Tripler, with the consummate bureaucrat's instinctive suspicion of novelty, had predictably rejected earlier proposals along the same lines ("It is now too late to raise, drill, and equip so elaborate an establishment. There is nothing new in the plan, nothing not thought of and well weighed years ago"). But McClellan, an inveterate logistical organizer if nothing else, approved Letterman's proposal at once, issuing General Orders No. 147 essentially adopting Letterman's plan verbatim. Letterman also hastened the requisition of a much-improved four-wheel ambulance to replace the infamous two-wheel gut-busters.

There had been no opportunity to carry out so extensive a reform in the turbulent weeks that followed during the withdrawal from the Peninsula. South Mountain and Antietam would be the first real test.

CAMP RELAPSE

It is a truism that disease killed more soldiers than did bullets in wars prior to the twentieth century. A visitor from the twentieth or twenty-first century to an army camp in the Civil War would have had no trouble identifying the reason. The sheer squalor of the men and the grounds they occupied had to be seen to believed, which no doubt explains the failure of reenactors' encampments and museum dioramas to reproduce the ubiquitous reality of army camps which "fairly wallowed in abominable filth," as one inspector reported.

Coming from a world in which cooking, cleaning, and laundering were almost universally regarded as women's work, the soldiers who now had to fend for themselves looked upon any nicety or refinement in these necessary tasks as fussy or effeminate. It was the natural inclination of many young men freed from the restraints of domesticity to simply let themselves go, and live like bears, or worse. Anthony Trollope, visiting the Army of the Potomac camps around Washington, noted the resentment of the Northern volunteer soldier of the presumption "that he is to be treated like a child in the nursery—that he must change his shirt so often, wash himself at such and such intervals, and go through a certain process of cleansing his outward garments daily." It was worse among men from rural areas or the towns of the West, Trollope observed, to whom "indifference to appearances is . . . a matter of pride. A foul shirt is a flag of triumph. A craving for soap and water is as the wail of the weak and the confession of cowardice." It was a milestone when Letterman succeeded after nearly a year in his position in having an order enforced that men must change their underwear once a week, and change their shirts and bathe twice a week.

Letterman also struggled for months to enforce orders requiring men to use latrines and to bury kitchen waste, stable manure, and blood and offal from slaughtered animals. Regulations required pit latrines to be dug and covered with fresh earth each day, but in practice they were so repellent, nothing but a pole to sit on suspended over a slit in the ground, that many soldiers out of revulsion or modesty ducked into any available spot instead. It was a constant war for surgeons to "police" a camp to follow basic sanitary rules. In places beyond their control, or where an army remained for any length of time, conditions invariably went downhill fast. "Men were in the habit of going out into the bushes, and not infrequently some 30 or 40 feet from some of their tents and relieving themselves," reported Grant's surgeon during the prolonged siege of Vicksburg; "in fact, human excrement has been promiscuously deposited in every direction."

Worst was the sprawling tent camp in Alexandria, Virginia, established to house sick and wounded soldiers hastily evacuated from the Peninsula along with assorted stragglers and deserters rounded up in the ensuing chaos. Demoralized, weak, undisciplined, many suffering from intestinal disorders, the 7,000 inhabitants of "Camp Convalescent"—promptly renamed "Camp Misery" or "Camp Relapse" by its inhabitants—fouled the surrounding area with abandon. An inspector from the Sanitary Commission reported finding the three-acre campsite completely encircled with "a broad belt, on which is deposited an almost perfect layer of human excrement."

Dysentery and other diarrheal illnesses became the No. 1 killer in the army, followed by typhoid, pneumonia, and malaria. In all, about 1 in 12 Union soldiers died of disease during the war, versus 1 in 25 from battle wounds; in the Confederate army the corresponding figures were 1 in 8 and 1 in 14. Dysentery was such an inevitable feature of army life that, Holmes recalled, he expected it "every time I went back" following his furloughs home recuperating from battle wounds. An estimated 99.5 percent of Civil War soldiers contracted diarrheal diseases at some point.

No theory of disease had yet correctly identified the causative agents of bacteria, viruses, and parasites behind these ailments, or the role of contaminated water, flies, and mosquitoes in transmitting them. But the belief that foul smells were to blame—the "noxious effluvia" and "miasmas" that hovered over rotting food, uncovered excrement, decaying corpses, putrid swamps, and the exhalations of crowded men—at least pointed vaguely enough in the right direction to suggest effective preventive measures that could break the chain of transmission. The Sanitary Commission printed and distributed to surgeons and officers thousands of copies of pamphlets ("Rules for Preserving the Health of the Soldier") counseling cleanliness in cooking utensils, burying of waste, fresh air in sleeping quarters, and avoidance of malarial swamps—along with an equal helping of contemporary medical old wives' tales, such as wearing flannel belly bands, not eating baked bread until it had thoroughly cooled, and warding off dysentery by sleeping on freshly cut pine boughs.

One area where Letterman had no difficulty enlisting the cooperation of the soldiers was in his efforts to improve their diet. The standard-issue ration of coffee, hardtack, and salt pork was as much a nutritional as a culinary disaster, neither alleviated by soldiers' creative attempts at variety by combining the components in every conceivable permutation—hardtack crumbled into coffee, hardtack fried in salt pork, raw salt pork sandwiched between hardtack. The only medically recognizable benefit of the basic diet was that boiling water for the ubiquitous coffee incidentally sterilized pathogens. The only thing that could make the soldier's standard ration worse was the salt beef sometimes substituted for pork, which was so vile, reeking, and hard as wood that it was more the object of sport than consumption. Pickled with so much salt and saltpeter, it required soaking in a brook overnight before it could even be cooked. Soldiers exercised their wit inventing humorous employments for chunks of army-issue salt beef, or staged elaborate mock funerals for especially hideous specimens, solemnly marching it to the company latrine for internment followed by a volley of rifle fire over the "grave."

Express companies made regular deliveries of boxes sent by wives, mothers, and sisters packed with homemade preserves, pies, cakes, cookies, and candies, and sutlers did a brisk business relieving men of their $13-a-month pay selling dubious cheese, butter, canned condensed milk, and molasses cookies at outrageously inflated prices, but what soldiers seemed to crave more than anything was onions and potatoes. ("List of articles wanted," began one Massachusetts soldier's letter to his wife during the Maryland Campaign, "Bermuda onions and a few potatoes, they are 50 cents a peck here," then, almost as an afterthought, a request for dried beef and chocolates.)

Enough had been learned from trial and error aboard ships of the British Royal Navy about the causes of scurvy and its prevention to know that the diet of the Civil War soldier was a catastrophe in waiting. Immediately upon arriving at Harrison's Landing, Letterman detected unmistakable signs of the disease—listlessness, fatigue, bleeding gums—and ordered tons of tomatoes, potatoes, onions, squash, cabbage, and other fresh vegetables, along with 1,500 boxes of lemons, to attack the problem. It would remain a challenge throughout the war to maintain a supply of fresh vegetables to hundreds of thousands of men on the move, and subsequent experiments with substituting bricks of desiccated vegetables or potatoes were a double failure: the troops gagged on them (one likened the cooked product to a dirty brook with leaves floating on top) and the drying process and long cooking time needed to reconstitute these "desecrated vegetables," as soldiers dubbed them, essentially destroyed their entire vitamin C content, rendering nil their contribution as a scurvy preventive.

Letterman became something of a bore on the subject, acknowledging that the authority of medical staff over commissary matters was "entirely advisory," but relentlessly reminding medical directors of each corps that it was nonetheless their "imperative duty" to raise with commanders as often as necessary this matter "indispensable to the health and consequent efficiency of the troops," and "not to relax your efforts" to see that fresh vegetables are provided—at a minimum, potatoes three times a week and onions twice. Regimental surgeons in turn were ordered to record, in their official weekly sick reports, how often such issues had been made. It was a small but telling demonstration of Letterman's mastery of bureaucratic procedure, combining moral authority with whatever bureaucratic levers were available to make good a want of actual legal authority.

HEROIC MEASURES

The piles of amputated arms, feet, hands, and legs that vividly feature in so many descriptions of Civil War field hospitals were a gauge both of medical knowledge during what has been termed "the very end of the medical Middle Ages" and of military technology at the very beginnings of its era of modern lethality. The Minié ball was capable of rendering horrific damage to the human body. Its hollow conical shape, soft lead composition, and relatively slow speed guaranteed it would flatten, spread, and deform when striking flesh and bone, sometimes breaking into multiple fragments that could drill gaping exit wounds and leave inches-wide voids in shattered bones.

Many surgeons initially thought the wounds they were seeing must be the work of a diabolical weapon like an exploding bullet. Those did exist: the Union army purchased some 10,000 experimental explosive Minié balls, which subsequently fell into Confederate hands. Fashioned with a chamber filled with fulminate connected to an internal fuse ignited by the discharge of the gun, they either exploded in flight into a lethally jagged chunk of flying metal or even more destructively exploded after penetrating the body. Six well-documented cases of explosive bullets were recorded in the

Minié balls deformed on impact with the human body, from The Medical and Surgical History of the War of Rebellion

monumental *Medical and Surgical History of the War of Rebellion* that the surgeon general's office published after the war. But most of the cases of "explosive" bullets were simply ordinary Minié balls that had undergone the ordinary extreme distortion on impact that was in fact almost indistinguishable from the effects of an explosion.

In the cases of flesh wounds, the sensation of being shot was described as a sharp sting or a hot wire passing through the affected part, but when nerves were struck the pain could be excruciating, often seeming to come from a distant point where the nerves attached. More severe injuries, especially shattering damage to large bones or penetration of internal organs, invariably was followed by shock. Jagged fragments from exploding shells, varying in size from a few grains to many pounds, tended to cut through arteries inflicting "injuries of the gravest character," while injuries from solid shot ironically offered some of the benefits of surgical amputation:

"When the injury is not immediately fatal, as is not rarely the case when a limb is carried away by a projectile of considerable size striking directly," the *Medical and Surgical History* noted, "the surface of the stump will be found to be somewhat 'cleanly cut,' the skin and muscular tissues contused and dark with but little retraction; the bone fractured with not much splintering or comminution above the seat of injury; the arteries retracted and the hemorrhage slight." But even cannonballs largely spent of their force could cause fatalities through concussion or internal injury invisible from the surface.

Lacking sharp edges, smooth round musket balls sometimes remained embedded in the body for years without causing serious harm. The worst complications were when organic matter or other foreign debris was carried into the wound. Stones, splinters of wood and iron, debris from artillery caissons and carriages, pieces of breastworks were all dug out of wounded soldiers, along with buttons, coins, bits of pocketknives, shreds of clothing, the handle from a tin bucket, a piece of a ramrod, and ("not infrequently") teeth or bones of a wounded comrade that became lethal missiles in turn after being struck by a bullet or shell fragment.

Surgeons in 1862 understood little about the cause of infections, but they had ample evidence that the only effective tool in their reach to avert that often fatal outcome was prompt removal of a damaged limb. If no important vessels or nerves were affected, surgeons sometimes tried excising only the damaged portion of a bone, but the results were generally no better, and often much worse.

The pace of amputations during the war seems to have horrified not just later observers but contemporaries as well. No one could quite believe that all that butchery was really necessary, and newspapers and camp rumors regularly featured stories of drunk and incompetent doctors sawing off limbs with reckless abandon. "Many a one-legged or one-armed soldier to-day would have been saved the use of his limbs," insisted one Rhode Island soldier, "had it not been for the *grand opportunities for surgical practice* that were rendered our young army medical students just after a severe battle."

Huge advances in medical knowledge and surgical techniques, many the product of experience gained in the war itself, would indeed just a few years later make amputation seem like a barbaric anachronism. But, as Letterman observed after the Battle of Antietam—which would trigger a particular public outcry for the number of amputations performed—"if any fault could be found, it was that conservative surgery was practised too much, and the knife not used enough." He had been in too many hospitals to have any illusions about the fate of those who avoided the surgeon's knife. Of the 175,000 Union soldiers wounded in the war, 30,000 underwent amputation, with a 26 percent mortality rate: reasonable odds considering the alternatives.

The one saving grace of Civil War surgery was the almost universal use of anesthesia, usually chloroform or ether, to render the sufferer briefly unconscious while the grisly work was done. At the start of the war some conservative practitioners still resisted the innovation, insisting that anesthetics were dangerous and that the heightened emotional state of combat rendered patients insensible to pain, or, contrarily, that pain played a vital part in the body's natural response to shock. A handful of patients did die from overdoses of chloroform, and ether is also dangerously explosive, but the benefits so obviously outweighed the risks that the objections swiftly vanished. The exhaustive statistics and case studies that Hammond and Letterman took pains to have their surgeons record and file showed that 95 percent of major operations were performed under anesthesia during the war, providing a vast body of experience that secured its subsequent place in common medical practice.

UNLAUDABLE IGNORANCE

The great scourge of Civil War surgery was that in removing one source of infection surgeons introduced another. W. W. Keen, a new graduate of Jefferson Medical College sent by Letterman to General Hospital No. 1 in Frederick just before Antietam, recalled fifty-six years later with a shudder the standards of surgical practice of the time. Only a few years later the microbiological discoveries of Lister and Pasteur would revolutionize antisepsis. Keen, who would go on to become a distinguished medical professor and pioneering neurologist, could only say of his work in the Civil War, "May *le bon Dieu* forgive us for our ignorance."

> Utterly unaware of bacteria and their dangers, in our ignorant innocence [we] committed grievous mistakes which nearly always imperiled life and often actually caused death. . . . We operated in old blood-stained and often pus-stained coats, the veterans of a hundred fights. We operated with clean hands in the social sense, but they were undisinfected hands. We used undisinfected instruments from undisinfected plush-lined cases, and still worse, used marine sponges which had been used in prior pus cases and had been only washed in tap water. If a sponge or an instrument fell on the floor it was washed and squeezed in a basin of tap water and used as if it were clean.

Dressings were strips of linen rescued from the "family ragbag" or lint manufactured by "patriotic women" scraping old sheets and tablecloths. Moisture was deemed beneficial to wounds, so poultices of mud were sometimes applied. Hanging out the ends of the wound were anywhere from five to thirty silk ligatures, the ones tying off blood vessels marked with a knot, which after three or four days were "daily pulled upon to see if the loop on the blood vessel had rotted loose," Keen recalled. "When it came away, if a blood clot had formed and closed the blood vessel, well and good; if no such clot had formed then a dangerous 'secondary' hemorrhage followed and not seldom was fatal."

Infection was such a ubiquitous outcome that surgeons did not even recognize it as such in its common manifestation. The creamy white "laudable pus" from staph infections was regarded as a normal part of the healing process, so much so that when a wound healed by "first intention" without the appearance of pus at all it was viewed as an oddity. "Is it any wonder," Keen recalled, "that when my teacher of surgery, Professor Gross, wanted pus to illustrate his lecture he would turn to the orderly and say, 'Tomorrow, Hughey, I am going to lecture on suppuration. Go over to the hospital in the morning and get me a half tumblerful of pus!' And he always got it. Pus was always on tap."

Gangrene was another matter. Its first sign was the appearance of a thin, watery, bloody, and reeking discharge. "A slight flesh wound began to show a gray edge of slough," a surgeon described its ominous course, "and within two hours we saw this widening at the rate of half an inch an hour, and deepening, until in some horrible cases arteries and nerves were left bare across a devastated region." The exact causative agent of hospital gangrene, as the disease was known, is lost to history: it simply vanished with the advent of the antiseptic era. But it was probably a streptococcus variant of the kind loosely known as flesh-eating bacteria. That itself is something of a misnomer, since the havoc wreaked is not by the bacteria directly but by the toxins they produce. Savage methods were employed in an attempt to contain the spread of gangrene once it appeared: excising infected tissue again and again, cauterizing open wounds with corrosive acids or other excruciatingly painful chemicals. The mortality rate remained horrific, at least 45 percent.

No one ever forgot the stench of the field hospitals on the Antietam battlefield from hundreds of men with suppurating wounds. Yet the data meticulously collected there was a milestone in beginning to understand the cause and effective treatment of hospital gangrene. Letterman ordered that one assistant surgeon be assigned solely to keeping records in each regiment, and the individual case reports they filed, describing each patient's wound, treatment, and outcome, filled thousands of pages in the *Medical and Surgical History*, exhaustively catalogued and tabulated by location and type of wound, providing an enduring scientific record of the treatment of gunshot injuries and the diseases of the soldier.

The most striking fact was that gangrene all but vanished in hospitals with good ventilation. General Hospital No. 1 in Frederick consisted of a series of wooden wards hastily erected on the grounds of the old Hessian Barracks, a small stone prison built to hold captured British and German soldiers during the Revolutionary War. Keen reported a remarkable finding about the spread of the disease through the wards of wounded: "Attacks followed a few days of bleak, cold, and rainy weather," when windows were kept shut; "they improved immediately on the setting in of fine weather" when air again was allowed to freely circulate.

Families and friends who flocked to the battlefield seeking to remove a wounded soldier to a private house where they could presumably be better sheltered and cared for provided powerful evidence that reinforced Keen's finding. Letterman summarized the undeniable findings of this unintentional controlled experiment: "Within a few yards a marked contrast could be seen between the wounded in houses and barns and in the open air. Those in houses progressed less favorably than those in the barns, those in barns less favorably than those in the open air, although all were in other respects treated alike."

The very idea that diseases could be contagious was controversial; many doctors remained convinced that disease was fundamentally "constitutional," a product of the body itself under a state of debilitation or fatigue, best treated by stimulants such as coffee, quinine, whiskey, and a cheerful attitude. "No disease is so contagious, or so depressing to vital energy when taken, as inactivity and gloominess of mind," insisted one regimental surgeon, who sarcastically dismissed those who thought differently as suffering from "gangrene of the mind, for want of free ventilation of the brain." Even those who accepted the idea that diseases could be passed from one person to another through "contagion" did not think of disease as an external agent that could be targeted or killed, but rather as the product of putrid odors exhaled or produced by the body of an infected person that poisoned others who breathed the resulting bad air—thus the emphasis on ventilation as a preventive measure.

But mounting evidence from the war's hospital wards began to point clearly in the direction of a local causative agent as the culprit in gangrene. It almost always appeared in a wound without any preceding constitutional symptoms; and many nurses who tended gangrene patients developed erysipelas, a distinctive rough red infection of the skin that similarly manifested itself in a markedly local fashion, almost always on the thin skin of the face, or behind the ears, or in an existing cut elsewhere on the body.

The presence of a large body of patients, facing desperate odds of survival, and in no position to argue back at doctors exercising military authority, offered an unprecedented opportunity for genuinely scientific trials of new therapies. Middleton Goldsmith, a Union surgeon in a large military hospital in Louisville, was able to document the remarkable benefits of antiseptics, bromine in particular, in treating and preventing the spread of hospital gangrene. The serendipitous effectiveness of many powerful antibacterial agents in neutralizing odors had recommended their use to surgeons pursuing the war against "noxious effluvia." Goldsmith noticed that wards in which open pans of bromine were used to deodorize the air had markedly lower rates of hospital gangrene. In a careful report published in 1863, with thirty pages of case reports, he presented convincing evidence that treating affected wounds with a solution of bromine reduced mortality from 25 percent to literally zero. An experiment by another Union surgeon a few months earlier had even more dramatically established the directly contagious nature of hospital gangrene. Placing his mouth on the end of a glycerin-filled tube, Dr. Benjamin Woodward proceeded to suck the "putrid gas" from a patient's gangrenous wound until he almost "fainted with the stench." Then—unmistakably, this was the era before informed consent—he injected the recovered matter into the "perfectly healthy wound" of another patient, and placed him in a ward with no other gangrene cases. Within sixteen hours the healthy wound had turned gangrenous. (Although Woodward was able to save his experimental subject through subsequent treatment with bromine, he expressed "very little concern for the patient," a historian reviewing the documents noted.)

One of Letterman's other enduring contributions to medical science was to order his surgeons to carefully collect and preserve specimens of gunshot injuries for the Army Medical Museum that Hammond had just established in Washington, in an upper floor of the old Riggs Bank building near the White House. Keen was specifically detailed to help in the task after Antietam. Two barrels full of amputated limbs were subsequently shipped from the Gettysburg battlefield, including the leg of Union general Daniel Sickles, lost to a cannonball, and made enduringly famous by the general's regular visits to the museum after the war to show off to friends his shattered tibia and fibula. ("The general valued his lost leg away above the one that is left," Mark Twain, one such friend, remarked.)

Hammond was less successful in his efforts to drag the army pharmacopoeia into the modern era. His order to eliminate dangerous and useless mercury compounds, like the ever popular but much abused drug calomel, aroused the indignation of many surgeons. In the ensuing "Calomel Rebellion" his enemies saw an opportunity. Large, loud, and forceful, Hammond had accumulated no shortage of such enemies, including Secretary of War Stanton, who never forgave him for being appointed by Lincoln against his wishes. ("I'm not used to being beaten," Stanton told a confidant at the time, "and I don't like it.") Effectively ousted as surgeon general in September 1863, he was subsequently court-martialed on trumped-up charges of corruption, and dismissed from the service in 1864. His mentor gone, Letterman succumbed to the more prosaic toll of exhaustion, and left the service at the end of 1864 as well.

TRIAGE AND EVACUATION

"During World War II," said the chief U.S. surgeon in the European Theater, "there was not a day . . . that I did not thank God for Jonathan Letterman."

The enduring power of simple ideas rarely receives such eloquent testimonial, but Letterman's key management insights that transformed battlefield medicine indeed were simple ones. "You can't imagine how deeply we all are indebted to Letterman for telling us what to do and showing us how to do it," said one of his divisional surgeons-in-chief. The very idea of applying management principles to battlefield medicine was a breakthrough in itself: as Hammond had observed, the need was for "*some* system" where none existed. Although his complete system, spelled out in an order issued October 30, 1862, was not fully in place at the battles of South Mountain and Antietam, even in preliminary form it was a revolutionary improvement over the chaos of the Peninsula.

Along with a trained ambulance corps to evacuate and move wounded soldiers, Letterman devised a simple system with three levels of care. Designated medical officers would move forward with each brigade as it went into battle and establish a field-dressing station in as sheltered a spot as possible close to the front lines, to which the wounded would be carried by stretcher bearers and given whatever immediate attention was required, such as tying tourniquets or applying splints. From there the ambulances would transport them to field hospitals located farther to the rear, out of enemy artillery range, organized at the division level, thereby eliminating the problem of regimental hospitals that either sat idle or were overwhelmed with cases. By pooling resources at a higher level, and by directing the surgeon-in-chief to designate the three most able surgeons, regardless of rank, to perform all operations, Letterman observed, "it is hoped that the confusion and the delay in performing the necessary operations so often existing after a battle will be avoided, and all operations hereafter be primary"; that is, performed within the first forty-eight hours, which abundant evidence showed greatly reduced the mortality associated with amputations. Finally, to clear the field hospitals and allow the army to move, patients needing longer-term care would be transported to general hospitals permanently established in cities accessible by rail.

Smoketown hospital

Following the Battle of Antietam, a regularly scheduled service of ambulance trains rumbled over South Mountain on the National Road, stopping at Middletown for food and rest, then proceeding to Frederick. The town of Frederick, reported a newspaperman, had become "one vast hospital," with more than 7,000 patients, equaling in number the entire civilian population, distributed among seven general hospitals occupying some two dozen separate buildings. Boards were laid over church pews to accommodate cots, and two tent hospitals holding 1,000 men each held the overflow. Thousands more were moved from Frederick on trains to hospitals in Baltimore, Washington, and Philadelphia.

Although the seventy-one field hospitals at Antietam were still organized at brigade and regiment level, the proof of concept was clear and, by the Battle of Fredericksburg in December, Letterman's complete system was fully in place. The evacuation system at Antietam had succeeded in removing the wounded from the battlefield by 2 p.m. of the day after the fight, except for the army's left wing, where the ambulance system had not yet been organized and some soldiers lay without aid until nightfall. Letterman was able to clear all the wounded from the field hospitals in little over a week, save for 1,200 men unable to endure transportation owing to the severity of their condition, who were kept at two tent hospitals erected near the battlefield, at Smoketown and Locust Springs, which remained in use until the following March.

A parallel organizational improvement Letterman devised to alleviate the boom-and-bust of medical supplies at the regimental level followed close on the heels of the battle. Existing procedure called for each regiment to be issued three months' worth of equipment and drugs at a time, with the inevitable result that large quantities were lost or simply "thrown away by commanding officers" so the wagons could be used for other purposes, Letterman noted. At Antietam, the situation was compounded by the destruction of the Monocacy bridge, which was not repaired until four days after the battle, and only the timely arrival of trains of wagons dispatched by the Sanitary Commission bearing critical hospital and surgical supplies averted disaster in the field hospitals. Letterman's new system, in which stocks were maintained at the brigade level in wagons directly under the control of the medical department and distributed only on an as-needed basis, simply eliminated the problem.

Antietam would also apparently mark the first use of triage in the American army, an equally enduring and simple system, by which care was directed where it did the most good. The wounded were sorted into three categories: slightly wounded who did not need surgery or extensive immediate treatment, seriously wounded who did, and mortally wounded who were past help.

Letterman's system of field evacuation and a dedicated ambulance corps to support it would be adopted for the entire army by an act of Congress in March 1864, in turn becoming the model for every other army in the world. Nothing Letterman did after the war—a year managing an oil exploration enterprise that went bust, two terms as coroner of San Francisco, elected on the Democratic ticket—remotely equaled his accomplishments of eighteen months as medical director of the Army of the Potomac, another reminder of the strange virtues of war in effecting change impossible in peacetime, and in recruiting talent that would otherwise be lost in trivial and futile dissipation.

5

PASSION
AND IRONY

✷

Oliver Wendell Holmes Jr.

SIMMERING DOWN

"I remember just before the Battle of Antietam," Oliver Wendell
Holmes recalled years later,

> thinking and perhaps saying to a brother officer that it would
> be easy after a comfortable breakfast to come down the steps of
> one's house pulling on one's gloves and smoking a cigar to get
> on to a horse and charge a battery up Beacon Street, while the
> ladies wave handkerchiefs from a balcony. But the reality was
> to pass a night on the ground in the rain with your bowels out
> of order and then after no particular breakfast to wade a stream
> and attack the enemy. That is life.

The yawning chasm between expectations and reality experienced in the first year of the war was almost too great for most
Americans to comprehend at once. All wars begin, or at least before
the twentieth century did, in a flush of enthusiasm and excitement:
rage militaire the French term this ailment. American boys of the mid-
nineteenth century, their resistance weakened by tales absorbed in
childhood of romantic courage of a nation born in revolutionary
war, and left uninoculated by any corresponding dose of reality in

the intervening decades of anti-militaristic peace, succumbed to the fever in droves. In his boyhood home on Beacon Hill, Holmes read the same novels of Sir Walter Scott that, Mark Twain later facetiously opined, were "responsible for the war," having filled the libraries of Southern planters in particular, and the minds of a generation, with romantic tales of knights and chivalry and the glory of brave deeds.

Like boys let out of school—in Holmes's case literally so, since he had abruptly left Harvard two months before graduation to enlist, immediately after the surrender of Fort Sumter—the first eager volunteers regarded going off to war as a lark and an adventure instead of an excellent way to die a gruesome death. Holmes was handsome, confident, privileged, idealistic, so certain of the cause and his part in it that he had not even bothered to ask permission of the college authorities before leaving, and initially spurned an offer from Harvard's president to return and collect his degree, his absence forgiven. "I am in bully condition," he wrote his mother after a week of militia drill and camping out on an island in Boston harbor, "and have got to enjoying the life much."

The high words with which parents saw their boys off to the war ("Die if it must be, but never prove yourself a coward") and which filled the newspapers when they did begin to fight ("the order was carried out in gallant style") and to die ("sacrificed upon the altar of their country") could have come right out of the pages of chivalric romance, too. The persistence of words and phrases that to later generations cloy with sentimentality, the mock-heroic, and the mawkish was one measure of how hard expectation died.

The first inklings that war was not going to live up to its billing arrived in the form of sheer boredom soldiers encountered in camp life. "This slow perishing in blank inaction day after day," a Virginia private lamented, "is more than men can endure." Holmes would rank "to endure being bored" as one of the three "great lessons" the army had taught him. He also discovered how little this was comprehensible to the folks back home, who had undergone no parallel experiences to intrude upon their storybook ideas of war. In Boston recuperating from the third of the three wounds he would suffer during the war, the first two of which had almost been fatal, he had incautiously defined war as "an organized bore"—"to the scandal," he said, "of the young women of the day who thought that Captain Holmes was wanting in patriotism."

Volunteers who arrived with an expectation of continuity with life as they had known or conceived of it received another quick disillusionment; it was a source of never-ending amusement to the veterans to watch new recruits undergo the inevitable process of "simmering down," shedding one by one all of the trappings of civilization they and their families had optimistically packed them off with: shoe brushes and shoe polish, clean handkerchiefs, extra socks, mittens, comb and brush, shaving gear, knife and fork, patent water filter, flannel underwear, buttons and thread, photo album. Life as a soldier was simpler and cruder than anything imagined, a standing mockery to any preconceived picture of a noble crusade adorned with heroic deeds. A young artilleryman from New York was instructed by one veteran in the simple rules of survival on the march. Stick to your gun through thick and thin. Fill your canteen at every stream. Do not pick up anything but food and tobacco. Get food, honestly if you can, but get it: cut haversacks from dead men, steal from the infantry. Rather than the pinnacle of chivalry and knight errantry, army life was a nadir of dog-eat-dog existence.

Edward Wightman, that New York artilleryman who related the lessons imparted by his older and wiser companions, was one of the few Civil War letter writers trained as a writer, a college-educated journalist who was determined to send home "truthful sketches," as he told his brother, and he looked on his fellow soldiers with an eye unclouded by sentiment:

> The privates, of course, are not such people as you or any sensible man would choose, or perhaps I should say could endure, as associates. As a mass they are ignorant, envious, mercenary, and disgustingly immoral and profane. Being as they are here

free from the restraints of civil law, they give loose rein to all their vices and make a boast of them. In our whole regiment, I know no private who will not curse and swear and but few who will not when circumstances favor, rob or steal.

Almost every one drinks to excess when the opportunity offers, chews, and smokes incessantly, and swears habitually, "army habits," they say, "that are to be thrown aside the moment we reach home."

Holmes, who had gone to war filled with a Boston Brahmin's conviction in the superiority of class and intellect along with an unquestioned assumption that zeal for the cause and a gentlemanly bearing were sufficient qualifications to lead men in battle, lost those heroic illusions, but gained some practical wisdom. He later recalled one of the other great lessons the army taught him: that "however fine a fellow I thought myself in the usual routine there were other situations . . . in which I was inferior to men that I might have looked down upon had not experience taught me to look up." Lofty ideals were no match for practical ability.

Nothing more contrasted with prewar ideas about the heroism of war than the sheer squalor of disease and battlefield wounds. The ignominy of dying from dysentery in the throes of bloody diarrhea, or from one of the epidemics of childhood diseases like measles and mumps that swept through the army camps, was the antithesis of manly valor. Battlefield deaths were often no better, nothing like the dramatic tableaux of unbloodied men sinking into the arms of comrades on Bunker Hill in the paintings they had grown up seeing in picture books and popular prints. Frank Wilkeson, a young New York volunteer who wrote one of the vanishingly small number of Civil War memoirs that even attempted to capture the squalor, meanness, and incompetence that marched side by side with courage, resilience, and idealism, entitled one chapter "How Men Die in Battle," and proceeded to describe exactly that, totally unsparing of Victorian sentimentality: men with their bowels hanging out in

*Carte de visite of Oliver
Wendell Holmes Jr.*

ribbons, thighs fleshed to the bone and bleeding to death, or stag-gering in circles with blood streaming from their head only to be picked off by Confederate sharpshooters.

"I made up my mind to die," Holmes remembered, as he drifted in and out of consciousness in the rude hut of a hospital where he was taken after he was shot in the chest in his first brush with the enemy, at the Battle of Ball's Bluff almost exactly a year before Antietam. In an ambulance bumping down the road, he saw the hideous wounds of his companion, a fellow officer of the 20th Mas-sachusetts: "Two black cavities seemed all that there was left for eyes—his whiskers & beard matted with blood which still poured black, from his mouth—and a most horrible stench."

Holmes was enough of an ironist to wryly recall years later how as he lay waiting to be carried across the Potomac from the battle-field he had briefly thought of the tale of Sir Philip Sidney offering his canteen to another wounded man saying, "Thy necessity is greater than mine," and had considered saying, "Have that other feller put in the boat first." He decided instead to "let events take their course": storybook heroism does not survive contact with the enemy. He was also amused by the high language of the story that appeared in *Harper's Monthly,* lauding his bravery for being shot "in the breast, not in the back; no, not in the back. In the breast is Massachusetts wounded, if she is struck. Forward she falls, if she fall dead." Words that he would recall with particular ironic amusement as he ran for life at Antietam with the rest of his regiment.

Learning to duck, run, and take cover was in fact one of the first ways in which battlefield reality imposed itself. At the start of the war it had been considered a great thing for a mounted officer to ride out in front of the lines to urge his men forward, and demonstrate his contempt for danger. By the summer of 1862 the chivalrous inclination of soldiers on the other side to hold their fire out of respect for such splendid shows of courage had become one of the many casualties of the war. When Jackson heard of an incident in which one of his commanders had ordered his men not to shoot at a Union officer conspicuous for such gallantry, he sent him a peremptory order: "Shoot the brave officers and the cowards will run away and take the men with them." The commander of the 8th Alabama, in the midst of the relentless fight for Bloody Lane at Antietam, was amazed at the courage of one Union soldier who calmly retreated back over the hill in front, coolly turning and firing every eight or ten steps, then at last out of ammunition, slapping his backside in a parting gesture; but not so much so that he refrained from shouting to his men, "I will give the man a furlough that will shoot that rascal!" He acknowledged afterward that he was sorry not to have better appreciated the "gallantry of this man," but "the bravest of the enemy were the men I wanted to kill—they set bad examples, and that was no time for sentiment."

The words of inspiration given green troops—that moving forward conferred the greatest protection in battle—did not offer comfort for long to soldiers who saw the best men die one after another. Ambrose Bierce described in his usual sardonic manner the procedure by which an aide was sent forward to deliver a message to "some commander of a prone regiment in the front line": "It is customary in such cases to duck the head and scuttle away on a keen run, an object of lively interest to some thousands of admiring marksmen. In returning—well, it is not customary to return."

There had been hints at South Mountain of a more brutal form of hardening to come: the shooting of the enemy's unarmed color bearer, even as he lay on the ground helpless; the sport played by some Union soldier who shoved a biscuit in the mouth of a dead Confederate whose body was caught upright against a stone wall; the unsentimentality of the dying Confederate who, in an inversion of the sorts of words that thousands of soldiers had literally uttered as they lay wounded in the first months of the war, Holmes included—"tell my mother I died a brave boy," "tell them I'd done my duty," "tell them my mother and my country's flag were last in my thoughts"—instead told the Ohio soldier who found him in the woods, "Won't you take a message to my mother? Tell my mother it's her fault I'm here."

After the war Bierce wrote a series of astonishingly dark and ironic short stories trying to convey some of the unheroic truths about battle to a reluctant audience; "denied existence by the chief publishing houses," they were privately printed with the financial assistance of a businessman acquaintance only in 1891. All are shocking for their cynicism and unsparing details of what bullets do to a man's body; none is as deeply disturbing as "Chickamauga," which grotesquely juxtaposes the incomprehension of a small boy setting off into the woods with his wooden sword to play soldier and the horrors of the actual wounded from the battlefield he discovers there: their blood-streaked faces which he laughingly takes for those of circus clowns, the men crawling on all fours he thinks are inviting him to play horsie on their backs. It is, of course, a horrid allegory of the foolish naïveté of all boys who go off to war.

William Dean Howells, the editor of the *Atlantic Monthly*, recounted what James Garfield told him of the crushing blow his most deeply held beliefs had suffered in his first battle. "At the sight of those dead men whom other men had killed, something went out of him, the habit of his lifetime, that never came back again: the sense of the sacredness of life and the impossibility of destroying it."

HARDENING OFF

Anxious to put their courage to the test, many soldiers were eager for their first battle: "Seeing the elephant" was the stock phrase, and it captured the feeling of battle as a spectacle worth paying to see, at least once, anyway. What kept them going back into combat after satisfying that initial curiosity required a different kind of motivation. As Holmes recalled: "I was a devilish sight more scared in later engagements than I was in the first when one was keyed up to meet the unknown."

The growing ranks of stragglers and skulkers suggested that for many, one glimpse of the elephant was enough to cure both war fever and curiosity forever. "The sneaks in the army are named *Legion*," Edward Wightman reported in a letter home, "and they are shameless enough to proclaim their cowardly practices openly. When you read of the number of men engaged on our side, strike out at least one third as never having struck a blow." He later revised that estimate to one half. Practiced skulkers would report sick the morning of a fight, hide in the woods, and show up afterward claiming they had been separated from their regiment in the heat of the fight, or (a favorite ploy) "tenderly carry away the first wounded." The rich assortment of derisive nicknames they earned underscored their ubiquity: sneaks, shirks, skulkers, malingerers, skedaddlers, beats, coffee-boilers, and, perhaps more humorously derisive, "coffee-coolers."

But much of the apparent rise in disillusionment reflected a different breed of soldier entering the ranks from the second year of war on, rather than a loss in determination among those who had responded to the first call for volunteers in 1861. Frank Wilkeson, who ran away from home at sixteen and lied about his age to volunteer late in the war, was astonished to find himself herded into the state penitentiary in Albany, where those who had enlisted to collect the bounty, as much as $1,000 by that point, were being held under armed guard so they wouldn't run—"a den of murderers and thieves," where he was mercilessly mocked and abused for innocently averring that he had joined out of patriotism.

Wilkeson in his memoir artfully suppressed details of his background to emphasize the sense that he was relating the perspective of the common soldier: he was in fact from a wealthy and prominent family in Buffalo, his father a renowned journalist and war correspondent; he had been educated at Phillips Academy and joined the army after his brother was killed at Gettysburg, none of which he reveals. But along with a brutally frank depiction of corruption, incompetence, vice, and suffering in the ranks, he offers a convincing portrait of the determination of the soldier who enlisted out of idealism to see the war through. "I cannot afford to give three years of my life to maintaining this nation and then giving them Rebels all they want," said one Union volunteer. "The conviction of Northern soldiers that they fought to preserve the Union as a beacon of republican liberty throughout the world burned as brightly in the last year of the war as the first," concluded James McPherson from his reading of thousands of soldiers' letters and diaries. If anything, "their searing experiences" refined ideological belief into "a purer, tougher" form. The day after Antietam, a New York volunteer who had survived that introduction to battle wrote, "When I was a boy I never thought I should be called upon to fight for my country. But I am no better to die for liberty than any one else. If I lose my life, I shall be missed by but few; but if the Union be lost, it will be missed by many." If they were cynical about the jingoism of civilians, they still reserved to themselves the right to be fighting for a higher purpose. Of a friend killed at Gettysburg, Holmes would write, "Henry had the real flame of patriotism & not the newspaper stuff."

Holmes was in a distinct minority among Union soldiers, even among his fellow Harvard men in the 20th Massachusetts, for his abolitionist views: his close friend and collegemate Henry Abbott, whose death leading the regiment at the Wilderness would for Holmes become a luminous memory of duty heedless of its ends, was far more typical for his ugly contempt of the abolitionist cause altogether, and of those who, he sneered, were abasing themselves before "the shrine of the great n——er." But the cause, "the glorious Cause" of the Union, as many still called it, was to them just as much one worth fighting for, to the end.

Holmes himself was not referring to slavery, or not just slavery, when in the spring of 1864 he referred to the war as "the Christian crusade of the 19th century . . . the cause of the whole civilized world"—the only belief, he said, that made it possible for him to keep going. Fighting for the Union sounds as airy to us today as fighting for the flag. Southerners who asserted they were fighting for matters "real and tangible"—protecting their property and homes from invaders—were puzzled why their enemies would fight for things that seemed "abstract and intangible." But to Holmes's generation, the example of sacrifice of the Revolutionary generation and the responsibility to the ideals of republican government they bequeathed *were* things of real substance. It was not just the rights of Americans to continue to enjoy liberty, religious freedom, and the other blessings of free government that were at stake, they insisted; the war was a test of whether republican government *anywhere* could survive. This indeed made the Civil War a "cause of the whole civilized world," a struggle not merely of local but universal import. An Irish-born carpenter in a Massachusetts regiment, Peter Welsh, remonstrated to his wife at home and his father-in-law back in the old country for suggesting he had no stake in the war he was fighting in. "I have as much interest in the maintenance of the integrity of the nation as any other man," he retorted. "This is the first test of a modern free government . . . if it fail then the hopes of millions fall and the designs and wishes of tyrants will succeed—the old cry will be sent forth from the aristocrats of europe that such is the common lot of all republics."

Many Christian leaders of the North saw the Union even more as the cause of Christ. Inklings of the coming solidarity of the entire human race—"a world of men, equal, brotherly, united, and holy," joined in "one language and one family," in the words of the Reverend Gilbert Haven of Boston—were already to be seen in America's embrace of "emancipation, equalization, unification," and its advance of English as a universal tongue. To abandon that march to unity was to turn a back on the coming of the millennium that America's creation itself foretold. "All governments based on the few, by the few, and for the few, are hostile to the government of Christ, and must be abolished before His glory fully comes," Haven declared. "Union, not for ourselves alone, but for all men, was our strongest, our most general feeling."

That these were not empty words was borne out by the striking fact that 136,000 Union soldiers, more than half of those who had volunteered in 1861 and whose three-year enlistments were set to expire in the summer of 1864, reenlisted. And an overwhelming majority of Union troops, 78 percent, cast their votes for Lincoln that fall, rejecting the Democratic Party's call for peace negotiations and with that the man they had nominated, their still-admired former chief, George McClellan.

USES OF CONTEMPT

The other force that sustained the soldiers of the Union army was a growing assurance of their own competence. If the war was going to be brought to an end, they were the ones to do it and no one else, a powerful and empowering realization.

Holmes's disdain for the empty phrases and admonitions from the armchair generals back home bore some similarities to the feel-

ing of courage betrayed that seared soldiers of the First World War
like Siegfried Sassoon, whose most virulent poems imagined taking
revenge bloody on the jingoistic civilians and their safe and shallow patriotism. Yet there was a subtle but all-important difference.
The Union veterans saw themselves less as victims of the war than
as taking charge of the war, their cynicism an expression of superiority rather than nihilism, their hardness a mark of professional
dispassion rather than callous indifference. Wightman recorded one
humorous expression of this businesslike attitude to war when he
and a companion were granted a pass into the town of Sharpsburg
a few weeks after Antietam. Entering the small tavern and hotel,
which was riddled with holes from Union shells, they were greeted
with hostile glares directed at their uniforms from the half dozen
obviously pro-Southern locals awaiting their Sunday dinner. After a
few minutes of stony, tobacco-juice-spitting silence, one of the civilians burst out, with a gesture at the heavily damaged room, "You
men did this yer!" Wightman's comrade, "surveying the premises
with the air of a mechanic who had done a nice job," responded
with a complacent, "Yas-as!"

As for the armchair generals, Wightman wrote home shortly
after the battle, "Foot soldiers cannot endure the criticism of the
citizens on horseback. Permit me to say that I think the soldiers
of the Republic fight her battles better than the uninformed citizens." They were also learning that they fought her battles better
than their officers. Nothing gave Wightman and his comrades more
satisfaction than mocking their supposed commanders, whom they
had long ago surpassed in real courage and competence. "In the
present state of affairs they were merely an incumbrance," he wrote
near Petersburg in the spring of 1864. "Their labors were limited to
scaling themselves behind trees and shouting, 'Go in, boys, give it
to em!'" He offered a litany of poltroonery: their colonel hid during
a battle and offered his resignation; the senior captain pretended to
be sunstruck during a raid and was dismissed in disgrace; the next
captain in line mysteriously disappeared for several hours when sent

to skirmish; the third-ranking captain, in a perfect display of the inversion of roles now at work, was fired on by his own men for running away and ordering a retreat. Wilkeson gleefully recounted watching a colonel who had cowered from the battle surreptitiously tearing open a rifle cartridge and rubbing his face with gunpowder to make it look like he had been in the fray.

In another camp a recitation of officers' cowardice became a literal ritual every evening at dark, a call and response of contempt echoing over a half mile:

"Who got behind the tree?"

"Lef-tenant Brown!"

"Who tried to run from the guards and got nabbed?"

"Colonel Williams!"

"Who played off to ride in the ambulance?"

"Captain Smart!"

Veterans in the ranks took humorous satisfaction in their hard-won superiority and self-reliance in telling ways, large and small: mocking the emptiness of the honorary brevet ranks handed out for bravery (soldiers took to referring to army mules as "brevet horses" and camp followers as "brevet soldiers"); roaring in laughter at gawking civilians or other noncombatants scurrying for their lives from dangers they themselves calmly faced day after day; sporting with green newcomers by lifting a blanket from the face of a horribly mangled corpse to watch them blanch as they passed by; hooting at any official reports from headquarters not confirmed by the "camp-walkers," a grassroots source of news carried from campfire to campfire and generally far more reliable and accurate than anything officers told them.

Their hard-headed realism, significantly, had little place for the kind of compensatory rumors eagerly seized upon by soldiers of later wars who had come to see themselves as hapless victims, desperate for some miraculous deliverance from their fate. Confederate soldiers on the losing end toward the last months of the war would be more susceptible to magical thinking of this kind, circulating tales of impending peace or the sudden collapse of the enemy, but even many of them retained their skepticism. (Having heard twice in a month that Grant had been killed, a Confederate artilleryman drily observed, "Grant is *still* dead, but comes to life occasionally.")

Wilkeson described the old soldiers' far more gruesome satisfaction in seeing skulkers get their terrible due. One of the most shocking passages in his memoir candidly recounts his unadulterated glee witnessing a camp of "coffee-boilers" caught in Confederate artillery fire.

> Shot howled past and cut large trees down, and they fell with a crash among the frying-pans and coffee-pots. . . . Through the dust and smoke and uproar I saw men fall, saw others mangled by chunks of shell, and saw one, struck fairly by an exploding shell, vanish. Enormously pleased, I hugged my lean legs, and laughed and laughed again. It was the most refreshing sight I had seen for weeks.

In assuming a professional attitude toward the business of killing, the veterans also redefined courage. Where officers early in the war had paraded their defiance of danger to inspire the troops, Wightman's own similar act later in the war was an expression of pure contempt, motivated by nothing but self-respect. Falling back from a rebel fieldwork following an arduous attack over rough ground under heavy artillery fire during the siege of Petersburg, he coolly turned his back and retreated at a steady pace. "I would not have double-quicked a step to save a thousand lives," he said.

For the most part, though, courage as the soldier now saw it was no longer even about facing death fearlessly, but rather about a simple willingness to stick to a job that had become unbearable. "An army's bravest men are its cowards," Bierce ironically opined of the shirkers who "unflinchingly" faced the firing squad rather than return to their regiments. An Illinois regiment for its part cheerfully tolerated one of their number who ran at every battle, but who always came back and tried it again the next time. "He was a coward," offered one of his comrades, but "a good coward." They had, rather, come to agree with the definition of courage that Dwight D. Eisenhower would offer two great wars later: "The acceptance of unendurable conditions."

If it had indeed become "the business of the soldier to kill," in Bierce's words, "mechanical, dull, dogged machine-work" in the words of another soldier, it was by the same token impersonal and cool. "The soldiers who were doing their best to kill one another," Holmes later wrote, "felt less of personal hostility, I am very certain, than some who were not imperilled by their mutual endeavors." Later, during the First World War, Holmes remarked that he agreed with the English officer who said that "he didn't hate the Germans, the people at home did that, he only wanted to kill them." That, Holmes thought, "is the usual feeling of men at the front."

"I hate to hear old soldiers telling what heroes they were," he told a gathering of veterans of his regiment thirty-five years later. "We did just what any other American, what the last generation would have done, what the next generation would do if put in our place." War, he told one of his young Supreme Court clerks a half century later, is "a real horror while it is going on," but "you simply do it because you have to." To Holmes the enduring lesson of battle was that that was the only thing a man *could* do: "file in and do your damndest," leaving the uncontrollable to fate, and not troubling oneself with the worry "that the cosmos would collapse" if you fail.

At the level of any one man's personal experience things usually happen without reason; death is always random and often cruel and squalid; the brave died first. Those were inescapable lessons of war. But it was a mark of the idealism that still divided Holmes's generation from those of later wars that these thoughts steeled him for life. He would come to see battle as one of the sublime experiences of life—he also listed among these climbing the Bernese Alps, a storm at sea, a total eclipse of the sun, and "women." Yet even in its terrible and often pointless mismatch of means to ends, war affirmed the ability of men to strive for great things. "In our youth our hearts were touched with fire," he declared in his most famous distillation of how the war had set him and his other surviving comrades apart. These were thoughts that stayed with him for the rest of a long life, in which he would gain renown at age forty as the author of the single greatest work of legal scholarship by an American, his treatise *The Common Law*, and from age sixty-two to ninety as a Supreme Court justice of unequaled brilliance and originality.

But first he would have to be shot through the neck at Antietam.

BAYONETS IN THE SUN

By candlelight at 3 a.m. the morning of September 17, Holmes scribbled a brief letter to his "Dearest Parents," its light-hearted tone at odds with the late hour he was devoting to the task and the approaching dawn that was to bring the expected battle. "I don't talk seriously for you know all my last words if I come to grief— You know my devoted love for you—those I care for know it— why should I say any more—It's rank folly pulling a long mug every time one may fight or may be killed. . . . I have lived on the track on which I expect to continue travelling if I get through—hoping always that though it may wind it will bring me up the hill once more. . . ."

He added: "All of us feel a deuced sight more like a fight than in that forlorn peninsula."

No one felt more like a fight than did Hooker. It was not until mid-afternoon on the sixteenth that Hooker at last received orders from McClellan to move into attack position, and at 4 p.m. the First Corps began moving across the Antietam over the uppermost of the three bridges that crossed the creek, and by a nearby ford just below the upper bridge at Pry's Mill. From its mouth where it empties into the Potomac about three miles south of Sharpsburg, the Antietam bears slightly east of north along its upstream course. A large bow in the Potomac bulges westward around the town, leaving a large triangle of land that widens at its top. South of town, where the angle closes, the hills separating the two streams rise 200 feet over the Antietam's banks in sharp ravine-cut slopes, but they smooth out to the north, and there, on Lee's left, McClellan determined to strike on ground that offered more room for maneuver.

Palfrey's description of Hooker summarized the explosive forces compressed into his personality: "Brave, handsome, vain, insubordinate, plausible, untrustworthy." But no one doubted his fighting qualities. Riding in advance close to his skirmishers, as was his habit, he was soon joined by McClellan and his staff.

"I said to the general," Hooker reported, "that he had ordered my small corps, now numbering between 12,000 and 13,000 (as I had just lost nearly 1,000 men in the battle of South Mountain), across the river to attack the whole rebel army, and that if reinforcements were not forwarded promptly, or if another attack was not made on the enemy's right, the rebels would eat me up." McClellan returned to his headquarters at the Pry house and sent orders to Sumner to have the Twelfth Corps follow Hooker across the Antietam that evening. They did not get under way until 11:30 p.m., reaching their bivouac behind Hooker's position at about 2 a.m. But McClellan turned down Sumner's plea to have his own Second Corps move into position across the creek as well. Ordered to remain securely behind the Antietam at the ford by Pry's Mill, the Second Corps was placed where it could not possibly launch any simultaneous attack with Hooker in the morning, but only act as a reserve. Deliberately or not, McClellan's decision also had the effect of further fragmenting the command structure by separating both of the corps that were to open the attack, Hooker's First and Mansfield's Twelfth, from their respective wing commanders, Burnside and Sumner.

Hooker's advance across the Antietam was known at once to Lee from cavalry pickets stationed along the creek, who were driven back by Hooker's skirmishers as they advanced. McClellan's plan was for Hooker to be in position to strike Lee's flank at dawn. But the intense skirmishing and probing attacks that the move set off,

Situation at daybreak, September 17, 1862

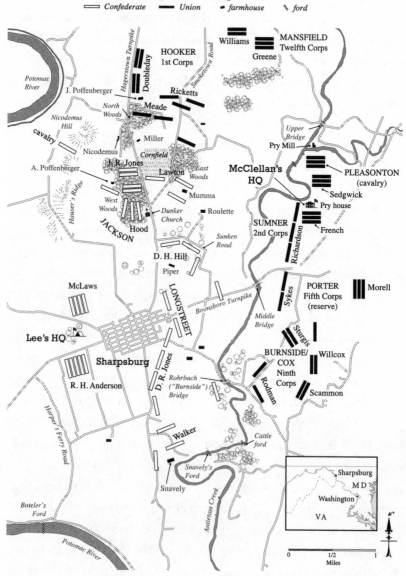

which continued well past midnight, gave away any surprise as to McClellan's intentions, while the Union commander's corresponding failure to carry out any cavalry reconnaissance of his own left Hooker in near total ignorance of Lee's precise disposition of his forces. The result was that when dawn came Lee had formed his lines facing almost due north, perpendicular to the Hagerstown Turnpike, presenting a front, not a flank, to Hooker.

At about 9 p.m. a soft but steady rain had begun to fall. In a futile gesture that added to his soldiers' misery but did nothing to regain the lost element of surprise, McClellan ordered no campfires be lit, leaving the men to chew coffee grounds silently in the dark. The exchange of musket and artillery fire died away around 3 a.m. Hooker reported to McClellan that the fight would be "renewed at the earliest dawn," and again urged that reinforcements be sent forward to reach him before the attack began. To no one in particular, Hooker muttered loud enough for the *New York Tribune*'s reporter George Smalley to hear, "If they had let us start earlier, we might have finished tonight."

Alpheus S. Williams, who would be thrust into command of the Twelfth Corps just a few hours into the next morning's fight, would never forget the night. "So dark, so mysterious, so uncertain; with the occasional rapid volleys of pickets and outposts, the low solemn sound of the command as troops came into position, and withal so sleepy there was a half-dreamy sensation about it all; but with a certain impression that the morrow was to be great with the future fate of our country." Across the lines, many of the men near enough that they could hear the voices from the other side, "the soft, smothered sound of the summer rain" left a similarly indelible impression on Confederate general James Longstreet's memory of that night on a field "on which was to break in the morning in the storm of iron and lead."

Across open, level ground, thousands of men on opposing sides formed in lines three-quarters of a mile long and separated by a thousand yards, supported by dozens of guns with clear fields of

fire for canister and case shot, the fight that began the Battle of
Antietam at dawn on September 17 was as savage as any in the war.
Hooker's veterans of the humiliation at Second Bull Run fought as
if they meant to end the war that morning. As they moved through
the thirty-acre cornfield south of the Miller farm, Hooker caught
sight of the glint of bayonets from between the rows of ripening
corn, an entire sea of men standing at "support arms," their rifles
held vertically in the crook of their elbows.

For the next two hours possession of the cornfield would seesaw
back and forth in relentless attacks and counterattacks, the Confederates supported by a murderous enfilading artillery fire from guns
placed on the Nicodemus Heights to the west, while the Confederates were shelled in turn from twenty-four long-range 20-pounder
Parrot rifles across the creek near McClellan's headquarters, along
with thirty-six guns that crept forward with the Union advance.

Reporters had been banned from the army by Halleck after a
series of leaks on the Peninsula, but Smalley had wangled his way
into a temporary appointment on Sumner's staff, while one of his
assistants had somehow scrounged an outdated pass signed by
Burnside that was enough to get him through the lines.

Hooker, looking about for a staff officer, noticed a remarkably
cool-looking young man sitting quietly on his horse watching the
battle unfold a few hundred yards ahead.

"Who are you?" he asked.

"Special correspondent of the *New York Tribune*, sir," replied
Smalley.

"Will you take an order for me? Tell the colonel of that regiment
to take his men to the front and keep them there," pointing to a
hard-pressed section of the line.

Smalley gamely went forward and delivered the message to the
skeptical officer, who rebuffed him, insisting that orders had to
come from a proper staff officer. "Very good," Smalley replied, "I
shall report to General Hooker that you refuse to obey."

"Oh, for God's sake don't do that!" the colonel quickly amended his response. "The Rebels are too many for us, but I had rather face them than Hooker." When Smalley reported back, the general grunted, "Don't let the next man talk so much," and sent him off on another errand.

An officer of the 6th Wisconsin described the veritable madness that gripped his men as they rushed toward the little white Dunker church that would be a focal point of much of the battle, and were hurtled back with equal force by the rebel counterthrust.

The men are loading and firing with demoniacal fury and shouting and laughing hysterically, and the whole field before us is covered with rebels fleeing for life, into the woods. Great numbers of them are shot while climbing over the high post and rail fences along the turnpike. We push on over the open fields half way to the little church. The powder is bad, and the guns have become very dirty. It takes hard pounding to get the bullets down, and our firing is becoming very slow. A long, steady line of rebel gray, unbroken by the fugitives who fly before us, comes sweeping down through the woods around the church. They raise a yell and fire. It is like a scythe running through the line.

In his official report, Hooker would state that in most of the field "every stalk of corn . . . was cut as closely as could have been done with a knife, and the slain lay in rows precisely as they stood in their ranks a few minutes before." By 7:30 a.m. the losses on both sides were staggering. Many regiments had lost more than half their number killed and wounded; in one Texas regiment it was four-fifths. In Jackson's three divisions that had been fed into the fight, total casualties were one-third, one-half, and three-fifths. Casualties in Hooker's First Corps were almost 3,000, a third of their number, the survivors by this time in disarray and largely done as an attacking force.

No effort had even been attempted to coordinate the First Corps'

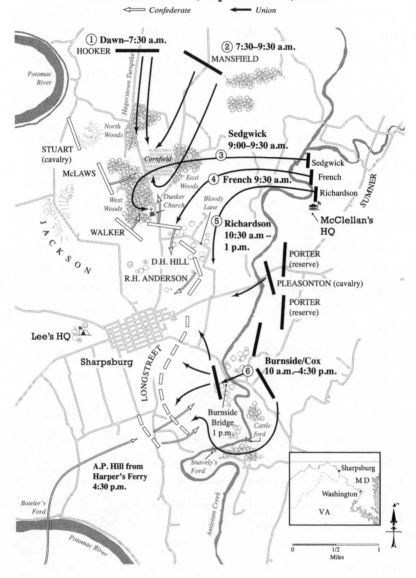

Battle of Antietam, September 17, 1862

◁▭ *Confederate*　　◀━ *Union*

attack with the Twelfth Corps, which still remained in reserve to Hooker's rear, a mile and a half to the northeast. Now, rather than augmenting the force of Hooker's initial blow, they were called to relieve him. Just as his attack was fizzling out, the Twelfth Corps marched up on Hooker's left. Half of its 7,000 men consisted of five newly raised regiments less than three weeks from home who had never fired a shot at an enemy before.

Mansfield ordered his entire corps to move up in columns of companies, each regiment forming into a narrow rectangle one company wide by twenty deep, the companies separated by just six paces. Williams protested that dozens of men could be killed by a single shell in such an exposed formation, and asked to place them in line of battle as they advanced. Mansfield had been an engineering officer in the old army. This was his first infantry command, and his nerves were showing. He had kept Williams up nearly all the night, awakening him over and over with some new instructions so that Williams did not get more than two hours' sleep. Now he insisted that "all the new regiments would run away" unless kept tightly together, and refused to alter his orders.

The issue was settled soon enough when Mansfield was mortally wounded and Williams assumed acting command. He had managed to get some of the green troops in line by having them assemble along a fence that ran perpendicular to the Hagerstown Turnpike. But any attempts at further maneuver dissolved into a shambles. "In attempting to move them forward or back or make any maneuver they fell into inextricable confusion and fell to the rear," Williams wrote in a letter home after the battle. "They were easily rallied . . . ready and willing, but neither officers nor men knew anything, and there was an absence of the mutual confidence which drill begets. Standing still, they fought bravely."

But standing still was no way to win a battle, and despite some furious fighting by the men of the old regiments which drove the enemy past the morning's battleground in the bloody cornfield, Williams's men were held in check at the north edge of the woods near the Dunker church, which would be known ever after as the West Woods. During this time, Hooker was wounded by a musket ball that passed through his foot as he rode near the front line, a conspicuous target dressed in his immaculate uniform astride a white horse. Losing blood rapidly, he was carried off on a stretcher and taken to the Pry house across Antietam Creek. With Hooker's departure from the field the fight seemed to go out of what was left of the attackers. Around 9:30 a.m. the sound of musketry, which had seemed to Williams as if every stone and brick house on Broadway had collapsed simultaneously, died away.

Francis Palfrey, who would soon traverse the same bitterly contested ground, reported that the "worst sight of all was the liberal supply of unwounded men helping wounded men to the rear. When good Samaritans so abound, it is a strong indication that the discipline of the troops in front is not good, and that the battle is not going so as to encourage the half-hearted."

"IN DRIBLETS"

At the Pry house, Edwin Sumner had been kept pacing the yard and cooling his heels on the front steps for more than an hour before McClellan emerged from his bed at 7 a.m., his aides having refused to allow his sleep disturbed. McClellan had told Sumner to have his men ready an hour before daybreak, but not to move until further orders. With the sound of a ferocious battle underway, but still no orders, Sumner had grown increasingly anxious. As he would later testify to congressional investigators, he had seen no point in launching an attack "in driblets."

A signal flag station in Hooker's rear was able to communicate by direct line of sight with the Pry house headquarters, and initial reports of Hooker's advance played to McClellan's caution. "All goes well. Hooker is driving them," McClellan commented. It was not until 7:20 a.m. that he at last ordered Sumner to set his Second Corps in motion. The men waded the creek, two feet deep in places, paused to wring out their dripping socks, and began the two-mile march to the front. It would take them nearly two hours to enter the fray, as a series of increasingly urgent messages arrived now from Williams, reporting Mansfield's death, Hooker's wounding, and the deteriorating situation: "Please give us all the aid you can. It is reported that the enemy occupy the woods in our advance in strong force."

From atop the hill at the Pry house, McClellan and his staff sat in chairs carried out from the house and watched what they could see of the action through telescopes braced on posts. With McClellan as always was Porter. There was a clear view of the center of the battlefield toward the Dunker church, but the flanks were hidden by the hills, leaving the billows of smoke and reports of cannon the only "eloquent" messengers of what was taking place to the right, in the words of one staff officer. They had a clear view of the troops of John Sedgwick's division in the lead of the Second Corps, Holmes's 20th Massachusetts among them, as they moved up the rise on the far side of the Antietam: "With flags flying and the long unfaltering lines rising and falling as they crossed the rolling fields," the staff officer recalled, "it looked as though nothing could stop them."

Sumner's "favorite idea," said Williams, was to place infantry in three tightly spaced lines. He was an old cavalry officer and that was the way cavalry deployed for maximum shock effect. But it was madness for infantry, where a second line was intended to form a reserve, out of range of the enemy musket fire, to maintain steady pressure on a defender if the first line gave way. Holmes, whose regiment was at the far left of the second line, saw the helplessness of their situation, just as vulnerable to enemy bullets and artillery as the front line but unable to return fire without hitting their own men in front. Describing the scene to an old friend seventy years later, he explained that Sumner had "shoved our second line (I am talking of *lines* not ranks), a *quasi* reserve, up so close to the front line that we could have touched them with our bayonets."

His natural impetuousness exacerbated by the delay, Sumner threw his men into action at once without listening to Williams or pausing to learn the location of the rebels. Williams wrote his brother-in-law a week after the battle lamenting the want of "coolness by some of our commanding generals," who "threw away our power by hasty and impulsive attacks at the wrong points. Hundreds of lives were foolishly sacrificed by generals I see most praised, generals who would come up with their commands and pitch in at the first point without consultation with those who knew the ground or without reconnoitering or looking for the effective points of attacks." There was no doubt whom he meant.

Lee, with an aide leading Traveller as he still could not hold the reins in his splinted and bandaged arms, had ridden forward earlier in the morning to assess the situation, and placed a second line of artillery on high ground to the west of the West Woods known as Hauser's Ridge. As Sumner's men entered a small meadow to the north of the woods the guns opened fire, shells passing through the tight lines. In the woods a more appalling surprise awaited them. Sumner had brashly assumed the lull in musket fire meant the rebels were fought out and in bulling straight ahead he was flanking the remaining enemy facing the remnants of the corps that had preceded him.

It was not a deliberate ambush he had walked into, but it might as well have been. Taking a calculated gamble, Lee had correctly read McClellan's inaction on the rest of the field and quickly shifted a division and an additional brigade from Longstreet's command on the right to the West Woods, where they were joined by McLaws's division, just arrived from Harper's Ferry that morning. Deploying along a cart path that led from the A. Poffenberger farm to the Dunker church along the base of the small hill on which the West Woods stood to the north, they were well concealed by limestone ledges and woods.

A few minutes after halting along the post-and-rail turnpike fence at the west end of the woods, Sumner's men were hit by a flank attack from the five brigades of rebels. Unable to fire without hitting their own men, unable to wheel to the left in their close-ordered lines, all that Holmes's regiment along with the rest of the division could do was retreat with alacrity when Sumner gave the order. Many of Sumner's men had been issued twice the usual number of cartridges, eighty rounds to a man, but the regiments in the second line lost scores of men without even being able to fire their guns once in return, while enduring the same fate as the front line. "We got hit as much as they did, but of course could do nothing," Holmes wrote.

A man in the 15th Massachusetts recounted the chaos of being shot at seemingly from all directions at once. "The bullets actually came from the rear," he recalled in amazement in a letter home a week later. Some of those bullets came from men of a New York regiment that began frantically firing right through the left wing of the Massachusetts regiment crowded closely in front of them.

My God, such confusion. All hands ran for dear life. The rebs chased us like the Devil for about a half or 3/4 of a mile when our batteries opened on them with grape and they give up the chase. They were very foolish for they might of drove us clean into Pennsylvania as well as not. I be Damned if I should have stopped had they come for us. *No God Damned Southerner is a going to catch me unless he can run 29 miles an hour.* That's my gate. Well no Capt. had any Company. No Col had any Regmt. No Brigadier had any Brigade.

As he ran, Holmes was struck by a round that went clear through his neck. The bullet somehow managed to miss nerves, spinal cord, and carotid artery by a fraction of an inch. Holmes was able to make his way on foot before collapsing at a small field hospital at the Nicodemus farm a few hundred yards to the north of the woods, his sense of irony enough intact that he recalled "chuckling to myself," he later wrote, about the *Harper's* article that had been "flamboyant on my first wound at Ball's Bluff—about Massachusetts hit in the breast etc. I thought to myself this time I am hit in the back, and bolting as fast as I can—and it's all right—but not so good for the newspapers."

The rebel counterattack was halted only when one of the Second Corps batteries dashed from the rear into the meadow south of the cornfield and unlimbered their six Napoleon smoothbores, loaded with canister. The cannoneers furiously yelled at the fleeing Union soldiers to get out of their line of fire. At last unable to wait any longer, they blazed away regardless. "Some of our men, I have no doubt, were killed," wrote one of the artillerymen in a letter to his girl back home, "but it was better to sacrifice a few of their lives than to allow the rebels to capture our battery."

The Nicodemus house for a while lay between the two lines and its windows were shattered by shellfire that, in the words of one of Holmes's wounded comrades who lay on the floor near him, "ploughed up the wounded in the yard outside." Remarkably, the house itself was not hit. Late that afternoon ambulances carried the wounded off to the Union field hospital at Keedysville, a few miles to the east.

William G. Le Duc, a staff officer, wired Dr. Holmes with the news of his son's wound; he later told the doctor how he had found the young officer lying unattended at the hospital and had importuned a surgeon to tend to his wound. But the surgeon "shook his head," and "said his duty was to try to save those who had a chance of recovery." Letterman's triage system, correct in principle, was mistaken in this particular case. Le Duc asked if there was anything he could do. "Wash off the blood, plug up the wound with lint, and give him this pill of opium, and have him keep quiet," the surgeon impatiently replied. "I'm glad it's not a case for amputation," Holmes wisecracked, "for I don't think you'd be equal to it, Le Duc."

Sedgwick's division took 2,200 casualties in twenty minutes, nearly half its numbers. The veterans of the 15th Massachusetts would in afteryears erect a flamboyant tribute to themselves, a marble sculpture of a fallen lion recalling the 330 of their ranks who fell that day, a third killed or mortally wounded, ignoring the irony of marking the spot where they ran for their lives.

Holmes valued more than any such outward show the quiet tribute paid to his regiment, the 20th Massachusetts, which never erected any monuments and did not write any letters to newspapers extolling its feats. A brigade commander complimented the unit saying, "The twentieth have no poetry in a fight"; they just went in and did their job.

Holmes's more sentimental keepsakes he hid away in his private papers and personal safe deposit box, where they were found when he died: a note hastily scrawled on the floor of the Nicodemus farmhouse reading, "I am Capt. OWHolmes 20th Mass son of Oliver Wendell Holmes M.D. Boston," written when he feared he might lose consciousness or die and so "be unable to tell who I was," as he explained in an accompanying note; and two musket balls wrapped in a small paper parcel with a note in his hand, "These were taken from my body in the Civil War." The futile but beautiful heroism of battle was more important to him as a lesson in the irony of life than as a matter of triumph.

6

WAR AT THE
OPERATIONAL
LEVEL

James Longstreet

OFFENSIVE DEFENSE

This was not the battle James Longstreet wanted to fight.

After the war he would write of Lee and McClellan, "Both were masters of the science but not of the art of war." But that was a matter of definition. If the science of war encompassed deliberate, thoughtful planning, the employment of force to maximize advantage, choosing the time and place of battle to attain a clear strategic objective, then Longstreet was the only one of the three to master either its art or its science.

Like his close friend in the antebellum army Ulysses S. Grant, who had been one year behind him at West Point, Longstreet had done poorly enough at the academy to end up in the infantry, being more interested in horsemanship and earning demerits for insubordination and general rule-breaking than academic study. Like Grant he served with distinction in Mexico; like Grant he "thought to settle down into more peaceful pursuits," as Longstreet put it in his memoirs, in his case staying in the army (while Grant left for a precarious career as a farmer and businessman), but securing a safe appointment as a paymaster and so giving up "all aspirations of military honor."

Stationed in Albuquerque in the fraught months leading up to secession, he and his fellow officers would assemble on the flat roof of the quartermaster's office the day the monthly mail was due, watching for the dust of the approaching mail wagon visible five or ten miles in the distance. The son of a South Carolina planter, Longstreet did not profess to suffer any agony of conflicting loyalties in resigning his commission and accepting an appointment as brigadier general in the service of the Confederacy, though he was apparently touchy enough about the point of honor involved that he fudged in his memoirs the fact that the latter had preceded the former.

He was an unlikely apostle of ideas about military operations that, even viewed a century and a half later, stand out from those of his peers for their strikingly modern character. He was no intellectual; the flash of intelligence that some caught in his eyes made less of an impression than the burly ursine cheerfulness his 6-foot 2-inch, 220-pound figure suggested. At West Point his love of pranks contrasted sharply with the brooding seriousness of his friend "Sam" Grant. His memoirs betray no reading of military history or effort to systematize his own thinking on the matter. But he had the rare trait of dispassion, and the ability to profit from it along with experience.

Lee called him "my old war horse" after the Battle of Antietam, and the contrast with Lee's other wing commander was striking, and revealing. Jackson was relentless and remorseless, getting results with a determination and zealotry that imbued his campaigning with the humorless fanaticism of a religious crusader. He had been physically sickened at the sight of the first corpse he had seen on a battlefield in Mexico and steeled himself ever after with an armor of sanctimonious certainty that bordered on cruelty. He brought charges against officers for failure in battle, ordered deserters shot, ten in a day on one occasion. Sinners against the "army of the living God," he called them, and angrily brushed aside appeals for mercy from their officers, barking, "Is the accused a soldier? Did he desert? If so, *he must die!*" He added on one occasion: "And officers who obtrude for them deserve to be hung!" He once proposed arming his infantry with pikes instead of muskets, and openly advocated raising "the black flag" and giving "no quarter to the violators of our homes and firesides." ("The Bible is full of such wars," he offered by way of justification for murdering prisoners.) He viewed illness and even battlefield wounds as weakness, if not outright cowardice. "He places no value on human life, caring for nothing so much as fighting," his fellow Confederate general George Pickett observed in a letter to his wife, "unless it be praying." But the success that Jackson's stern discipline bought had a mesmerizing hold. "As a leader," acknowledged Longstreet, "he was fire."

Longstreet himself saw battle through a completely different lens. As preternaturally cool as any man who ever sat unblinkingly on a horse while shells burst over his head, he bowed to no one in personal courage. He seemed to personally defy the realities of the battlefield's new lethality, a one-man demonstration of the traditional belief that courage conferred the best protection, repeatedly exposing himself to harrowing dangers and somehow emerging unscathed. But he saw no point in throwing away men's lives in glorious charges that paid no larger dividends. "Exactly the kind of grandeur which the South could not afford," D. H. Hill agreed; though many of his fellow Confederate generals did not.

That was all the more true given the long odds the Confederacy faced. Success, Longstreet believed, could be attained only from husbanding the resources he had, employing them where they would do the most good. That informed both his dispassionate view of the business of battle and his realistic empathy for the common soldier which Jackson so manifestly lacked. Longstreet would write of the straggling and absenteeism during the Maryland Campaign, "To those who have spent their lives near the ranks of soldiers and learned from experience that there is a limit to physical endurance, explanation is not called for; to those who look upon the soldier as a machine, not even needing oil to facilitate motive power, I will say, try to put yourselves in the soldiers' places." A good workman does not blame his tools.

Whatever intangible gifts of tactical intuition he possessed, he had also learned from experience the pivotal value of intelligence, coordinated action, and biding one's time on the tactical defense, allowing the enemy to dash himself to pieces first, then swiftly and devastatingly counterattacking at the decisive moment. At Second Bull Run he had done just that, thrice dissuading Lee from launching a corps-sized attack, holding a solid defensive line along the cut of an unfinished railway as Pope's men attacked in waves, first sending a probing division-size reconnaissance-in-force forward to search for a gap in the Union lines, calmly repositioning his artillery to create a critical opening. Only then did he send his entire corps wheeling to the left, pivoting on a line anchored on Jackson's corps to his left, catching the fleeing enemy on the flank and pressing him back a mile in one blow. He only failed to cut off and capture Pope's entire command when Jackson failed to come to his support.

The essence of Longstreet's emerging thinking was the combination of strategic offense with tactical defense. Maintaining the initiative of the offensive forced the enemy to scramble and react: that much of Lee's invasion of Maryland had already proved a success. But there was no point in throwing away the huge advantage of the tactical defense that modern firepower was beginning to confer: when it came to actually fighting, far more sensible to maneuver to a position that would force the enemy to attack, on one's own terms. Of Lee he pointedly observed, "He found it hard, the enemy in sight, to withhold his blows."

Longstreet thought taking Harper's Ferry "a venture not worth the game." Sitting at Hagerstown on September 13, he likewise argued vehemently against Lee's decision to fight a delaying action at the South Mountain passes, proposing instead to unite forces at once behind the Antietam at Sharpsburg, where the combination of his and D. H. Hill's brigades would be able to make a strong defensive stand while simultaneously threatening McClellan's flank should he try to move down Pleasant Valley to relieve Harper's Ferry.

After the fall of Harper's Ferry, McLaws's freed-up force posed a double danger to McClellan, threatening his flank and rear should he try to move on Sharpsburg, and in turn posing an even greater strategic dilemma by moving via the Weverton Gap back to the east side of South Mountain, which would place him squarely between McClellan and Washington. (Alternatively, McLaws thought, Lee could have united his entire force at Harper's Ferry and Maryland Heights as a "stronghold," forcing McClellan "to have attacked us in some strong position of our own choosing, and with less wear and tear of our men, and less prospect of general disaster, than now seemed imminent.") Longstreet thought that "prudence would have gone with the bolder move" of sending Jackson's entire command through Weverton onto McClellan's rear. Anything, however, was better than the decision to send McLaws up the Virginia side of the river to join Lee at Sharpsburg, thereby abandoning altogether "the beautiful point of strategic diversion" that Sharpsburg represented *only* in conjunction with such an ongoing threat to the security of McClellan's lines of communication and rear. Ironically, Longstreet wrote, the situation's "charms were changed to perplexities" by the Confederate success in taking Harper's Ferry and Lee's moves that followed from it.

Soviet military theorists of the early twentieth century would introduce the term "operational" to define the level of military planning that lies between the tactical and strategic, and that crucially ties the two together. The need for a new word reflected historical neglect. Longstreet's emphasis on when and where to fight was a precocious instance of operational-level thinking, which focuses on shaping battles to advance the larger strategic goals of a campaign.

The battle for the South Mountain gaps had at least a discernible purpose in advancing the aims of Lee's incursion into Maryland; Longstreet's idea to maintain the threat to McClellan's rear would have more seriously constrained the Union commander's options while setting conditions to fight from a position of advantage. By contrast, Lee's decision to make his stand at Antietam was a throwback to an almost ritualistic kind of chivalrous combat, a battle for the sake of battle that ignored the operational level altogether.

Arriving on the field on the fifteenth, Longstreet had quickly sized up his sector on the hills east and south of the town, ordering his battery commanders simply to "put them all in, every gun you have, long range and short range," and having them go to work at once to convince McClellan he faced a much larger force than he did while buying time for Jackson to rejoin. McClellan had obliged, spending the day personally and methodically supervising, and frequently then altering, the placement of every one of his artillery positions.

Although Lee had employed fieldworks extensively on the Peninsula, and although he had had time to dig in on the Antietam battlefield, he did not. But at the bottom of a sloping orchard and cornfield in front of the Piper farmhouse, which Longstreet had chosen as his headquarters, a mile south of the Dunker church and just to the east of the Hagerstown Turnpike, ran a zig-zag farm lane sunken over the years from the heavy passage of farmers' laden wagons. A line of fence rails ran along the cornfield in front. The lane formed a natural trench and breastwork for Longstreet's men, who were about to face an even more horrific fight for control of the center of the Confederate line, as the other two divisions of Sumner's Second Corps now moved forward in the clockwise-turning engagement that moved around the battlefield from north to south.

BLOODY LANE

If McClellan had a plan, he did not bother to put it in writing, call a conference of his corps or division commanders to explain it, or take the necessary steps to see that it was carried out. He left two flatly contradictory accounts of what his plan was. In his official report a month after the battle, he stated that his intention was to launch the main attack on the right and "to create a diversion in favor of the main attack, with the hope of something more," with an attack on the left by Burnside's corps. "As soon as one or both of the flank attacks were fully successful," he stated, he intended to "attack the centre with any reserve I might then have on hand."

In a subsequent account published a year later, Burnside's attack, which he now claimed he had ordered at 8 a.m., had become instead of a diversion a military fantasy. In McClellan's revised telling, Burnside's men were supposed to have crossed the south bridge over the Antietam—the only place where the Confederates held a line right against the stream—and fought their way up the high bluff that rose 150 to 200 feet in less than half that distance, then "having carried their position to press along the crest toward our right." The idea of crossing a bridge commanded by fire from heights which completely covered its narrow approaches at no more than pistol range, and which could rake from front to rear any column of men that did start across it, might have been justifiable as "a desperate sort of diversion," allowed Cox, whose men were to draw the task. But no one who knew the impregnable position held by the enemy there could have entertained for a second the idea that "a serious attack upon it was any part of McClellan's original plan."

In any case, the order he dispatched to Burnside was not sent until 9:10 a.m. Obscured by trees and hills from the Pry house, Burnside's headquarters was unable to communicate by signal flag until later in the day when a signal station was established in his rear, so the message had to go by an aide on horseback. It was not received until around ten. The reason for McClellan's failure to have Burnside move earlier—when a diversion might have still done some good tying down Longstreet's divisions on the Union left during the fighting on the right—was manifest in the first line of his order, which noted the just-received news of the arrival of two of Franklin's divisions, ordered up only that morning from Pleasant Valley, where they had pointlessly remained after idly watching McLaws slip off more than twenty-four hours earlier. Still oddly anxious over the theoretical possibility of a Confederate dash into his rear, he had waited until word arrived that Franklin was within a mile and half of the battlefield before setting Burnside forward.

Meanwhile, Sumner's remaining two divisions launched what would become a three-hour ordeal attempting to dislodge Longstreet's men deployed along the sunken road. Wave after wave of brigade-sized assaults followed the same harrowing course, cresting a gentle rise about 100 yards from the lane where the Union assaulters were immediately pinned down in the corn and grass, kneeling or lying flat as they exchanged relentless volleys punctuated by desperate charges. One Ohio soldier remembered thinking that the constantly fluttering grass around him were crickets hopping about, until a fellow soldier laughed when he remarked on it. Then he knew it was bullets. A hundred years after the battle a boy searching for relics near the sunken road after a heavy rain found a .69 caliber Confederate Minié ball that had been deformed on impact and fused to a .58 caliber Union bullet, the opposing projectiles having collided in midair amid the dense opposing hails of lead.

Longstreet had arrayed the defenders to create what a modern soldier would recognize as a "kill zone," a box of converging fire that trapped any attacker attempting to cross. Additional lines of troops positioned on the rise behind the lane were able to fire over the heads of the men in the trenches, adding to the withering volleys that caught the Union troops in front. Batteries of Confederate artillery placed farther up the hill to the rear, by the Piper farm, poured case shot and shells into the mix. Neither men nor chivalry survived long under such conditions. "You wouldn't shoot a wounded man!" exclaimed a captain of the 1st Delaware as a sergeant of his regiment took aim at a Confederate soldier limping toward them using his musket for support. A second after he slapped down the sergeant's rifle the Confederate shot the captain dead, and was in turn immediately killed by a volley of fire.

One Union battery about 500 yards to the northwest was able to answer the Confederate guns and also enfilade the defenders in the lane, shooting a thousand rounds of canister, solid shot, case shot, and shell, while the Mumma farmhouse, set ablaze by the Confederates to prevent its being used by Union sharpshooters, burned behind. At one point a Confederate infantry charge on the battery was beaten back in hand-to-hand fighting.

The long-range guns across the Antietam were hindered from offering any direct support of the Union attack, their view of the lane and the slope in front obscured by intervening hills. They could, however, sight with occasional accuracy on the puffs of smoke from the Confederate guns to the rear, and the ensuing artillery duel began to take a slow toll: the ammunition caisson for one Confederate gun blew up from a direct hit in a spectacular explosion.

Yet the inability to quickly marshal the vast and for the moment elsewhere unused firepower of Union artillery painfully underscored the limitations of the Union command structure and planning on the offensive. Nearly a hundred Union guns of other corps sat idle a mile or a little more to the north, while the battle at the sunken lane raged for hours.

At a critical point Longstreet, whose "eyes were everywhere" in the fighting, his chief of staff would later write, rushed forward with his staff when the artillerymen manning two guns in the Piper orchard were picked off by sharpshooters. Holding the reins of his officers' horses, Longstreet sat placidly chewing an unlit cigar while his aides worked the guns, Longstreet ordering double charges of canister which made the guns leap ten to twelve inches in the air with each shot, until replacement artillerymen scrambled up the hill to take over the work.

At about 1 p.m. the Union attackers finally broke through the line. Several well-timed but horrifically costly counterattacks Longstreet ordered against the Union flank had held off earlier charges. But now the line crumbled and fell back half a mile to the Hagerstown Pike, where Longstreet was able to rally a few guns and the remnants of his broken regiments. One of McClellan's staff officers, D. H. Strother, could not at first understand what he was seeing as he watched from a knoll near McClellan's headquarters as the Union brigades swept forward.

> As the smoke and dust disappeared I was astonished to observe our own troops moving along the front and passing over what appeared to be a long, heavy column of the enemy without paying any attention whatever. I borrowed a glass from an officer, and discovered this to be actually a column of the enemy's dead and wounded lying along the hollow road. . . . Among the prostrate mass I could easily distinguish the movements of those endeavoring to crawl away from the ground; hands waving as if calling of assistance, and others struggling in the agonies of death.

Some 5,500 lay dead and wounded from the fight for what would ever after be known as Bloody Lane, roughly equally distributed between the two sides. Franklin, abandoning his usual caution, repeatedly pressed McClellan to send in his 10,500 newly arrived and fresh troops; together with a renewed attack by Sumner, they could sweep into the West Woods with a thrust from the north into the heart of Lee's fatally weakened center and end the battle right there.

But Sumner, shattered from the morning's events, rebuffed the idea, sending McClellan's young staff officer Lieutenant James Wilson back to headquarters with a message for the general. "I have no command" left, Sumner insisted; his men were utterly demoralized; he could only advance if McClellan were willing to risk "not being able to rally a man on this side of the creek if I am driven back." McClellan all too readily gave way, reporting "it would not be prudent" to make the attack.

Wilson, a twenty-five-year-old graduate of the West Point class of 1860, was so beside himself at the pusillanimous decision that he buttonholed George Smalley at McClellan's headquarters and asked the reporter if he would beseech Hooker to take command of the army and do what McClellan would not. This was nothing short of mutiny, Smalley pointed out. Wilson said he knew it. "We all know it," he said. But it was the only chance. Smalley said he could not possibly carry such a message. Wilson pleaded with him at least to sound Hooker out about whether he could return to the field at all, even in command of his own corps, "and let us know what his views are. The rest we will do." The wounded general, who had been carried to a room in the Pry house, swore a blue streak to Smalley about the dragging progress of the battle, but said there was nothing he could do. "I am perfectly helpless."

Along with Porter's and Franklin's divisions that he was jealously husbanding as a reserve against the ever-looming specter of defeat, McClellan placed Pleasonton's entire cavalry in the center with some vague idea of a grandiose Napoleonic charge to be unleashed at the climactic moment, against a broken and fleeing enemy. Around noon he had cautiously inched a section of Pleasonton's horse artillery over the middle bridge, supported by a squadron of cavalry. But when Pleasonton explained he needed infantry support, McClellan responded that there was "no infantry to spare"—then astonished his cavalry commander by asking, "Can you do any good by a cavalry charge?" Attacking infantry with massed cavalry was an idea only a few centuries out of date, made obsolete by the advent of the musket. Pleasonton demurred.

In the middle of it all, McClellan as always found time to telegraph Washington, and his wife, with boasts of triumph and hedges for failure. At around 1:30 p.m. he wired Ellen, "We are in the midst of the most terrible battle of the age. So far God has given us success but with many variations during the day. . . . I trust that God will smile on our cause." He wrote out a telegram to General-in-Chief Halleck calling the battle not merely the greatest of the war but "perhaps of history," adding, "I have great odds against me," the "small reserve" of Porter's corps all he had left to attack Lee's center when the crucial moment arrived—if it ever did. "It will be either a great defeat or a most glorious victory. I think & hope that God will give us the latter," he wrote on the telegram blank. Then perhaps realizing that that was too much preemptive excuse-making even by his own standards, he crossed out the last two sentences, and wrote instead, "I think & hope that God will give us a glorious victory."

The frustrated commander of the lead division of Franklin's Sixth Corps, William F. "Baldy" Smith, had already reached a different conclusion. McClellan's refusal to send in his corps at the moment when it could have turned the tide of the battle, he thought, was "the nail in McC's coffin as a general."

BURNSIDE'S LAMENT

As Hooker later testified to the congressional Joint Committee on the Conduct of the War, McClellan had given him the clear understanding that "simultaneously with my attack" there would be an attack on the "rebel army in the centre and the left." Instead, Burnside's advance now became the obsessive focus of all McClellan's hopes for retrieving the morning's failures. Cox had set the Ninth Corps in motion at once on receiving McClellan's mid-morning attack order, harried both by the unanswerable Confederate artillery and sharpshooters concealed and protected by the heavily wooded bluff above, and by a stream of increasingly importuning messages from McClellan to speed things along. "Tell him if it costs 10,000 men he must go now!" an aide heard McClellan tell a messenger.

The approach to the bridge ran along an exposed road that paralleled the bank for about 300 yards, a mere 50 to 150 feet away from the Confederates above. The first regiment that attempted it fell back with a third of their number dead or wounded within minutes from the intense rifle fire that rained down on their flank. A company tried to wade the creek below the bridge, only to be picked off in the water one by one. When yet another messenger arrived from headquarters with a hurry-up order, Burnside responded with restrained irritation. "McClellan appears to think I am not trying my best," he told the messenger. "You are the third or fourth one who has been to me this morning with similar orders."

If Burnside was not exactly "sulking," as more than one writer has alleged, he had been placed in an awkward position by McClellan's deliberate sabotage of his authority. Cox offered to return to his division and allow Burnside to resume immediate command of the Ninth Corps after McClellan detached Hooker's corps from his control on September 15. But Burnside refused to waive his precedence as wing commander. McClellan then grossly aggravated the provocation by officiously sending his own engineers and staff to place Burnside's divisions and artillery for him upon their arrival at the Antietam battlefield the next day.

Later that night—Cox believed this was again Porter's mischief at work—McClellan dictated an official rebuke reprimanding Burnside for failing to have his men in place on time, when in fact they had been delayed by McClellan's own staff modifying their initial instructions. Burnside understandably concluded that he had been reduced to a figurehead, and resigned himself to ceding all important command decisions to McClellan, merely passing on his orders without comment to Cox for execution.

Uncertain of the limits of his own authority and responsibility as acting corps commander, Cox similarly felt undermined by McClellan's interference in judgments normally left to corps and division commanders. He was hampered, too, in having to rely on his own small divisional staff, members of Reno's Ninth Corps staff having been granted leave after South Mountain to carry the body of their fallen general to Washington. Under the strained circumstances Cox declined to exercise the initiative he otherwise might have, and later said he would have. Most notably—and disastrously—he did not carry out his own reconnaissance of the ground, accepting a report from McClellan's engineers who had located a ford a half mile below the lower bridge. In fact that ford was impassable, apparently having been confused by McClellan's officers with information local farmers provided of another crossing, Snavely's Ford, farther downstream. The division Cox sent to cross the ford to try to flank the Confederates on the bluff spent nearly three hours locating the correct ford and moving into position, weathering the fire of rebel sharpshooters. The lead unit, the 9th New York, crossed just about the time two Union regiments stormed across the bridge upstream.

A private in the 9th, when the regiment leapt forward to storm a line of Confederate artillery silhouetted ominously on the ridge line above, recalled experiencing a strange sensation that he had read Goethe describe, under a similar moment of extreme mental strain in battle: "The whole landscape for an instant turned slightly red." A lieutenant in the same regiment, Mathew J. Graham, remembered lying on his back on the grass, wondering if he raised his hand in the air how many seconds it would take for one of his fingers to be shot off, when the colonel appeared and, to his utter incredulity, gave the order to get up and move forward. But up they went, the well-disciplined men closing ranks automatically as they advanced, the length of the regiment's line steadily contracting as men fell dead or wounded.

McClellan in his first order to Burnside had assured him "you will be supported" once he secured the bridge. Again McClellan quailed at the moment of decision. By 4 p.m., Cox's four divisions had crossed the Antietam and were driving Longstreet's battered defenders back to the Harper's Ferry road south of Sharpsburg, now threatening to cut off Lee's rear and the ford across the Potomac. At that moment a column of soldiers appeared in the distance on the road: after a moment of confusion caused by the blue uniforms they had donned from the spoils of Harper's Ferry, they proved to be 3,300 men from A. P. Hill's division, who had marched the seventeen miles from there in eight hours. Moving into battle without pausing for breath, they hit Cox's left flank.

Hill's undetected arrival was another product of the unaccountable blunder of McClellan's outmoded idea of holding his cavalry in reserve in the center, thereby ignoring what one Union cavalryman acerbically noted was "the practice of centuries" to employ cavalry to patrol an army's flanks to guard against just such surprises. Among the Union troops sent flying back from Hill's counterattack was yet another woefully untrained regiment thrown hastily into battle. The 16th Connecticut, as its regimental history would record, "had received no drill, no discipline, and few instructions even in marching." Mustered into service on August 21 and sent to Washington, it had caught up with its brigade only the day before the battle. In the chaos of Hill's counterattack the inexperienced line officers of the 16th struggled to hold their men in some semblance of order. "Tell us what you want us to do and we'll try to obey you," one officer yelled in desperation to the regiment's colonel. Their ensuing dash to the rear set off a cascading crack down the whole line.

When a messenger from Burnside galloped up to McClellan's headquarters requesting assistance, one of Porter's division commanders heard Porter vehemently argue to McClellan against any idea of sending in his 5,500 men—most of whom had not fired a shot that day: "Remember, General! I command the last reserve of the last Army of the Republic." Porter later denied the account, but as the historian James McPherson observed, his denial is not persuasive. Smalley was an eyewitness to the scene, and recounted seeing Porter slowly shake his head when the question was put to him.

McClellan in a dispatch to Pleasonton at the same time said as much: rebuffing his request for infantry to support an advance beyond the Middle Bridge in aid of Burnside's still advancing right and center, McClellan said that he could spare none of Porter's troops, as they were "the only infantry the General-in-Chief has now to rely on in reserve." He repeated the same in the reply he ordered Burnside's messenger to carry back: "Tell Gen. Burnside this is the battle of the war. He must hold his ground till dark at any cost. . . . I can do nothing more. I have no infantry. Tell him if he cannot hold his ground, then the bridge, to the last man! If the bridge is lost, all is lost!" As Cox would later mordantly write, "troops are put in reserve not to diminish the army but to be used in a pinch." But convinced to the end that his enemy vastly outnumbered him, McClellan dared not part with the force he needed to cover his retreat if all were indeed lost, as he feared.

The sun set over the heartbreaking irony of a savage battle fought to a tactical draw, both sides in possession of lines not far from where they had begun twelve terrible hours earlier. It had been "the old McClellan method" all over again, Josiah Favill, a young officer in the 57th New York, wrote in disgust in his diary. "Fighting in detail, one corps at a time, the rest of the army looking on," no effort made at any point to engage the whole line simultaneously. Longstreet, with the eye of a commander who grasped the resilient principles of military operations that those more vain, bloodthirsty, or impetuous were blind to, in his memoirs reduced the story of McClellan's failure to two sentences:

> General McClellan's plan of the battle was not strong, the handling and execution were less so. Battles by the extreme right and left, divided by a river, gave us the benefit of interior lines, and it was that that saved the Confederate army, for it became manifest early in the day that his reserves were held at the No. 2 [i.e., middle] bridge, which gave us freer use of our inner lines.

He added: "We were so badly crushed that at the close of the day ten thousand fresh troops could have come in and taken Lee's army and everything it had."

"AS THICK AS AUTUMN LEAVES"

Everyone expected the battle to resume the next day, but the eighteenth passed in comparative quiet, burial parties exchanging the dead and wounded. At daylight on the nineteenth the Union army crept forward, to find the enemy had vanished overnight.

The obvious toll lay on the ground, spread across a miles-long front. "The days after the battle are a thousand times worse than the day of the battle," wrote the surgeon of the 5th New Hampshire, Dr.

William Child, "and the physical pain is not the greatest pain suffered. . . . No one can begin to estimate the amount of agony after
a great battle." Of his 450 patients at the Smoketown tent hospital,
four-fifths had suffered amputations. "Many die each day. Some are
doing well." Edward Wightman, visiting his wounded comrades at
Smoketown, was equally struck by the varying ways men faced their
suffering. "Some appeared to have been opened by bullets merely to
let out a superabundance of good nature and to make a vent for the
egress of their philosophy; but others habitually wore an expression
of pain and depression."

Alpheus Williams rode over the field two days after the battle,
and was able, in a long letter to his daughters a few days later, to
rise above the usual hollow cliches in trying to paint a picture of the
terrible scene.

The rebel dead, even in the woods last occupied by them, was
very great. In one place, in front of the position of my corps, apparently a whole regiment had been cut down in line. They lay
in two ranks, as straightly aligned as on a dress parade. There
must have been a brigade, as part of the line had been buried. . . . In riding over the field I think I must have seen at least
3,000. In one place for nearly a mile they lay thick as autumn
leaves along a narrow cut below the natural surface, into which
they seemed to have tumbled. Eighty had been buried in one
pit, and yet no impression had apparently been made on the
unburied host. The cornfield beyond was dotted all over with
those killed in retreat.

The wounded Rebels had been carried away in great numbers and yet every farmyard and haystack seemed a large hospital. The number of dead horses was high. They lay, like the
men, in all attitudes. One beautiful milk-white animal had died
in so graceful a position that I wished for its photograph. Its
legs were doubled under and its arched neck gracefully turned
to one side, as if looking back to the ball-hole in its side. Until

you got to it, it was hard to believe the horse was dead. Another feature of the field was the mass of army accouterments, clothing, etc. scattered everywhere or lying in heaps where the contest had been severest. . . .

But I am well and bear it better than anyone.

The casualty figures compiled and so carefully tabulated in the years immediately following the battle underreported the dead by thousands. At least 2,000 of those listed as wounded would subsequently die of their wounds, and many of the 1,700 reported missing were almost certainly missing because they too were dead, scattered among hasty anonymous graves on the battlefield. Incorporating these revised figures, the best modern estimates put the total dead at Antietam at 6,500 and the wounded at 15,000 to 16,500. Casualties in both categories were almost equally divided between the Union and Confederate sides.

The less obvious toll would emerge more slowly, over days, years, and decades that followed. After the slaughter of his men in the West Woods, the colonel of Holmes's regiment, W. Raymond Lee, fell to pieces, unable "to do any thing," one of his officers reported. The day after the battle he mounted his horse and rode off without saying a word to anyone. George Macy, another officer of the 20th, found him later that afternoon "just like a little child wandering away from home," without a cent in his pocket, having had nothing to eat all day, his clothes covered in his own excrement, about to bed down for the night in a stable. Macy gave him some money, found an empty room in a house, put him to bed there stark naked to recover. Lee resigned his commission two months later.

Others kept their sanity but adjusted their perceptions of reality in a desperate attempt to accommodate their searing experiences, a process of forgetting that would envelop the whole war in a misty haze of sentiment in decades to come, as old veterans reworked their memories. The traumatized men of the 16th Connecticut who ran under fire were shaken enough at first to admit the truth. "As for myself," wrote one private, "I am a big coward." Another frankly admitted that after firing one shot he had run with the rest of the regiment, "Bull Run fashion." But within two weeks he was calling those of the regiment who had died "heroes," explaining that the *real* cowards "were the ones who stayed back in the hour of trial"— not even trying to face the enemy as he had.

McClellan slept well the night after the battle and, awakening the next morning, telegraphed Washington that the battle "will probably be renewed today." But to his wife shortly afterward he deferred the matter, as usual, to God. "It is all in his hands," McClellan wrote, "where I am content to leave it." He added: "Those in whose judgment I rely tell me that I fought the battle splendidly & that it was a masterpiece of art."

Later in the day he was struck by an excruciating neuralgia attack, which he attributed to "the want of rest & anxiety," and which reduced him to riding in an ambulance and banished any thought of renewing the attack. Consulting only with Porter, he concluded, as he explained in his official report, that "with less than an absolute assurance of success," he could not in good conscience "risk a battle . . . at this critical juncture." Finding the rebels gone the following morning, he expressed nothing but relief. "We may safely claim a complete victory," he exultantly telegraphed Halleck. "The enemy is driven back to Virginia. Maryland and Pennsylvania are safe."

Passing by the town of Sharpsburg on the afternoon of the nineteenth, McClellan was greeted with a far more subdued response from his men than he was used to. The soldiers of Porter's corps who had been kept out of the battle altogether swung their hats and cheered. But Hooker's corps was deafening in its silence. "A change had come over the army," reported war correspondent Charles Carleton Coffin, who witnessed the scene. "I am thoroughly disgusted with the management of the army," Thomas Welsh, commander of the Ninth Corps brigade that had carried the right wing of the attack nearly to the outskirts of Sharpsburg, wrote his wife afterward. "It makes me sick to contemplate the result. The whole

Rebel Army—could have been captured or destroyed easily before it crossed the Potomac—but indeed it seems to me that McClellan let them escape purposely."

McClellan's fecklessness aside, Lee's ability to get away pointed up fundamental limitations in command, organization, logistics, and even psychology in armies on the offensive at that point of the Civil War, which, added to the growing resiliency of the tactical defense, ensured the inconclusiveness, and accordingly bloody prolongation, of the conflict. Directed mostly at "targets of opportunity," as one modern military analyst, John Erath, noted, battles in the war's first two years lacked the strategic focus that could even make victory decisive—although the opportunity presented, and lost, at Antietam came very close. Even when one side succeeded in attacking an unprotected flank or battering its way through in a near-suicidal frontal assault, the result was rarely a rout. While the armies of 1862 lacked the command and communications to consistently carry out coordinated offensive operations on a scale larger than a brigade, their hierarchical organization into subordinate units of corps, divisions, brigades, regiments, and companies generally allowed even a broken and fleeing army to maintain its coherence, regroup, and retreat in good order to a new defensive position. An army in retreat fell back on its own interior lines and supply lines, an automatic advantage over a usually exhausted pursuer who would be running beyond any preparations to send men, ammunition, and provisions forward.

And there still remained a reticence even among the more hardened veterans at this point in the war to shoot at a fleeing foe. Men fought with ferocity within the limits of formal battle, but still recoiled at killing in what seemed cold blood. And then there was the fact that men did get sick of it all, and resented civilians who from the comfort of their armchairs did not even begin to understand their sickness. Alpheus Williams, while he bemoaned the chance to destroy Lee's army that had slipped past, resented the impatient calls of those who knew nothing of such things "demanding" in the newspapers an immediate advance. "No sooner is one story of bloody fights grown cold," he complained, "than the outcry is for another. Men and women who groan and sigh over a railroad accident which kills two and wounds six, seem to delight in the glowing description of a battle which leaves upon a single field 20,000 killed and four times as many wounded. Strangely inconsistent is poor human nature! . . . "

MAKING GENERALS

"How ignorant our generals were of all the principles of generalship," Emory Upton lamented after the war. It was a direct if still slow-to-evolve consequence of the war that its endemic problems of poor staff work, inadequate reconnaissance, inability of commanders to coordinate the movement of units and the employment of artillery, cavalry, signals, and intelligence, would bring the first glimmers of modern reform to the U.S. Army. The failures, Upton saw, had come from the very conception of the role and training of commanders. "People blame poor generals," Upton observed, "but what has our government ever done to make a general?"

Change might have come faster had not the lessons of James Longstreet's example been subsumed in postwar revisionism fueled by unreconstructed Southerners marching under the banner of the Lost Cause, determined to make a scapegoat of him for the Confederacy's defeat. The operational concepts Longstreet employed at Second Bull Run and Antietam would be put to devastating effect by the Confederate army in later battles like Fredericksburg and ignored with devastating failure at Gettysburg. At Fredericksburg, Longstreet centralized the control of artillery to bring synchronized fire of dozens of cannons emplaced on, behind, and on both flanks of his line, all focused on a 400-yard-deep open field that Union troops had to cross, uphill, to reach his three brigades of infantry securely behind shoulder-high stone walls and trenches. Wave after wave of brigade-sized attacks were ordered by Burnside, now in command of the Army of the Potomac, convinced that just one more blow would break through. "As courageous and hopeless as anything in the war," James McPherson said, it proved the impregnability of a properly coordinated defensive line commanding a well-prepared kill zone. Union forces suffered 13,000 casualties and the Confederate lines held.

At Gettysburg, Longstreet failed to convince Lee of the folly of attempting the same hopeless show of courage. "All we have to do is file around his left and secure good ground between him and his capital," Longstreet pleaded. He spoke in unusually personal and emotional terms. "I have been a soldier all my life," Longstreet said, "and it is my opinion that no fifteen thousand men ever arrayed for battle can take that position."

But Lee had impatiently gestured to the Union brigades lining the ridge above and replied, "The enemy is here, and if we do not whip him, he will whip us"; any maneuvering would be taken by the men as a demoralizing retreat. Pickett's everlasting contribution to the lexicon of synonyms for futile courage followed, with the cost of 6,500 casualties in one hour. "It is all wrong, but he will have it," Longstreet sadly said. He wrote afterward, "I could see the desperate and hopeless nature of the charge and the hopeless slaughter it would cause. . . . That day at Gettysburg was one of the saddest of my life." If not Lee, then the Union soldiers who had faced Longstreet earlier had learned the lessons of war he had proved. "The moment I saw them," recalled one of Holmes's comrades in the 20th Massachusetts as Pickett's men began their charge, "I knew we should give them Fredericksburg."

Longstreet's cardinal sin after the war was to accept defeat. He wrote a letter to the newspapers urging Southerners to acknowledge reality, "abandon ideas that are obsolete and conform to the requirements of law," and, like him, accept Reconstruction, and Black suffrage. "It will ruin you, son, if you publish it," warned his Methodist minister uncle, to whom he had shown a draft.

Appealing to Lee to write a letter of support in the maelstrom of abuse that followed, Longstreet received a stiff reply five months later, leaving him out to dry: Lee "avoided all discussions of political questions," his old comrade informed him. Soon Longstreet was the cause of all the Confederate army's defeats. The keepers of Lee's "sacred memory," including his former artillery chief the Episcopal Reverend William Pendleton, invented a series of outright fabrications accusing Longstreet of disobeying Lee's command to attack earlier, thereby losing the Battle of Gettysburg, and with it the cause of Southern independence.

When James Longstreet died in 1904 the good ladies of the United Daughters of the Confederacy voted *not* to send flowers to the funeral. His recognition as a great general far ahead of his time would have to await the clearer judgment of military professionals once the cobwebs of the Lost Cause were cleared away, and reminiscing Confederate veterans had sputtered their last.

7

LAID
IN OUR
DOORYARDS

Alexander Gardner

THE WHITE HORSE

The Confederate officer's hauntingly beautiful milk-white horse that had attracted Alpheus Williams's eye as it lay dead on the Antietam battlefield was destined for a new kind of fame, unknown before in war. Williams could have had his wish for a photograph of it just three weeks later, when an exhibition opened at Matthew Brady's "National Portrait Gallery," at the corner of Broadway and 10th Street in New York City, announced by a small placard hanging at the door bearing the title, "The Dead of Antietam."

The forty-five photographs exhibited, with copies of stereoscopic views available for purchase at fifty cents apiece, were the first actual images taken of American dead on a battlefield, the first such photographs of the realistic horrors of war to be widely viewed anywhere in the world. Brady's talented associate Alexander Gardner and another assistant had hurried to the battlefield and arrived in time to capture scenes that would become some of the most famous pictures of the Civil War: heaps of corpses in Bloody Lane, in front of the Dunker church, scattered along the fences of the Hagerstown Turnpike, an endless line of Confederate dead gath-

"Is This Death," photograph by Alexander Gardner of a Confederate officer's white horse, killed at Antietam

ered in a row awaiting burial, and the Confederate officer's eerily lifelike white horse.

Newspapers had sought to satisfy the insatiable thirst for details of the war with extra editions and assembly lines of engravers who worked overnight to produce woodcuts ready for the morning's press based on pencil drawings dispatched by deft sketch artists accompanying the troops. But the immediacy of Gardner's photographs was something completely different, as more than one contemporary observer recognized. At least a small door of conventional evasion had been forever shut. "We recognize the battle-field as a reality, but it stands as a remote one," wrote a columnist in the *New York Times* after viewing the exhibition.

The dead of the battle-field come up to us very rarely, even in dreams. We see the list in the morning paper at breakfast, but dismiss its recollection with the coffee. There is a confused mass of names, but they are all strangers. . . . Our sensations

might be different if the newspaper carrier left the names on the
battle-field and the bodies at our doors instead. . . .

Mr. Brady has done something to bring home to us the terrible reality and earnestness of war. If he has not brought bodies
and laid them in our dooryards and along the streets, he has
done something very like it.

The American craze for both photographs and news predated
the war. In 1860 there were more than 4,000 newspapers in America, twice the number in Britain, and every large city had multiple
competing dailies. There were eleven in New York, twelve in Philadelphia, eleven in Chicago, ten in St. Louis. Total newspaper sub-
scriptions averaged 2.3 per household in 1860, and, in all, American
newspapers printed and sold a billion copies a year.

Three days after the surrender of Fort Sumter the *New York
Tribune* began publishing an evening edition, which it continued
throughout the war, to catch up with the arriving news of the day;
the *New York Herald* countered with extras each afternoon at one
thirty, three, and four o'clock. The more slapdash *New York Express*
churned out so many extras that the wisecrack in newspaper circles
was that no one had ever seen its regular edition. The taboo against
Sunday editions fell almost as quickly, with the major papers in
New York, Chicago, and even proper Boston ignoring the protests
of clergymen and launching Sunday papers in the first two months
of the war. New York railroads instituted special express trains to
deliver the Sunday editions, met by crowds at each station.

Hordes thronging newspaper offices awaiting the latest editions
and the telegraphed reports posted on a board outside became a
fixture of life in the war. It became a kind of addiction in itself. Dr.
Holmes told of a friend who would dodge through side streets on
his way to pick up the noon extra, "afraid somebody will meet him
and *tell* him the news he wishes to *read*, first on the bulletin-board,
and then in the great capitals and leaded type of the newspaper";

and of another acquaintance, "an eminent scholar" who admitted he had "fallen into such a state that he would read the same telegraphic dispatches over and over again in different papers, as if they were new, until he felt as if he were an idiot." Dr. Holmes wryly compared it to the Roman populace's bread and circuses: "They must have something to eat, and the circus-shows to look at. We must have something to eat, and the papers to read. Everything else we can give up."

More subtly, Dr. Holmes observed that the feeling of an entire nation bound together by rail lines and telegraph wires—"a network of iron nerves which flash sensation and volition backward and forward to and from towns and provinces as if they were organs and limbs of a single living body"—had altered the very sensation and perception of events. It was the awakening of a "sense," wrote Louis Starr in his history of news reporting in the Civil War, "that Americans have come to know more intimately, perhaps, than any other people: that mystic sense of common destiny which is conveyed by news of great events reported everywhere and in profusion almost simultaneously with their occurrence."

George Smalley's coverage of the Battle of Antietam would in retrospect be another milestone along that road to the immediacy of events, his 7,000-word story which appeared two days later in the *Tribune* remarkable for both the speed and honesty of its reporting. He had taken the job to get out of a financial hole he had dug for himself as a young lawyer in Boston. Son of a Congregational minister, graduate of Yale and Harvard Law School, he was recommended to the *Tribune's* editor by his future father-in-law, the abolitionist leader Wendell Phillips. At Antietam he saw more of the action across the entire battlefield than anyone present that day. His horse was shot twice by enemy bullets. After dark he commandeered his assistant's horse and rode all night to Frederick, where he arrived at 3 a.m. and began an unsuccessful hunt for the telegraph operator. At seven the operator appeared and, seated on a log outside his office, Smalley began to write out a short preliminary dispatch, handing each page to the operator as it was finished. He would later learn that the message had been diverted by operators down the line to Washington, where it was delivered directly to the War Department. He tried to engage a special train but was told that was impossible without permission of the military authorities. He was finally allowed aboard a military train that afternoon, and with ten minutes to spare in Baltimore caught the express to New York. Writing all night, he arrived in the press room at 5 a.m. on the nineteenth, where the entire staff of compositors was waiting to set his piece into type, working from what Smalley later described as the most illegible manuscript they had ever seen.

He scooped all the competition but, more important, he produced the finest battle account of the war, forgoing the usual empty jingoism ("On to Richmond!" "Great Victory!") for an accurate and sober depiction of its horrors ("the dead are strewn so thickly that as you ride over it you cannot guide your horse's steps too carefully"), indecisive result ("night closes on an uncertain field. It is the greatest fight since Waterloo—all over the field contested with an obstinacy equal even to Waterloo"), and tactical mismanagement ("still more unfortunate in its results was the total failure of these separate attacks on the right and left to sustain, or in any manner co-operate with each other").

Newspapers had as yet no way to publish photographs. But the invention of the glass negative plate a few years earlier had already created a huge mass market for portraits of famous figures, stereoscopic views of exotic scenery, and, beginning in 1859, carte de visite album cards that would provide a ubiquitous record of the war in the form of soldiers' personal portraits distributed to friends, relatives, and sweethearts. The price of a portrait dropped from as much as $750 for a life-sized "Imperial" format image (a staggering $30,000 in today's currency) to 25 cents (about $10). Gardner shrewdly anticipated the coming demand for portraits of war leaders and common soldiers alike by contracting with a commercial photographic supplier who could print copies by the thousands.

Alexander Gardner,
self-portrait, 1863

Though Gardner possessed a keen commercial acumen that his employer lacked—Brady resisted even hiring a bookkeeper, and the records of the business were in perpetual chaos—he shared with him an abiding conception of the photographer as artist, not mere technician. Growing up in Glasgow, Scotland, Gardner had worked as a jeweler's apprentice, a bank manager, and a newspaper proprietor before turning to photography. He came to America intending to found a utopian community in Iowa based on the socialist teachings of Robert Owen, a plan forcibly abandoned when many of its members succumbed to tuberculosis. In America he forsook the Presbyterianism of his youth for the dreamy mysticism of Swedenborgianism, and with his flamboyant beard, insouciantly dressed in an artist's smock, he could have passed for any Bohemian rebel against bourgeois convention.

The time required to set up and expose a shot, and the technical demands of the photographic process itself that remained very much in the fore at that time, reinforced Gardner's tendency to think of his works as artistic compositions. It was inescapable that he and his fellow photographers of the dead in battle looked to classical models. A photographer who accompanied British troops in the late 1850s, an Italian-born Englishman named Felice Beato, was probably one of the first to take a picture of dead soldiers; a British officer recalled Signor Beato "in great excitement" coming upon a group of slain defenders of a fort in China grouped about a gun and declaring the scene "beautiful," begging that the bodies not be moved until he could capture them in a photograph.

Many who viewed "The Dead of Antietam" remarked on the stark realism of the images. Dr. Holmes, himself a keen amateur photographer, wrote in the *Atlantic* that Gardner's images had brought back all of the emotions and horrors he had experienced searching the battlefield himself for his wounded son. "Let he who wishes to know what war is look at this series of illustrations," he wrote. "The honest sunshine 'Is Nature's sternest painter, yet the best,'" laying bare "what a repulsive, brutal, sickening, hideous thing" war is.

But in fact Gardner's images in telling ways honored artistic conventions of death, and the captions he wrote to accompany them reinforced this notion, describing the figures of the dead as if "cut in marble," or "sleeping their last sleep," or "calm and resigned . . . as though they had been caught in the act of prayer." The caption he appended to the famously lifelike white horse was *Is This Death?*

Gardner insisted that while "verbal representations . . . may or may not have the merit of accuracy," photographic depictions will be accepted "by posterity with an undoubting faith." But for all their self-declared realism, there was much that Gardner's images omitted. They captured none of the terrors of battle itself, only its aftermath, and even that in a carefully modulated manner. He never showed corpses decapitated or disemboweled or missing limbs, much less any that had been partially devoured by marauding pigs or dogs, an occurrence often remarked on by soldiers. Scarcely any

"Confederate soldiers as they fell near the Burnside Bridge,"
photograph by Alexander Gardner

of his photographs dwell on the wounded and their mutilations and agonies. And, as some remarkable detective work by the photographic historian William Frassanito discovered, in later battles (Gettysburg in particular) Gardner had clearly dragged corpses around the battlefield to pose them to his artistic satisfaction, always to conform to some idealized representation of death. One has to look closely at his images of dead soldiers at Antietam to notice one of the grimmer but unremarked-on realities that his photographs did sometimes capture: the inside-out-pockets of the Confederate dead, showing that their corpses had been systematically looted.

And then, as the historian Mark Schantz observed, there is little evidence that people who viewed Gardner's photographs were traumatized by them. Both the sensitive *New York Times* columnist who visited the exhibition and Dr. Holmes were swift to draw from them not a lesson of the madness or unsupportable cruelty of war but rather moral affirmations of patriotic resolve. "But there is poetry in the scene that no green fields or smiling landscapes can possess," the *Times* writer insisted. "Here lie men who have not hesitated to seal and stamp their conviction with their blood—men who have flung themselves into the great gulf of the unknown to teach the world that there are truths dearer than life, wrongs and shames more to be dreaded than death."

And while Dr. Holmes acknowledged that "the sight of these pictures is a commentary on civilization such as a savage might well triumph to show its missionaries," he immediately added, "Yet through such martyrdom must come our redemption. War is the surgery of crime."

There were less pleasant hints that for more than a few visitors to Brady's Gallery, part of the allure lay in the vicarious horror they were permitted to safely share by looking on these curated scenes of the dead. Some of Gardner's captions bore more melodramatic titles, playing to sensationalism: "A Harvest of Death," "Slaughter Pen," "SILENCED FOREVER!" As the *Times* writer observed of the "crowds of people . . . constantly going up the stairs" to the exhibit hall, "there is a terrible fascination . . . that draws one near these pictures and makes him loth to leave them. You will see hushed, reverend groups standing around these weird copies of carnage, bending down to look in the pale faces of the dead, chained by the strange spell that dwells in dead men's eyes."

GAWKERS AND GHOULS

Nearly all of the thousands of gawking civilians who descended on the Antietam battlefield in the days after the fight stopped to pick up souvenirs. "The country people flocked to the battlefield like vultures, their curiosity and inquisitiveness most astonishing; while my men were all at work, many of them stood around, dazed," wrote a young officer in the 57th New York who had been detailed to bury the dead. A few offered to help, bringing supplies or food for the wounded or offering to carry them to hospitals in Frederick or Hagerstown. But most of the tourists "scattered over

"Maryland and Pennsylvania farmers visiting the battle-field of Antietam," illustration by F. H. Schell in Frank Leslie's Illustrated Newspaper, *October 18, 1862*

the field, eagerly searching for souvenirs in the shape of cannon balls, guns, bayonets, swords, canteens, etc." Even the sophisticated Dr. Holmes, while professing to find "something repulsive" in the remains of battle strewn about like the remnants "of some hideous orgy," joined the relic hunters with apparent unselfconsciousness. "A bullet or two, a button, a brass plate from a soldier's belt, served well enough for mementos of my visit," he reported, also pocketing a letter written by a dead Confederate soldier.

The desire for a vicarious—if brief—experience of the battlefield swept up many. Dr. J. Franklin Dyer, the army surgeon in charge of the field hospital at the Hoffman farm, where he had seven surgeons to look after hundreds of wounded, was as disgusted at the daily sight of relic-collecting citizens roaming the fields as he was by the apparently glory-seeking civilian aid workers who quickly appeared on the scene and departed just as quickly when faced with the prospect of actually caring for the bloody dressings and pus-filled stumps of the wounded. "Surgeons have come from Baltimore and other places, but I am sorry to say they do not care to stop and do the work," he wrote in his journal. "We would have been glad if those surgeons who visited the army soon after the battle had remained to assist us, but they did not seem willing to remain and dress stumps." The wounded men found they were just another stop on the tour. A wounded Massachusetts sergeant said of these battlefield visitors: "They stare at us but do not find time to do anything."

A more ghoulish species of memento found its way into the hands of some civilians. Although discounted at first as Union exaggerations and rumors, stories of rings or other keepsakes carved from the bones of the enemy dead by Confederate soldiers and sent to admiring female relations back home are documented by enough reliable sources, including the letters of Confederate soldiers themselves, to give them credence. A soldier in the 21st Mississippi, the son of a planter, wrote his parents after Antietam that there were hundreds of Union dead lying in the area of the battlefield they controlled before retreating. He asked them to tell his sister, "I thought of collecting her a peck of Yankee finger nails to make her a sewing basket of as she is ingenious at such things but I feared I could not get them to her." Dr. Lewis H. Steiner, a Sanitary Commission inspector who had been in Frederick during its occupation by Lee's men, witnessed what he described as "one of those incredible incidents . . . which have been occasionally reported in our papers, but have always been disbelieved": a Confederate officer riding up to a group of young women (whom he took for "Southern ladies") and declaring, "Ladies, allow me to make you a present. This is a ring made from the bone of a dead Yankee."

Such relics probably said less about the hardened soldiers who fashioned them than the civilians at home for whom they offered the same morbid fascination as Gardner's photographs, with the same once-removed distance from the realities of war. What there was little to no appetite for, however, were the kinds of breathtakingly honest representations of the sheer bestiality of war that only a few of its participants ever attempted to put into words. With the possible exceptions of only Ambrose Bierce and Frank Wilkeson, no one wrote as graphically or realistically about war as John De Forest, a well-educated Union veteran from Connecticut who in 1867 published the novel *Miss Ravenel's Conversion*, a romance set against the events of the war that includes some horrifyingly vivid battle and hospital scenes. Along with unsparing descriptions of brains leaking from bulging wounds and grotesquely ironic deaths on the battlefield, he portrays the sheer terror of the soldier's inner experiences and the baseness that war drives men to as the trappings of civilization are stripped away, offering unsettling accounts of cowards and skulkers, drunk officers, venal surgeons remorselessly stealing the port, brandy, and peaches intended for their patients.

The book, unsurprisingly, was a flop. The *Atlantic Monthly*'s editor William Dean Howells praised it, and later urged De Forest to read Tolstoy's *War and Peace* when it appeared in English translation in 1886. De Forest wrote back to Howells:

> Let me tell you that nobody but he has written the whole truth about war and battle. *I* tried, and I told all I dared, and perhaps all I could. But there was one thing I did not dare tell, lest the world should infer that I was naturally a coward, and so could not know the feelings of a brave man. I actually did not dare state the extreme horror of battle, and the anguish with which the bravest soldiers struggle through it.

As Ambrose Bierce found, it was probably even less palatable to reveal that war is sordid and meaningless than to reveal that it is bloody and horrifying. Some of his most searing tales involve hideous burlesques of the brave death, exactly what Gardner's photographs so artfully conceal. His flippant treatment of battlefield gore ("I had not previously known one could get on, even in this unsatisfactory fashion, with so little brain," he writes of a sergeant dying convulsively as his brains hang out in strings) was one thing. The idea that the truth about war as soldiers knew it made conventional civilian ideas about courage literally meaningless was, however, the inspiration for his darkest humor, as when he dismisses as "a womanish fellow" one of his men who suggests putting the sergeant out of his misery by putting a bayonet through him: "Inexpressibly shocked by the cold-blooded proposal, I told him I thought not; it was irregular, and too many were looking."

One of his bitterest sendups is of the idiotic sacrifice of life by those trying to act out the expectations of civilians who will never really understand what war is. In his tale "Killed at Resaca," the protagonist is a young officer who coolly takes outrageous risks to display his courage. At the climax of the story, he charges forward on his horse directly at the enemy line, triggering a massive battle, with devastating artillery exchanges, as his comrades rush forward in an unsuccessful attempt to save him. The punchline comes with the narrator's discovery, after the end of the war, of an overlooked letter among the dead officer's effects. In a woman's hand, signed "Darling," the writer states that she had a heard a tale from a mutual acquaintance that he had been seen crouching behind a tree in an earlier battle: "I think he wants to injure you in my regard, which he knows the story would do if I believed it. I could bear to hear of my soldier lover's death, but not of his cowardice."

Bierce concludes, "These were the words which on that sunny afternoon, in a distant region, had slain a hundred men. Is woman weak?"

Soldiers themselves would become complicit in obscuring truths they had encountered; some of this was a natural inclination to forget trauma, but more was the mighty force of nostalgia. At the end of "What I Saw of Shiloh," Bierce evokes a complete circle of irony to make this point. Marveling at the way time left only memories of what had been beautiful, exotic, and adventurous in his wartime experiences, while "the danger and death and horrors" had faded, he says he "would willingly surrender an other life than the one that I should have thrown away at Shiloh," if a similar magical transformation could be wrought upon the ugly dullness of present-day life.

DEATH COMES HOME

The sheer numbers of dead at Antietam might have carried with them some shock of truth about the real nature of war, except that death on such a scale was hardly anything new. The time-honored description of the Battle of Antietam as "America's bloodiest day," the routine comparisons of the thousands killed there to far lower casualties suffered even in the worst fighting in later wars, such as the Normandy landings on D-Day, reflect a modern reaction to the scale of death that was not shared by those living in a world where death was a pervasive and constant companion. It was not that Americans of 1862 did not suffer and grieve when a son or husband died in battle; they did. But they did not see it as an outrage against the order of the universe. Because experience had taught them that was what happens, even the young often die, and deeply ingrained custom eased reconciliation to this truth.

In a world just on the cusp of the modern revolution in sanitation and medicine that would greatly extend life-spans and transform expectations about life and death, a third of children born in America in 1850 died before reaching age nine. Sermons admonished parents to be prepared to part from their children, while instruction for even small children dwelt upon death in a way that to modern eyes seems positively morbid ("Death is the only thing certain in the world," nine-year-old Clara Barton, sitting in a Massachusetts schoolroom in 1830, carefully copied over and over in her penmanship book), but which underscored the acceptance of death, and its uncontrollable inevitability, as an integral part of nineteenth-century life. As the historian Mark Schantz has argued, antebellum America was a "death-embracing" culture in ways we today can scarcely fathom. Poetry, novels, art, sermons, personal letters, all placed death at the center of antebellum life: It was literally topic No. 1. Americans in the mid-nineteenth century "understood that death awaited all who were born and prized the ability to face death with a spirit of calm resignation," wrote Schantz. "They believed that a heavenly eternity of transcendent beauty awaited them beyond the grave." In short, they entered the Civil War "with a cluster of assumptions about death" that "facilitated its unprecedented destructiveness."

They were certainly no strangers to mass death that struck without warning. Even the stunning toll of carnage during the war was routinely equaled by epidemics of cholera, yellow fever, typhoid, and other routinely fatal illnesses common in antebellum America. An outbreak of yellow fever in New Orleans in the summer of 1853 killed 12,000 in a few weeks; epidemics in New York and Chicago regularly tripled the normal death rate of about 2 percent of the population per annum. Those in the prime of life were never spared. In the years immediately before and after the war, 1 in 5 American men aged twenty to twenty-four did not survive a decade; during the war years the comparable figure was 1 in 4, not the kind of increase to make people recoil at the numbers per se.

Even under the strained circumstances of war, soldiers and their families went to extraordinary lengths to maintain the rituals of the "Good Death" that had sentimentalized and idealized death in a culture where death was ubiquitous, domestic, and familiar. Reading dying soldiers' letters and the lines of condolence sent by their officers and comrades, the historian Drew Gilpin Faust observed, one can almost see a checklist in the minds of the writers as they sought to place death in familiar consoling terms: "The deceased had been conscious of his fate, had demonstrated a willingness to accept it, had shown signs of belief in God and in his own salvation, and had left messages and instructive exhortations for those who should have been at his side." Although Faust suggested that the war overwhelmed these traditional means of understanding and accepting death, Schantz drew almost the opposite conclusion: the lengths families went to to keep these customs alive even under nearly impossible circumstances emphasize their enduring power and importance—and were precisely what made it possible for Americans of the Civil War era to accept a degree of loss and suffering that would have been unsupportable to later generations.

Most striking is the determination of families, at least those who could afford it, to recover the bodies of those killed in battle, and so maintain the ritual of seeing and bidding farewell to a loved one and providing a suitable place of burial close to home. After surviving Antietam, now marching south in the pursuit of Lee's army, a New York soldier wrote his parents, "If I get shot I don't want you to go to the trouble of sending for my body. It is all nonsense. It will do no good. It can return to its native dust as easy and as well in Dixie as anywhere." But however soldiers felt, the importance and solace their families drew from being able to maintain the customary ways of death was evident in the arduous treks countless family members made to recover the bodies of a dead son or brother, and the burgeoning business in zinc- and lead-lined coffins and embalming that the Civil War set off.

Elation is not the reaction people today would associate with locating the severely decomposed remains of a dead son. But Edward Wightman's father was wholly typical in the account he left of his long and ultimately successful quest to bring his son's body back for burial in the family plot in Connecticut. A Yale-educated lawyer, Wightman senior left a long account of his journey to North Carolina hoping to find where his son, killed during the final assault on Fort Fisher in January 1865, lay. No detail is spared: his purchase in Moorhead City of a pine coffin, all he could locate there; his excitement when he came upon a barrel of pitch to seal the seams, plus the rosin needed to crudely preserve the remains for transport; and then his rapture upon discovering at last along a line of mounds a wooden board bearing a crude inscription made by a small lamp-black brush, Sergt Major 3d N.Y. V.—E. K. Wightman. "O, how my heart leaped with joy!!!" he wrote of that moment.

The surgeon and commanding officer try to dissuade him from attempting to return with his son's body with nothing but a pine coffin to carry it in: given its state of deterioration, he should really wait until he could send a lead coffin. But he was adamant. "General, a long and tedious journey from New York City I have just performed to this place, to obtain the body of my son . . . if it not be counter to God's will I will never leave Federal Point without taking the body of Edward with me." The ability of soldiers and their families to endure the suffering and death around them was portrayed by many as an uplifting act that affirmed the sanctity and justice of their cause. As the historian Nicholas Marshall found, "The culture was at least partially successful in folding the experience of war into an effective process of coping with suffering and dying."

Yet there could be no doubt the war was testing the limits of what such rituals could do. "Burying the dead after a Civil War battle seemed always to be an act of improvisation," Faust noted. No advance preparations were ever made; coffins were practically unheard of; at Antietam, as elsewhere, some of the dead lay for weeks unburied, the grisly work left to burial details made up of reluctant soldiers sometimes assigned the task as punishment, contrabands, or local farmers hired after officers despaired of any other solution. The condition of even intact corpses left exposed for days and then shoveled into mass graves, much less those mutilated or atomized by shells, made a mockery of any antebellum notions of death, "Good" or not. A Sharpsburg man who was paid ten dollars a day by a group that had come from Massachusetts to search for their missing boys never forgot the awful moment they located the son of one, "partly buried, one foot sticking out. I do not want to witness such a scene again."

Any expectation of reverence was extinguished in revulsion. Union soldiers assigned to bury the Confederate dead at Fox's Gap, where the hot days had made the job particularly horrific, could only manage to do the work staggeringly drunk. Though it would be played up as a Yankee atrocity story in later years (still repeated on the large and histrionic North Carolina monument erected at Fox's Gap in 2002 by Confederate sympathizers), the burial of fifty-eight Confederate dead in an unfinished well was an act less of contempt than urgency and necessity on impenetrably stony ground. Shallow mass graves, of both Union and Confederate dead, littered the fields of Antietam.

Anonymity was the final blow to any comfort grieving relations could hope to draw from the customary rituals surrounding death: relatively few of the bodies were even marked by name. A private in the 15th Massachusetts, Roland Bowen, explained with stark frankness to the father of a friend killed at Antietam, who had asked to know "the particulars" of his son's death, how he had been buried. "I fear they will do you no good and that you will be more mortified after the facts are told than you are now," Bowen replied. "Still you ask it and whether it be for the better or worse not a word shall be kept from you." After looking over hundreds of bodies in vain, Bowen wrote, he had caught up with a burial party just as they had placed his friend in a long shallow trench along with scores of others. He was able to provide at least the numerical position of the corpse among those deposited two deep. "Perhaps you don't know how we bury the dead," he wrote.

The trench is 25 feet long, 6 feet wide and about 3 feet deep. The corpses were buried by Co., that is the members of each Co. are put together. Co. H was buried first in the upper end of the trench next the woods. They are laid in two tiers, one top of the other. The bottom tier was laid in, then straw laid over the head and feet, then the top tier laid on them and covered with dirt about 18 inches deep. . . . Mr. Ainsworth, this is not the way we bury folks at home. I am sorry, but I was too late to have it different. Then there is a board put up at each end of the trench with a simple inscription, "15th Mass. buried here." There is 39 men in the trench with Henry. . . . Some of our men had their clothes taken off by the rebels. Henry did not have anything taken but shoes and what was in his pockets.

Even in the face of such disruptions to the antebellum culture of death, the war's toll never, however, became a source of serious opposition to the war itself from grieving families. The Northern Copperheads who called for peace never made halting the slaughter a reason, focusing instead on infringements to civil liberties and high taxation the war had brought, the unequal burden they asserted fell on the poor through the military draft, and (most of all) their revulsion at abetting the emancipation of the Negroes.

In some ways, the war had even made death *more* palatable, by providing a readily understandable meaning to what the bereaved always struggled to understand as God's purpose when young men died in the prime of life. Dr. Dyer wrote in his journal three weeks after Antietam, "When I had charge of the Hoffman Hospital, every day fathers and mothers, wives and brothers, came looking for their friends. Many of them learned for the first time of their death, but I never heard one of them in the bitterness of their grief reproach any one for influencing them to engage in the war."

James McPherson concluded from soldiers' letters that religious belief increased as the war went on. But it was a fatalistic and often superstitious Christianity, equal part faith in God's protection and resignation to one's fate that rested in his hands. Edward Wightman reported that even "the hardest characters among us" believed in the protective powers of a pocket Bible or prayer book. His fellow soldiers had nothing but jeers for the "theoretical Christianity" offered by preachers, he related, but "a real earnest practical Christian" who shared the soldier's lot was respected.

Wartime faith was certainly a departure from the kind of enlightened humanitarianism that New England Unitarians before the war were sure would in due course infuse all of mankind, a religious belief based on God's gift of rationality and goodness. The madness of war was a living rebuke to any such notions, and whether the war ultimately affirmed or undermined religious belief, it unmistakably marked a growing rift between religion and science: the Unitarians' tranquil reconciliation of the two found fewer takers, and the rational pragmatism that Holmes and many like him carried from the war was to become the distinguishing feature of American secular culture in the century to follow.

Just as the army had made no provisions for burying the dead, it had no system for tracking their fate or notifying families. That was a failing that sheer numbers did at once drive home. Immediately after the war the government established a U.S. Burial Corps, to locate, identify, and rebury the Union dead. The national cemetery that would be laid out at Antietam in 1867, its deliberately neat rows of identical white headstones in a parklike setting a pointed contrast to the haphazard shallow temporary burials across the farms and woods of the battlefield, was a tangible act of apology and assumption of public responsibility for the previously private ways of death. Inevitable cases of mistaken identity endured as a lasting reminder and rebuke of the former neglect. Out of wry humor, or perhaps simple gratitude at being spared a similar fate, a Pennsylvania private every year sent flowers to be placed on the grave of the unknown soldier at Antietam Cemetery mistakenly marked with his name.

REMAINS

In 1892, a wall of the German Reformed Church in Keedysville, which had been used as a field hospital during the Battle of Antietam, cracked and the foundation beneath gave way. On investigation, the cause was found to be a pile of severed limbs that had been buried in a pit against the foundation wall.

For years after the battle, farmers kept turning up bones, unexploded shells, and other debris of battle when they tried to plow their fields. Plowing itself was an ordeal even apart from any unpleasant discoveries it brought to the surface: the ground, as one farmer complained in a damage claim submitted to the U.S. government, had been "beaten down as hard as a turnpike road" by the passage of troops, horses, and guns, and the earth broke only into "great clods and lumps," unsuitable for planting. On the Roulette farm near Bloody Lane, acres of ground were occupied by 700 dead and acres more left unplowable. Many of the Confederate dead were not removed until the 1880s. "It was a common thing to see human bones lying loose in gutters and fence corners for several years," one local recalled, "and frequently hogs would be seen with limbs in their mouths."

Sharpsburg and its surrounding farms and villages were the first well-settled area of the North to be the scene of fighting, and its citizens experienced realities of war and its aftermath on far more intimate terms than the readers of newspapers or viewers of Alexander Gardner's photographs. Members of the Pietist and pacifist Dunker sect who farmed a number of the large parcels near the church that would be the center of the battlefield had watched smoke rising from South Mountain after they returned home from church on Sunday the fourteenth, and many had fled with what livestock they could move; others hid their horses in cellars and hoped for the best. Many other civilians took refuge in the limestone caves along the C&O Canal. All returned to find their crops trampled or foraged to the ground, stock and horses gone, larders stripped bare, houses, barns, and yards filled with the wounded. "Every door in town was broken open," a Confederate soldier recounted, "and everything that could be eaten . . . consumed." No civilians were killed, apparently, but buildings in Sharpsburg, including the small tavern and hotel, were "perforated like a honeycomb" by the shelling, with only five dwellings in the entire town escaping damage.

In the weeks that followed, epidemics seeded by the traversing armies swept through the civilian population: smallpox and typhoid fever, the latter taking the Roulettes' twenty-month-old daughter along with many others. A highly contagious and highly fatal equine infection known as glanders, carried apparently by the Union army's mules and horses, felled farmers' animals that had not fallen into the hands of Confederate or Union forces, adding to the piles of dead horses requiring disposal. Samuel Mumma, whose farmhouse near Bloody Lane had been burned to the ground by the rebels, dragged fifty-five dead horses left from the battle on his farm to the East Woods and burned them there, only making a small dent in the problem.

Many local citizens spent years seeking compensation for their losses, but establishing what the Union army had taken or destroyed to the satisfaction of government examiners proved an arduous process, and no compensation was offered at all for damage done by the Confederates. Phillip Pry, owner of the house that had been McClellan's headquarters, filed claim after claim for his losses— horses, cattle, sheep, hogs, 800 bushels of wheat, 2,550 of corn, 8,000 fence rails, rent for 85 acres of pasture—but received only a fraction, and ten years after the war he sold out and started anew in Tennessee.

The sheer quantity of discarded war materiel proved more a disposal problem than a boon to civilians left to clean up the mess. Shattered wagons and caissons, shredded haversacks, battered canteens, broken rifles, scraps of scorched harness, heaps of empty cartridge boxes were gathered up and burned or pitched down abandoned wells. The bayonets that one Mumma descendant recalled, a century later, her grandmother had always found handy as fireplace pokers were an exception to the general inutility of the abandoned piles of junk. A local newspaper reported that on Christmas Day, three months after the battle, residents of South Mountain entertained themselves throwing unexploded shells into a bonfire (DANGEROUS SPORT, the paper chided in its headline), but for years after, more grim accounts of fatal accidents regularly appeared when the curious or careless came in contact with leftover ordnance, or farmers hit them with plows and threshers. The teenaged son of the pastor of the German Reformed Church in Sharpsburg was killed when he tried to hammer open a shell; more than one citizen was severely injured trying to melt the valuable lead out of artillery rounds. Meanwhile so many boys in Middletown availed themselves of the opportunity to equip themselves with free rifles, with inevitable consequences, that the town council was compelled to adopt an ordinance barring anyone under the age of sixteen from carrying or discharging a firearm.

As recently as 2013 live unexploded shells were still turning up in the fields around Sharpsburg, each prompting a call to the military's demolition experts, who are able to consult a handy official U.S. Navy publication, *A Field Guide for Civil War Explosive Ordnance*, for correct procedures on identifying and defusing some of the more deadly and enduring reminders of that day in September.

As those with memories of what war was like died or moved away, the land itself healed over to conceal its scars, abetted by the earnest and ever-ironic work of preservationists. The Dunker church, abandoned by its dwindling congregation, its brick walls picked apart by souvenir hunters, collapsed in a windstorm in 1921. After serving as the site of a gas station, souvenir stand, and lunch counter, the property was restored with a facsimile of the original structure reconstructed atop the old foundation in time for the centennial of the battle in 1962. Visitors today see a beautiful, whitewashed little church, standing like all the surviving farmsteads within the park's boundaries neater and better maintained than they ever were when marked by the wear and tear of life. Alexander Gardner caught occasional glimpses of real life behind his portraits of death: sheets and long-johns strung out on a farmhouse porch to dry, pickets askew on a backyard fence awaiting mending, overgrown brush in yards of working farms where other daily chores demanded greater attention. The strange and utter deadness of vacant but immaculate farmhouses and barns there today is the absence not only of life but of death; all witness they once bore to the destruction of battle obscured by time, paint, and the anachronistic primness of twenty-first-century lawn care.

8

WOMAN'S WORK

Clara Barton

"PURSUED BY A SHADOW"

It was the Battle of Antietam that launched Clara Barton's fame as "The Angel of the Battlefield." But she was an angel pursued by demons that even her later triumphs could never exorcise.

In the spring of 1852, recently turned thirty, she looked to the future and saw a vast emptiness stretching out before her. She had broken free of the "long shackles" of home—the same image she would use a decade later to describe overcoming the army's reluctance to permit a woman into the field—only to find more of the same. "It will be a quiet resting time," she wrote in her diary, "when all these cares and vexations and anxieties are past and I no longer give nor take offence. I am badly organized to live in the world. . . . I am weary of all that's so wrongly called life."

At home she had spent years "wishing myself dead," she confessed to her nephew once, a feeling that never really left her in all her later fame. "The lives of us all are at best only a kind of slow suicide," she wrote in 1876 during one of her regular, multiyear episodes of near-total mental and physical collapse. Throughout her life, boredom and idleness would always bring a torrent of old fears rushing back, the crippling doubt that she was not giving all she was capable of, and even worse that the world did not care. "Nothing makes me so sick of life as to feel that I am sacrificing it—and it is sacrificed when one is pursued by a shadow from which they cannot escape."

There were shadows enough from childhood in a central Massachusetts mill town: an insane sister who had to be kept locked in a room with barred windows, a mother given to swearing and cheeseparing miserliness like some demented character in a Dickens novel, buying only rotting vegetables and baking stacks of apple and mincemeat pies that she would hide away until they grew moldy. Described by a school friend as a "rather thick-set girl" with "heavy low eyebrows," Clara was more than usually tormented by adolescent self-consciousness of her appearance, and would periodically starve herself to try to lose weight. Her wondering great-niece recalled Aunt Clara in her seventies still agonizing over her looks, working assiduously to cover her age by dying her hair jet-black (while denying she did so), even stuffing tissue paper in her bust. To reporters, *Who's Who*, even census takers, she gave her birthdate as 1830, taking nine years off her age.

Despairing of what to do with their shy, sensitive, studious, tomboyish, and above all "incomprehensible" youngest daughter, her parents had consulted the famous phrenologist L. N. Fowler, in town to deliver a lecture; he advised "she has all the qualities of a teacher." She found satisfaction taming the rough and sullen boys in her classes by giving them unaccustomed respect, winning their respect in turn by proving she could be as tough as they were, playing ball with them at recess with an unfeminine adroitness she had learned from her older brothers; but she was always impatient once she had straightened out one school, and always moved on to another the next year. "I know how it will be at length," she wrote in her own despairing spring of 1852. "I shall take a strange sudden start and be off somewhere and all will wonder at and judge and condemn, but like the past I will survive it all and go on working at some trifling unsatisfactory thing, and half paid at that."

She had the kind of fierce sense of justice and egalitarianism that is often impersonal and domineering, and she often snapped at insufficient expressions of gratitude for her humanitarian endeavors. She freely opened her meager purse to pay for her consumptive nephew's "prairie cure" in the fresh air of Minnesota, but grew impatient at his complaining and refusal to obey instructions, finally telling his brother with savage irritation, "The child's disease must have removed from his lungs to his head." When late in the war she established an office to publish the names of missing soldiers to help provide information to families, she was equally indignant when some of the objects of her inquiries did not appreciate being found, having taken advantage of the war to slip off and start a new life somewhere else. She told off one soldier who had written to ask her to stop, curtly informing him that she would inform his family anyway: "It seems to have been the misfortune of your family to think more of you than you did of them, and probably more than you deserve from the manner in which you treat them."

The war had offered a strange sudden start that at last seemed equal to her restless energy and burning need to outrun the shadow. Visits to the soldiers encamped around Washington at the start of the war, to whom she brought pies, cakes, jellies, and sewing kits of her own making, fired larger ambitions. Soon she was collecting and distributing parcels sent by other women and relief societies from her hometown, moving from her rented room to a larger commercial space as the barrels and packing cases piled up; within six months she had three warehouses filled with donated supplies.

It had required "a long struggle," or so she later claimed, with her sense of decency and "the appalling fact that I was only a woman" before she dared seek permission to travel directly to the front to deliver items "for the comfort of the sick and wounded." But that was one of the many nods she would feel compelled, even years later, to make to Victorian propriety. In fact, she was burning to go. More than that, she was burning to be the first, and if she could arrange it, and she usually did, the only woman on the scene. She would later explain that she found herself "cramped and unhappy" alongside

Clara Barton in the 1860s

other workers, but what she really disliked was competition with or subordination to others. Much of her misery and duplicity grew from the impossibility of reconciling the social expectations of the role and conduct of women which she was unwilling to completely transgress, and her rightly perceived assessment of her abilities that the world was unprepared to fully employ, or even acknowledge. "If she had belonged to the other sex," said Henry Bellows, who as president of the Sanitary Commission did not always have reason to agree with or get along with her, "she would have been a merchant prince, a great general, or a trusted political leader."

No one knew that better than Clara Barton; barred from cultivating or at least displaying the professional ambition and executive skills that would earn a man applause and advancement, she poured her enormous energies into what were in fact little more than symbolic acts that appealed to the stereotypes of the time about where the natural genius of women lay. A half century after the Civil War, an old soldier angry at criticism of her management of the Red Cross reflected the public image she had so effectively fashioned for herself: "Clara Barton gave expression to the sympathy and tenderness of all the hearts of all the women in the world." A century after the war a monument erected to her memory at Antietam showed how little had changed, describing her work there as an "act of love and mercy."

Her undeniable physical courage, ability to endure great hardship, and resolute steadiness in the face of battlefield gore, suffering, and death were always recast in the postwar lectures that secured her fame as expressions of traditionally feminine traits of self-denial and caregiving. Like many humanitarians, she equated the value of the results with the earnestness of the effort, but at some level she was aware of the disparity between how hard she worked and how little she accomplished, and could never resist the temptation to exaggerate. The one wagonload of supplies she brought to Antietam became six; the two days she spent at Culpeper became five; her appointment looking after the nursing and diet of patients at one corps field hospital became the superintendency of nursing for the entire Army of the James, a position that did not exist. It was a pattern she continued in her humanitarian work after the war. A shocked aide found she had gone back through the lists of small sums of money distributed to starving and homeless refugees in Strasbourg, where she worked at the invitation of the International Red Cross during the Franco-Prussian War of 1870–71, and had added a zero to the end of each figure; she was covering up not peculation but only her failure to do as much as she had publicly claimed.

Her need to place herself at the center of action made her impatient of ever sticking to the steady attendance at hospital bedsides that thousands of women nurses devoted themselves to with far less fanfare in the war. During the war she routinely penned dramatic accounts intended for publication (they were addressed to an anonymous "My Dear Friend"), dated and composed as if written in the midst of battle, but which were not: notably one which she was supposed to have found the time to write during the Battle of Culpeper when, as she later claimed, she had gone five days and nights with but three hours of sleep. Her diary confirms she returned to Washington after two days, and promptly slept for twenty-two hours.

No matter. From 1866 to 1868 she was constantly on the lecture circuit, charging $75 to $100 per appearance, earning upwards of $1,000 a month, the equivalent of about twenty times that in present-day dollars, as she traveled from city to city on a hectic schedule. Lest any find themselves at a loss for a description of her appearance on the stage, she provided her own. "Easy and graceful, neither tall nor short, neither large nor small, head large and finely shaped with a profusion of jet-black hair with no manner of ornament save its own glossy beauty. She is well dressed. Her voice at first low and sweet but falling upon the ear with a clearness of tone and distinctness of utterance at once surprising and entrancing."

Her most popular lecture was "Work and Incidents of Army Life." Most of the "incidents" were unverifiable, many improbable on their face, but all well attuned to the melodramatic and sentimental tastes of the day: touching coincidences, hairbreadth escapes when a bullet tore through the sleeve of her dress and killed the man she was cradling in her arms to give a drink from a cup, a fair-haired dying boy pleading to see his beloved sister once more ere he depart the earth and Miss Barton—inadvertently; she would not consciously stoop to imposture—playing the part of "Dear Mary" to relieve his loneliness; gruff teamsters wiping away a manly tear at an act of unexpected kindness from her; wounded men, one minute demoralized and complaining, reacting to her womanly ministrations with "brave hopeful assurances" and a rousing cheer of renewed courage. "I bowed my head in penitence and humbly acknowledged that just rebuke upon all past ingratitude," Barton intoned. And finding to her amazement that the last three boxes of wine she had carried to Antietam were packed in cornmeal rather than sawdust, just when she had given up on finding anything to feed the wounded men lying nearby, she set to work at once, cook-

ing up bucketsful of gruel using kettles she scrounged in the farmhouse. "A woman would not hesitate long, under circumstances like
this," she explained of such housewifely resourcefulness.

The climax of her account of the Battle of Antietam in her "Work
and Incidents" lecture was the moment she opened the farmhouse
door of a field hospital she had driven up to with her supplies. There
she beheld Dr. James L. Dunn, whom she had assisted at the Battle
of Culpeper by cooking soup and supplying shirts for the wounded
men under his care. At the sight of her, the doctor "threw up his
hands" and was speechless, Barton recounted, but, recovering himself after a moment, declared, "God has indeed remembered us.
How did you get from Virginia here and so soon and again to supply our necessities, and they are terrible. We have nothing but our
instruments and the little chloroform we brought in our pockets—
have not a *bandage, rag, lint* or string and all there shell wounded men
bleeding to death."

Dunn had written a letter to his wife following the Battle of
Culpeper which he may or may not have intended to appear in the
newspapers, but it achieved enormous subsequent circulation. In
it he recounted Barton appearing in his moment of need, and said,
"I thought that night if heaven ever sent out a homely angel, she
must be one." In the clipping she pasted in her scrapbook Barton
crossed out the word "homely" and substituted in her own hand,
"holy." Her first admiring biographers dutifully followed her cue,
bestowing on her the epithet "the holy angel," or simply "the angel
of the battlefield."

She was an angel, however, who could not share the limelight
with anyone. Before traveling to Antietam she had sent away her
old friend and Washington landlady Almira Fales, actually the first
woman to travel to the front to aid men in the field. But Barton
insisted that Fales had run away at the first sign of danger at Second
Bull Run ("*I* know I should *never leave a wounded* man there if I knew
it, though I were taken prisoner forty times," Barton huffed). Dropping Fales in any case allowed her to add to the pathos of her arrival

on the field at Antietam: "I saw no other trace of womankind. *I was faint* but *could not eat. Weary* but could not *sleep."*

The Sanitary Commission, which often furnished her transportation and the stores she distributed, was, she privately complained, a humbug, "a fudge," apparently because its far better-organized and -planned operations threatened to expose the amateurishness and triviality of her own efforts by unflattering comparison. In her dramatization of her meeting with Dr. Dunn at Antietam she had declared that she had come with "everything," including lanterns to allow the surgeons to continue working at night, a bit of foresight that had again rendered the doctor speechless. But this was one of seventy-one field hospitals. The Sanitary Commission sent at least twenty-five times the tonnage of supplies and equipment to Antietam, sixty barrels of bandages, tens of thousands of towels and pillows and shirts, much-needed chloroform, tons upon tons of beef stock, canned meat, condensed milk, lemons, and farina for the wounded and sick.

In 1863, at Hilton Head, the sea island off of Charleston occupied by Union troops, she flatly refused to have anything to do with the women under Dorothea Dix, the tireless reformer of prisons and insane asylums who had been appointed superintendent of the thousands of female nurses now serving in the Union army. "What can I do?" Barton angrily wrote in her diary. "I should be out of place there . . . Miss Dix is supreme, and her appointed nurse is matron. . . . Should I prepare my food and thrust it against the outer wall, in the hope it might strengthen the patients inside? Should I tie up my bundle of clothing and creep in and deposit it on the doorstep and slink away like a guilty mother?"

In South Carolina that spring and summer she had the first and only true romance of her life, a passionate affair with a married officer that she knew would not last but swept her off her feet. She had had her share of admirers, drawn to her by her wit, intellect, and dashing horseback riding, but as a relative who knew her well in her twenties put it, "Clara Barton was a much stronger character than any of the men who made love to her that I do not think she was ever seriously tempted to marry any of them."

Instead she collected tame followers. Throughout her life she relied on a series of self-abnegating men who sacrificed their lives to support her work. She tended to write them out of the accounts of her accomplishments, too. Cornelius Welles, a Hartford minister who had been sent by a missionary society to Washington to help educate freedmen but who had been drawn to tend the wounded soldiers filling the city, traveled with Barton to Culpeper, Manassas, and Antietam, clearly an equal coworker at first. But soon she was referring to him as "my assistant," and he vanishes altogether from her accounts of Antietam, though he unmistakably was at her side throughout.

She described him later as "meek, patient, faithful," which seemed to be the necessary qualifications for the job. Another long-devoted assistant, who arranged her travels and took care of her correspondence at the Red Cross, was "helpful, faithful . . . and true." The most self-denying of them all was Julian Hubbell, whom she had met in Dansville, New York, during one of her regular extended rest cures at a sanitarium. A science teacher, twenty-six years her junior, shy and small, he devoted the rest of his life to her, obediently following her directions to go to medical school to make himself most useful, sharing her house, serving as her chief field agent for the Red Cross, usually referring to himself in the third person as "her boy." When at age fifty he fell in love with a beautiful and accomplished young woman, Barton worked relentlessly to break up the match, employing an effective and successful display of poor health, martyrdom, and needling reminders of the needs of the organization.

Barton's name to her less besotted aides was "The Queen," or "Great I Am." Yet all of her self-aggrandizing was less the pursuit of glory than of reassurance—reassurance that all her hard work had mattered. In London she dodged a meeting with Florence Nightingale, complaining that she, Clara Barton, was always being referred to as "The Florence Nightingale of America." Why isn't Florence

Nightingale "The Clara Barton of Britain?" she fumed. After she was ousted from the Red Cross for managerial and financial incompetence too large to ignore, visitors would sometimes find her at her home in Glen Echo, Maryland, working in the garden in an old cotton dress, to which pinned across the front were the medals awarded her by foreign royalty, including the Iron Cross bestowed by Kaiser Wilhelm I, for her humanitarian efforts around the world.

INFLUENCE AND INTUITION

In what she did and did not do, and what she did and did not tell the truth about, Clara Barton reflected the experiences of thousands of other women for whom the Civil War created new opportunities without abandoning old expectations.

European visitors in the first half of the nineteenth century were startled by American women's assertions of social equality, which they interpreted as a direct consequence of the expanding democratic values of the new republic. Women mingled with men on nearly all social occasions, which had not previously been the case; they traveled alone on steamboats and stagecoaches confident of courteous and deferential treatment from strangers; young girls, rather than being cloistered under the protection of their fathers' homes, learned from an early age to acquire self-reliance in dealing with a sometimes dangerous world. The ideal republican marriage, extolled by writers everywhere, was based on mutual love, compatibility, and respect, rather than property, dowries, and ownership.

Female literacy, especially in the North, soared in the decades following the Revolution, and the nineteenth century saw the founding of many academies for the education of women, focusing not on "ornamental" subjects like drawing, dancing, and music to amuse the male sex, but on the acquisition of such enlightened knowledge— grammar, arithmetic, history, geography—as would benefit society as a whole, both in their own possession and as the first instructors of their children. An anonymous poem at the dawn of the century captured the new republican spirit that made the rights—or at least the education and social standing—of women an inescapable question in a country established upon the rights of man.

> *Let us not force them back, with brow severe,*
> *Within the pale of ignorance and fear,*
> *Confin'd entirely by domestic arts:*
> *Producing only children, pies and tarts.*

Although the common law of coverture still placed all of a woman's property in the sole hands of her husband unless it was held in a specially created trust, many states in the decades following the Revolution passed new inheritance laws expanding the legal rights of widows, giving them outright control of at least a third of their deceased husband's real property so they could dispose of it as they chose (rather than holding it only as a life interest, as was previously the case), and all states but South Carolina liberalized divorce laws.

Yet few, even among the small number of women reformers pressing for more radical change, advocated equality for women in the worlds of politics and commerce. To do so, nearly all agreed, would violate women's "essential nature." In fact, and ever so ironically, the same democratizing forces that had dramatically elevated the status of American women in the first half of the nineteenth century had in some striking ways worked to confine that newly acquired status even more fixedly to the domestic sphere. That was one of the more shrewd observations that the French political theorist Alexis de Tocqueville made in his celebrated study of American society and democracy in the 1830s. In its exaltation of individual freedom of action and conscience, republicanism had weakened the ties between the family and society at large, elevating the importance of the private sphere. But, as Tocqueville observed, egalitarianism in public life, while fostering a kind of mutual tolerance and "virile confidence," drained the outside world of the traditional sources of authority that offered models of other important moral virtues, such as intelligence, self-denial, dedication, and loyalty. "Fancied equality" in the public sphere reduced human relations there to the materialistic and legalistic: "Souls remain apart."

In an oft-quoted conclusory passage, Tocqueville wrote, "Now that I come near the end of this book in which I have recorded so many considerable achievements of the Americans, if anyone asks me what I think the chief cause of the singular prosperity and growing power of this people, I should answer that it is due to the superiority of their women." But that was neither feminism nor gallantry. It was only because women took *no* part in public life that they were able, in Tocqueville's view, to be the true drivers of "democratic progress," the keepers and transmitters of finer values that had been excluded from democracy's public sphere. Democracy had made the home, and thus the women who kept it, that much more important to society.

Embraced by many activist women in the antebellum years, this picture of women exercising their "influence" through their natural yet exalted place in the home became a virtual "cult of domesticity," as modern feminist scholars have aptly termed it. It was *Godey's Lady's Book*, the most successful of the more than one hundred women's magazines that sprang up in antebellum America, which popularized that word "influence" to genteelly describe women's newfound assertion of power in the domestic sphere. All reinforced the message that the home was a refuge from the increasing rough and tumble of modern life, and it was woman's mission to cultivate it as a civilizing repository of virtues—sociability, morality, devotion, charity, kindness—that would otherwise be torn apart in economic and political competition in the "outside world." Catharine Beecher, sister of the author of *Uncle Tom's Cabin,* vigorous promoter of women's education, author herself of one of the first bibles of "domestic science," declared in 1846, "Let the women of a country be made virtuous and intelligent and the men will certainly be the same ... to American women, more than to any other on earth, is committed the exalted privilege of extending over the world those blessed influences which are to renovate degraded man." To sully themselves with business or politics would not only go against women's natural gifts of tenderness and refinement, but threaten their place as "God's vice-regent upon earth."

Although individual experiences varied enormously by class and circumstance, only about 10 percent of women in antebellum America brought in any cash income from employment outside the home. On a number of fronts economic opportunities for women actually contracted during the mid-nineteenth century as the physical separation of home and workplace that industrialization and the growing market economy ushered in emphasized the separate spheres of work and home, man and woman. Originally viewed as degrading to men, factory work was an almost exclusively female domain in the first half of the nineteenth century. But the New England textile mills that had offered temporary and respectable employment for girls and young women seeking to supplement their families' incomes for a few years, or save for their wedding trousseaux— albeit earning a fraction of the daily pay male laborers made—were by the 1850s already shifting to a permanent proletarian male workforce, most of them new immigrants.

Women who had worked as midwives in colonial America were pushed aside in the professionalization of medicine in the ensuing decades, though the male leaders of the field now allowed that women could play an even more important role nursing the sick within the confines of their own homes. Owing to their self-sacrificing and attentive natures, women made better nurses than men: "They are formed for days and nights and months and years of watchfulness," opined Dr. William A. Alcott of Boston, an author of many books on women's health. As the historian Ann Douglas Wood observed,

A rough bargain was being struck here as in so many other occupational fields at the turn of the nineteenth century. Women were exchanging some kind of professional expertise and official recognition for a domesticated version of the occupation in question, a version fed by official veneration but sapped by its distance from technological, scientific advance and its closeness to the hearth. In other words, women, told that they had been third-rate professional doctors, were promised that they could be first-rate amateur nurses. They could no longer be midwives, but they could be madonnas.

An estimated 20,000 women worked in the hospitals of the Union armies during the war. They included not only those enrolled by the Army medical bureau under Dix's superintendence, but thousands more employed by the Sanitary Commission or directly by regimental surgeons, plus thousands of others listed as cooks, laundresses, or "matrons," all of whose duties overlapped with those of nurses. They varied enormously in skill, aptitude, and dedication, but the one thing they all shared was a lack of formal education for the work: that there were no schools for training nurses until after the Civil War put the "madonnas" firmly in the majority among those who offered their services.

Surgeons generally preferred the Catholic nursing sisters, commonly if inaccurately referred to as the Sisters of Charity, who had the advantage of having actually worked tending the sick as a vocation, and (as Surgeon General Hammond observed when Lincoln inquired about the balance between Catholic and Protestant nurses) were "trained to obedience."

The far more numerous Protestant amateurs, seeking to make an army hospital a mirror of the home where they were used to reigning supreme, did not rank obedience a virtue. Many of them infuriated surgeons with their religious sanctimoniousness, defiance of routine, administration of "syrups" and other home remedies of their own devising, and insistence that a woman's "intuition" was the equal to any professional knowledge in deciding what their "boys" required. While often objecting to the brutality and roughness of surgeons and male attendants toward patients, which was

probably an accurate diagnosis, women nurses themselves not infrequently reinforced the equally brutal social stigma equating cowardice with unmanly weakness, delivered with an extra wallop of
female moral superiority. A stock tale in memoirs of women Civil
War nurses relates a dying soldier, overcome with agony and fear
of his impending end, being sternly chastised by the author along
the lines, "If you must die, die like a man, and not like a coward."
Then—the invariable happy ending—a rapturous glow suffuses the
dying soldier's face as he accepts Jesus at the last, and slips away
to eternity.

That do-gooders can be a nuisance was not a discovery unique to
Civil War surgeons, and many felt that an excessive concern for propriety among the more well-to-do volunteer nurses added another
order of irritation. Dix seemed to be more concerned about the
appearance of her charges than their abilities. Mary Livermore, who
directed the Northwestern Sanitary Commission, somewhat cattily
but one suspects accurately, observed of her, "She personally examined the qualifications of every applicant. The women must be over
thirty years of age, plain almost to repulsion in dress, and devoid of
personal attractions, if they hoped to receive the approval of Miss
Dix. She also insisted on good health and an unexceptionable moral
character. Many of the women whom she rejected because they
were too young and too beautiful entered the service under other
auspices, and became eminently useful. Many women whom she
accepted because they were sufficiently old and ugly proved unfit for
the position, and a disgrace to their sex."

Dr. Dyer of the 19th Massachusetts was probably typical of many
male surgeons in regarding what they saw as ignorance, meddling,
and self-righteousness of amateur nurses as more trouble than they
were worth. His last straw came after Gettysburg.

Most of the women quarreled with each other, each whispering
very quietly that they didn't want to associate with some others,
on account of their reputation not being good. It is singular that

each one was the only truly pious and virtuous one in the whole lot. A man wounded in the head wanted [a nurse] to wash and fix him up a little, as blood was dried on his face. . . . "My dear friend," said she, "I will read you a chapter from the Bible and that will do just as well." Rather doubtful.

Dyer was overjoyed to hear that Clara Barton herself had gone to South Carolina. "I hope she will stay there," he recorded in his diary. "She plagued me so that I had to get her out of the cook house and put one of my own men in charge."

In fairness to Dyer, he had as little patience with male do-gooders: "One night it rained very hard and only a part of the men had been brought under shelter. A lot of the Christian Commission got in one of the large tents and prayed very earnestly for some time that God would stop the rain, and made so much noise about it that the Doctor had to stop them. They could have brought all in in the time they were praying. These outsiders may have good intentions, but they don't know how to do anything."

But there was no doubt that women nurses held the upper hand when it came to keeping hospitals clean, patients neat and properly fed, clothes and bedding regularly laundered, and providing their "boys"—and most indeed were little more than boys, away from home for the first time—the maternal solicitude they secretly or not so secretly craved. (As Ann Wood pointed out, "There is pity, but there is an undernote of I-told-you-so, in the tone of these nurses when they describe, as Mary Livermore did, mutilated men deliriously screaming, 'Mother! Mother!'") "Our husbands, sons, and brothers need us, and want us, if the surgeons do not," one determined volunteer told Livermore when she tried to warn her of the resistance she would encounter.

And while there was always a note of the self-congratulatory in Civil War nurses describing having got their own way as "cutting red tape"—sometimes it was less red tape than necessary organization and routine that inexperienced outsiders simply failed to comprehend—they were definitely on to something. As outsiders they were able to question what those bound by the chain of command, deterred by careerism, or inured by custom had neither the authority, inclination, nor perspective to question. Outraged by corruption and mistreatment of patients at the Washington hospital where she was assigned, nurse Hannah Ropes, magnificently ignoring the chain of command altogether, marched off to see Secretary of War Stanton, who listened to her, nodded, and had the ringleaders, the chief surgeon among them, imprisoned.

Women had carried to their hospital work in the Civil War the inherent strictures, as well as the inherent moral authority, of their traditional place in the home. In their view they had not so much left the home as carried the home with them, and when the war was over nearly all returned to former lives. But that still had raised an interesting possibility about the place of women in society which would not quite go so quietly away. "If the world was a home," Wood pointedly asked, "where would their 'influence' end?"

LINT AND HAVELOCKS

Havelocks were a great early joke of the war. Inspired by a newspaper account of the eponymous headgear that one General Henry Havelock devised to protect British troops in India from sunstroke, ladies' aid societies across the North seized on the idea of manufacturing them by the thousands as a meaningful contribution to the Union war effort. "Sewing meetings" were organized to direct the work. During the first month of the war, one New York regiment received 1,200 of the garments. Resembling the white linen neck flaps of subsequent French Foreign Legion fame, havelocks were of doubtful utility in North America, unsoldierly in appearance, and served mostly to provide entertainment to their recipients, who devised new and humorous ways of employing them as nightcaps, turbans, and bandages. The "havelock fever," Mary Livermore recalled, vanished as quickly as it arose, only to be succeeded by an equally earnest "lint and bandage mania." Endless meetings to discuss "the lint question" were held, recipes for the best methods and materials for scraping lint from fabric were earnestly exchanged, and a further hundreds of thousands of woman-hours were devoted to a domestic manufacturing activity that, Livermore wrote, "one cannot forbear a smile" recalling in light of "how insignificant these items of relief proved in actual experience."

Philanthropy was another Civil War battlefield where amateurism came to die. Livermore was striking for being a woman at the vanguard of recognition that the female-dominated model of prewar charitable good works—"the chaos of individual benevolence," she called it—was utterly inadequate to something as big as a war. The wife of a Universalist clergyman, a committed abolitionist from the two years she had been a governess for a family in Virginia, Livermore had worked as a writer and newspaper editor before the war. After a shocking but courageous initiation to the horrors of war and battlefield surgery as a nurse in field hospitals, she had become co-director of the Northwestern Sanitary Commission in Chicago, convinced of the need for method, system, and order to take the place of the waste and misdirection of the "spontaneous" charity that had characterized initial efforts.

Women had played a significant part in charitable causes in the years before the war, a role generally approved of even by conservative men as in keeping with their greater piety, tender hearts, and sympathetic nature. Much of this work came under the auspices of religious organizations, which helped to make it acceptable: women predominated in church membership, had been conspicuous among those swept up by the Second Great Awakening. Aiding widows and orphans, fallen mothers, the sick and helpless and insane, and the worthy poor fell safely under the rubric of Christian service, one of the few areas where middle-class women could engage in activity outside the home without violating propriety or appearing to abandon their place in the "domestic sphere." Knitting socks for sick babies or sewing clothes for Fiji islanders, establishing a Home for

Unprotected Girls or an Asylum for the Repentant, women worked with other women in ways that combined charity with Christian moral uplift, which ministers encouraged and thoroughly approved.

But there were familiar limits. When women began to expand this foothold of charitable good works into moral causes such as abolitionism, temperance, and prison reform, that was something else entirely. Alleviating suffering was fine and womanly; seeking to prevent it through political change was intruding into forbidden realms. A few women reformers—notably the famous, or notorious, Grimké sisters, who began to give public lectures against slavery and supporting the rights of women—shocked the traditional-minded and led to swift denunciations, including by most of the male leaders of the abolitionist movement. A pastoral letter read from the pulpits of Massachusetts Congregational churches warned against "those who encourage females to bear an obtrusive and ostentatious part in measures of reform, and countenance any of that sex who so forget themselves as to itinerate in the character of public lecturers."

What was most striking about the U.S. Sanitary Commission was its thorough and deliberate rejection of the traditional view of philanthropy as charity. To its businesslike leaders, this was business, to be organized on a rational, professional, scientific, dollars-and-sense basis. The Reverend Bellows had sought out for the board of the commission prominent, practical-minded men in New York—lawyers, physicians, leaders of industry. The commission's Statistical Bureau gathered and compiled data to determine what was needed and where. The work of raising funds was turned over to professionals, and a paid staff of 500 employed to pack, ship, and distribute goods. Its managers and experts established eleven regional supply depots, designed and built hospital railcars and steamships to evacuate the wounded (in place of the woeful boxcars and cargo holds filled with straw), printed and distributed to army surgeons 50,000 copies of monographs on recent medical and surgical developments, and steadfastly refused to accept gifts or donations earmarked for individual companies or regiments, the bane of earlier efforts at systematic organization.

Explicitly refraining from the emotional appeals of traditional charities by refusing to dwell "as it might" on the "pathetic and touching incidents of its work," the commission instead appealed to "the practical good sense of the community" and the plain value to society of its efforts on behalf of soldiers in the field. This was as near complete a reversal as could be imagined of the womanly kind of amateur prewar charity—as a voluntary, spontaneous, benevolent act of religious obligation, aimed at alleviating individual suffering through the personal dispensation of sympathetic kindness.

It also wiped aside the prayerful self-congratulation that went hand in hand with that kind of alms-giving charity. Bellows sarcastically noted that in San Francisco "a society of 300 women of all the evangelic sects . . . meet 3 times a week to gossip over the infidelity and wicked character of the U.S. Sanitary Commission," whose paid agents were sneeringly referred to by members of the Christian Commission and other such traditional-minded dispensers of Christian charity as "hirelings." (Their own volunteers, by contrast, operated on "the system adopted eighteen hundred years ago by our Lord," working "in the apostolic spirit, for the apostolic pay.")

Having raised $5 million in cash contributions, $15 million in donated supplies, and millions more in free transportation and communications provided by railroad and telegraph companies, Bellows replied that God had perhaps recognized the wisdom of paying men and women for their work, and planning ahead. The war, he said, was "God's method of bringing order out of chaos."

WOMAN'S WAR

It was Clara Barton's particular misfortune that she could never make the leap to the world of order and method whose arrival the war did so much to accelerate. Everything she did remained personal, individual, ad hoc, and amateurish in the prewar way she knew. The Sanitary Commission spent $200,000 developing and maintaining a constantly updated Hospital Directory that recorded the names and whereabouts of 600,000 patients and systematically notified friends and relations of the wounded; Barton's Missing Soldiers Office, another of her almost purely personal endeavors, involved a hit-and-miss process of publishing lists in newspapers of missing soldiers and hoping a fellow veteran might recognize a name and reply with information, while she attempted personally to handle the hundreds of letters that poured in each day. Her postwar renown helped to publicize the ultimately successful campaign for the United States' accession to the Geneva Convention and the subsequent establishment of the American Red Cross, but her record as an actual worker and manager of the organization handed her enemies no shortage of ammunition. The members of the Red Cross board who finally succeeded in ousting her were able to point out that her name did not appear once in the 128 published volumes of official records in *The War of Rebellion*, and that the $15,000 she was awarded by Congress as compensation for her expenses operating the Missing Soldiers Office was supported neither by any written receipts nor even by plausibility, which led her successor as Red Cross president to conclude that Barton was "an adventuress from the beginning and a clever one."

At the Red Cross, Barton insisted on personally taking command in the field at each disaster the organization rushed in to address. The reverse side of her admirable willingness to set aside personal dignity and tackle any needed task from dishwashing to mopping floors was a near-complete inability to delegate responsibilities or develop a system for the work. "Decide I must attend to all business myself," she wrote in her journal. And so she ran from one crisis to the next, the Johnstown Flood, hurricanes in South Carolina and Galveston, Texas, as the business of the organization was left to its own meager resources. Fed up with her hand-to-mouth response to each new crisis, the far more professionally run Red Cross chapter

With her household entourage at Glen Echo, Maryland, in 1904

of New York, directed by doctors and experienced managers, raised funds and prestocked emergency supplies, trained nurses at its own hospital and school, and during the Spanish-American War shamefully eclipsed the national organization in the number of doctors, nurses, and supplies sent to Cuba. Barton privately castigated the New York group as "a nest of vipers." Publicly she ghostwrote a response to her critics explaining that Miss Barton's "extreme modesty and humility would never allow herself to make the full statement of work accomplished."

She had never distinguished between her own finances and those of the causes she threw herself into and both were perpetually in a state of disarray. For its relief work in Johnstown the Red Cross variously reported expenditures ranging from $40,000 to $250,000. The sprawling house she built in Glen Echo, using donated lumber left over from the Johnstown relief effort, combined rooms for herself and her retinue, offices for the organization's national headquarters, and storage for emergency supplies of blankets, bandages, and malted milk, while the title to the property remained in her name alone.

The utopianism which, along with amateurism, tinged many women's charitable causes before the war shaded over into a rich variety of crank enthusiasms for health and diet fads, dress reform, and spiritualism, and these too were legacies of Barton's antebellum past she never grew beyond. In later years she fell under the sway of a spiritualist, who, reading her subject without difficulty, conducted seances for her at which Abraham Lincoln, Ulysses S. Grant, and Kaiser Wilhelm spoke from the other side to praise her work and assure her of her lasting fame, all of which Barton enthusiastically recorded in her diary. In her will she left the Glen Echo property to the faithful Julian Hubbell, who not long after was swindled out of it all by a woman who showed up at the door claiming to be a medium sent by Barton to preserve her legacy. He ultimately won it back in a lawsuit that went to Maryland's highest court, which ruled that while belief in spiritualism did not in itself establish incapacity to make a valid deed, the simulated trances and supposed messages from the departed produced by the defendant amounted to fraudulent inducement.

In the end Clara Barton would be far more important as the symbol she made herself into, as a woman leading the way into a man's world, than for any of her actual accomplishments. Although keeping her distance for some time from the women's suffrage movement—she believed that educational opportunity for women was more important than the right to vote—she made a point of noting, in a Memorial Day speech in 1888, that the war had catapulted women far beyond what they might otherwise have achieved by that point. "Woman was at least fifty years in advance of the normal position which continued peace would have assigned her," she observed.

Oliver Wendell Holmes, during the worst of the grueling fighting at Cold Harbor, had written his parents, "I started in this thing a boy I am now a man." Many of the tens of thousands of women who worked in hospitals during the war had similarly discovered what they were able to endure, a source of confidence that remained even as they returned to more conventional routine. Mary Livermore remembered the shock and distaste she had first felt in seeing women in eastern Iowa in the sweltering heat of the summer of 1863 performing the heavy field work that was customarily the exclusive domain of men, driving teams pulling reapers through the wheat fields, binding and shocking, loading grain. But noticing how well they handled the horses, the precision and nicety and even artistic finish as they made up the sheaves, neater than the men field hands in fact did, she checked herself and realized they were doing work that God had meant them to, in an hour of need.

She had a greater shock when having worked with her female co-director on the massive undertaking of organizing the great fair in Chicago to raise funds for the Sanitary Commission—it would bring in $100,000 from the donated items, including a signed copy of the Emancipation Proclamation personally contributed by President Lincoln that sold for $3,000—the contractor for one of the exhibit halls caught her up short by asking, when it came time to sign the contract for the work, "Who underwrites for you?" He then explained what they had not known: that as married women, neither their signatures, nor even the cash they could offer as security, was worth anything without their husbands' assent. They had a long conversation with the man. As Livermore later movingly recounted,

Here was a revelation. We two women were able to enlist the whole Northwest in a great philanthropic, money-making enterprise in the teeth of great opposition, and had the executive ability to carry it forward to a successful termination. We had money of our own in bank, twice as much as was necessary to pay the builder. But by the laws of the state in which we lived, our individual names were not worth the paper on which they were written. Our earnings were not ours, but belonged to our husbands. . . .

We learned much of the laws made by men for women, in that conversation with an illiterate builder. It opened a new world to us. . . . I registered a vow that when the war was over I would take up a new work—the work of making law and justice synonymous for women. I have kept my vow religiously.

Livermore indeed became an effective leader in the women's rights movement after the war, and her experience was duplicated by others who had their confidence emboldened, their eyes opened, and their outrage stirred by their work during the war. Louisa Schuyler, a great-granddaughter of Alexander Hamilton, who became one of a dozen women managers in the Sanitary Commission's New York branch, called the commission "a great educator of women of the day," teaching her in particular, as a young woman in her mid-twenties, one never-forgotten lesson. It had, she said, "opened my eyes to the great value and the great power of organization—of which I had known nothing." After the war she secured the approval of the State of New York for an association to inspect its poorhouses, worked successfully to have the care of the insane transferred to hospitals, and opened one of the first nurses' training schools in the country, at New York's Bellevue Hospital.

The mere fact that women were paid for work, as nurses, cooks, sewers, and organizers and participants of charitable endeavors, which in the past was treated as a natural part of womanhood undeserving of compensation, opened their eyes to the economic value of what they contributed. A wondering British journalist wrote afterward that no conflict in history had been so much "a woman's war" as the American Civil War.

9

EMANCIPATION

Abraham Lincoln

"THE PRESIDENT'S LIFE-PRESERVER"

Watching him arrive at the battlefield of Antietam on October 2, Hooker's artillery chief Charles S. Wainwright thought Abraham Lincoln was "the ugliest man I ever saw." The burdens of war and office had done nothing to improve his looks, or the "uncouth and gawky" manner Wainwright thought the President so unpresidentially displayed as he unfolded his long legs, doubled up almost to his chin, and emerged from an army ambulance that had provided his transportation to McClellan's headquarters.

More sensitive observers recognized the depths of tragedy that lay in his countenance. Francis Carpenter, the artist who would spend six months at the White House painting Lincoln's portrait reading the First Emancipation Proclamation, thought his face in repose "was the saddest . . . I ever knew." There were days, the artist remembered, "when I could scarcely look into it without crying."

The weeks leading up to Antietam had been a time of "fearful anxiety" and "almost unendurable tension" to the President, his private secretary John Hay recalled. At Antietam, Lincoln asked to see "where Hooker went in" but when McClellan and his staff, riding ahead, arrived at the position, they waited and waited, McClellan dispatching one aide after another to search for the President, only to discover finally that Lincoln had suddenly changed his mind and driven back to camp without telling anyone. The entire First Corps,

Lincoln conferring with McClellan at his headquarters near the Antietam battlefield, October 4, 1862

lined up for a review by the President, waited four hours in vain. The next day Lincoln quickly reviewed the troops, riding the lines at a quick trot on a spirited coal-black horse, his face expressionless and his eyes elsewhere.

Throughout his life he suffered periods of black depression; his old law partner William Herndon recalled days when Lincoln would come into the office and sit for hours in a "terribly gloomy state," staring vacantly out the window in silence. On those occasions Herndon would pull the curtain down over the glass door and quietly leave, locking the door behind him, so as not to intrude on the privacy of "this unfortunate and miserable man."

The uproarious humor that was the far better-known part of his character was, to those who knew him well, the embodiment of Mark Twain's observation that "the secret source of humor is not joy but sorrow." As President he had abandoned his trademark habit of larding his public speeches with jokes and humorous stories (they were described as "Lincolnisms" as early as 1854), acknowledging their incompatibility with the dignity of the office, but in private his sense of humor remained a lifeline through trouble. "I laugh because I must not weep—that's all," he had told a friend during his circuit-riding days, alluding to a line from Lord Byron's poem "Don Juan" that he knew well. Carpenter once was waiting outside the President's office with one of Lincoln's old Springfield friends, and hearing the familiar laugh coming from within, the friend turned to him and said, "That laugh has been the President's life-preserver!"

Not everyone took it well. A European ambassador in Washington reported of the new American President that "his conversation consists of vulgar anecdotes at which he himself laughs uproariously." Driving across the Antietam battlefield, his companion Ward Hill Lamon tried to cheer him up by singing a few of his favorite comic songs, an unfortunate incident that gave his political enemies fodder for the charge that he was nothing but a buffoon who would mock even the Union dead.

As a lawyer and politician he had found anecdotes of the "this reminds me of the man who undertook to raise a very large number of hogs" variety invaluable for putting a client or adversary at ease, creating a diversion around a sticky point, or gently making a point by indirection. But Herndon saw a deeper source of Lincoln's wit, paradoxically, in his methodical and even plodding nature: "He was frequently at a loss for a word, and hence was compelled to resort to stories, maxims, and jokes to embody his idea, that it might be comprehended." Lincoln once explained to Herndon that he did not have the kind of quick intuition that allowed his younger partner to leap to a conclusion; he had to proceed by slow, logical steps, but the result, he said, was like a long-bladed jackknife that took longer to open, but was more lethal in the end.

He often invoked the will of Providence, but as with most men, Lincoln's God was made in his own image. There was none of the triumph and ready forgiveness that McClellan found in his role as

God's "chosen instrument"; Lincoln's was a brooding God, who placed upon him the burden of humility and the necessity of deliberation to comprehend His will. Lincoln's fatalistic sense of being controlled by events was merely projection onto the universe of his own methodical mind. His temperamental aversion to hasty decisions aligned perfectly with his politician's keen understanding of the need to bring public opinion with him, often by treading carefully and slowly along a razor's edge, buffeted by winds from each side. What some took for indecision or duplicity was Lincoln's way of preparing the ground and testing the waters of public sentiment.

MCCLELLAN'S BODYGUARD

Nowhere was that more so than in the cautious evolution of Lincoln's policy toward slavery in the spring and summer of 1862. Every choice he faced risked alienating some important faction on which the administration depended for support. His reinstatement of McClellan to the command of the Army of the Potomac and his revocation of an order by the Union commander occupying the sea islands of South Carolina and Georgia that decreed the abolition of slavery within his military department outraged the radicals of his Republican Party, who suspected McClellan's loyalty and were pressing for bolder action against slavery. His efforts to cajole the border states to accept compensated, gradual emancipation of their slaves now, a change that would "come as gently as the dews of heaven," rather than risk delaying and seeing slavery "extinguished by mere friction and abrasion—by the mere incidents of the war," was a clear enough hint, but found no takers.

Outraged conservatives warned that even such small steps would drive Unionist slaveholders to the Confederate side, while any suggestion that Lincoln meant to transform a war for the preservation of the Union into a war for the abolition of slavery would endanger Democratic support for the war altogether, strengthening the Copperhead faction within the party that was already denouncing the war as a failure and calling for a restoration of "the Union as it was" through negotiations. Even the relatively limited antislavery measures enacted by Congress in 1862, providing for compensated emancipation in the District of Columbia, barring slavery from the territories, and prohibiting the return of fugitive slaves by the army, had galvanized Democratic opposition, with 96 percent of its party's representatives voting no.

McClellan had made his own views clear enough, warning Lincoln and Stanton in July that "the nation"—by which he meant George McClellan and other "War Democrats" who shared his views—will support "no other policy" than one of strict noninterference with slavery, and that "a declaration of radical views, especially upon slavery, will rapidly disintegrate our present Armies." Privately, he expressed the racial contempt that undergirded much of antiabolitionist sentiment in the North, writing his confidant Samuel Barlow, a New York lawyer and Democratic Party power broker, "Help me to dodge the n———er—we want nothing to do with him. *I* am fighting to preserve the integrity of the Union & the power of the Govt—on no other issue." (Shortly after the war McClellan wrote, "I confess to a prejudice in favor of my own race & can't learn to like the odor of either Billy goats or n———ers.")

The opening that Lincoln inched toward as the summer wore on was the growing recognition by moderates that slavery was itself a source of power to the Confederacy; what they could not swallow as social reform they could as a war measure. The war had sharpened Lincoln's great gifts of compression and juxtaposition, his ability to express in a few well-chosen words, often of great simplicity, a point of much greater complexity and subtlety. In late July, answering a Louisiana Unionist, Lincoln went to the heart of why the war itself had turned slavery into a central issue. The mounting hardness of the war meant it could no longer be fought with "elderstalk squirts charged with rose water," he wrote. To the complaint that Union forces occupying New Orleans had interfered with the relations between master and slave, Lincoln retorted that there was no one to blame but those who continued to resist the authority of the government. The solution, he said, "does not lie in rounding the rough angles of the war, but in removing the necessity for the war." He asked: "What would you do in my position? Would you drop the war where it is? Would you deal lighter blows rather than heavier ones? Would you give up the contest, leaving any available means unapplied?"

Those in the South demanding a return to the "Union as it was," Lincoln said, could have it by ending the rebellion now. But, he warned, "This government cannot much longer play a game in which it stakes all, and its enemies stake nothing. Those enemies must understand that they cannot experiment for ten years trying to destroy the government, and if they fail still come back into the Union unhurt."

Replying to an excoriating editorial in Horace Greeley's *New York Tribune* in August denouncing Lincoln's pusillanimity for not proclaiming the abolition of slavery at once, Lincoln sent an open letter further preparing the ground for emancipation as a means to military success, explaining the point better in a few dozen plain words than a closely argued treatise might have done.

My paramount object in the struggle *is* to save the Union, and it is *not* either to save or destroy slavery. If I could save the Union without freeing *any* slave I would do it, and if I could save it by freeing *all* the slaves I would do it; and if I could save it by freeing some and leaving others alone, I would also do that.

To a group of Ohio clergymen who called on him on September 13 and told him it was God's will for him to proclaim a general emancipation of the slaves, Lincoln more pointedly replied, "If it is probable that God would reveal his will to others, on a point so connected with my duty, it might be supposed he would reveal it directly to me. . . . These are not, however, the days of miracles, and I suppose it will be granted that I am not to expect a direct revelation. I must study the plain physical facts of the case, ascertain what is possible and learn what appears to be wise and right." But he had, he told them, been thinking about the matter for months, and laid out to his visitors all of the objections to the idea: it would accomplish nothing in actual fact, no magistrate or judge could enforce it, it would be derided—like the supposed decree of the Pope against Halley's comet—as an impotent and vain gesture; there would be nothing to prevent the reenslavement of Blacks any place the Union army might be forced to pull back temporarily.

But as another of Lincoln's old Illinois friends recalled, Lincoln often did this, weighing and examining his ideas in the presence of others, not so much to impress his views on them, but "for his own enlightenment in the presence of his hearer." He had already drafted a proclamation, and presented it to the cabinet in July, in fact. But on the advice of Secretary of State Seward—which he acknowledged struck him with much force—he agreed to hold off until a Union victory would give it more credence, and not come off as "our last *shriek*, on the retreat," and placed the document back in his desk drawer. Antietam now gave him the chance he had been awaiting, and five days after the battle he again met with his cabinet to say the time had come. The preliminary proclamation issued that day declared that unless the Confederate states returned to the Union by January 1, 1863, their slaves "shall be then, thenceforward, and forever free."

"I wish it were a better time," Lincoln said. "The action of the army against the rebels has not been quite what I should have best liked." Prodding McClellan into bolder action remained as thankless a task as ever. No record exists of Lincoln's discussion with the general at his camp near the Antietam battlefield, which took place the week after the proclamation was issued, though in a letter he sent McClellan afterward he wrote, "You remember my speaking to you of what I called your overcautiousness." There had been rumors of discontented talk among McClellan's staff of "countermarching" on Washington and installing McClellan as a dictator to straighten out the mismanagement of the war. Lincoln made a point of cashiering on the spot one officer who had repeated the story that "the game" had been to allow Lee to get away in order to force a stalemate in the war as the only way to save the Union, through a compromise in which slavery would be preserved. While discounting the idea of McClellan's disloyalty, he wanted to put an end to such "silly, treasonous" "staff talk," Lincoln said.

But while it was true McClellan probably entertained no such notions himself, he clearly enjoyed the flattery of those proposing him for the post of dictator, repeating it to more than one companion, and he was also convinced that his brilliant victory at Antietam had placed him in a position to dictate terms for the retention of his services. "I feel that I have done all that can be asked in twice saving the country," he wrote Ellen three days after the battle. "If I continue in its service I have at least the right to demand a guarantee that I shall not be interfered with. I know I cannot have that assurance so long as Stanton continues in the position of Secretary of War and Halleck as general-in-chief." Between issuing bitter complaints that all he had received from Halleck and Lincoln were "fault-finding" messages couched in almost "insulting language," he sent word to Barlow to have the *New York Herald* "open your batteries" on Stanton, hoping to force his dismissal.

Learning of Lincoln's impending visit to the field, McClellan wrote his wife, "I do not yet know what are the military plans of the gigantic intellects at the head of the government." But he was inclined to think "the real purpose . . . is to push me into a premature advance into Virginia." As far as McClellan was concerned, "I look upon this campaign as substantially ended," he wrote on September 22. Not long after, he brought Ellen, their one-year-old daughter, and his mother-in-law to a farmhouse in Pleasant Valley for a two-week stay ("we are having a very quiet & pleasant time").

On the advice of his officers and Democratic confidants, he had refrained from any public criticism of the Emancipation Proclamation, instead issuing a general order reminding soldiers of their duty to respect the decisions of civilian authority—yet pointedly adding, "The remedy for political errors, if any are committed, is to be found only in the action of the people at the polls." Privately, he told his wife that he considered the proclamation "infamous," and that he was not prepared "to fight for such an accursed doctrine as that of a servile insurrection." It is "almost impossible," he said, "for me to retain my commission and self-respect at the same time."

But for now at least he retained his commission and command, biding his time composing a litany of justifications for his failure to pursue Lee across the river: he lacked horses and horseshoes; Lee's army numbered 150,000; he needed replacement draftees to fill out depleted regiments; he needed to secure the upper Potomac with permanent rail and road bridges at Harper's Ferry; he could not advance more than twenty-five miles down the Shenandoah Valley without first constructing two new railroads to secure his lines of supply, one connecting to Hagerstown, a second running south from Winchester.

As was often the case these days, Lincoln's best barbs were reserved mostly for himself. Looking down on the sprawling army camp from a hill by McClellan's tent early on the second day of his visit, he turned to his sole companion, Ozias Hatch, an Illinois politician, and abruptly whispered, "Hatch, Hatch, What is all this?" A bit puzzled, his friend replied that he believed it was the Army of the Potomac. "So it is called," Lincoln dryly replied. "But that is a mistake. That is General McClellan's bodyguard."

THE LAW OF NATIONS

It was a source of enduring wonder to Karl Marx that Lincoln's greatest acts took the form of documents that read like the "routine summonses sent by a lawyer to the lawyer of the opposing party," filled with "clause-ridden conditions," "legal chicaneries," and convoluted causes of action. "Nothing is simpler," wrote Marx in *Die Presse* upon the news of the Emancipation Proclamation reaching Europe, "than to show that Lincoln's principal political actions contain much that is aesthetically repulsive, logically inadequate, farcical in form and

politically contradictory." His proclamation abolishing slavery—
"the most important document in American history since the establishment of the Union," Marx unhesitatingly assessed it, which will
"secure Lincoln's place in the history of the United States and of mankind . . . next to that of Washington!"—was much the same, drafted
with all the eloquence of a lawyer's writ. "He gives his most important
actions always the most commonplace form."

Critics, notably the mostly anti-American and conservative British press, were quick to point out that the proclamation, in its legalistic "pettifogging," exempted from its terms the only places where
Lincoln actually had the power to enforce it, the border states, while
directing the emancipation of slaves where he did not. Others, Democrats at home most vocally, denounced the proclamation as an uncon-
stitutional usurpation of power, and even many who cheered Lincoln's
action saw the proclamation as a revolutionary act ("tantamount to
the tearing up of the old American Constitution," opined Marx), justified at best as an exercise of vague if inherent wartime powers of the
chief executive as commander-in-chief of the armed forces.

In Lincoln's eyes, however, the legalisms were the point; far from
violating the Constitution, the power of the proclamation lay in its
being situated within a carefully constructed framework of "antislavery constitutionalism," as the scholar James Oakes has described
it, a legal foundation stretching back to the Constitution's origins.
Notably, the proclamation did not merely treat slaves as enemy *property* that could be seized under the theory that they were "contra-
band" of war, the concept invoked since the first year of the war to
accept fugitives who made their way to Union lines; but rather that
they were *persons* entitled to freedom under well-established precedents of the laws of war—what legal scholars refer to as "the law of
nations"—as well as principles of English common law embodied
in the Constitution itself. Advancing to abolition through legally
available means was to Lincoln always the slower but surer route, as
well as the only means to ensure its lasting effect.

Lincoln had always regarded slavery with abhorrence, but had equally emphatically acknowledged that the Constitution gave the federal government no power to interfere with the institution in states where it existed. His opposition to slavery was simple, and moral. "If the Negro is a *man,*" Lincoln said in his first major antislavery speech, delivered in Springfield in 1857, "why then my ancient faith teaches me that 'all men are created equal'; and that there can be no moral right in connection with one man's making a slave of another."

To the argument that Blacks were marked for slavery by their skin color or intellectual inferiority, Lincoln retorted that would mean "you are to be a slave to the first man you meet, with fairer skin than your own," or "you are to be a slave to the first man you meet, with an intellect superior to your own." All of the justifications for slavery were just "the same old serpent," he said, nothing but the assertion, "you work and I eat, you toil and I will enjoy the fruits of it."

In running for president in 1860, and during the first year of the war, Lincoln reiterated his acceptance of the fact that "Congress has no power over slavery in the states." In his first inaugural address he quoted his own previous utterances on the subject: "I have no purpose, directly or indirectly, to interfere with the institution of slavery in the States where it exists. I believe I have no lawful right to do so, and I have no inclination to do so."

But even if the Constitution did not permit such direct "interference," it affirmed several fundamental principles that could be built on to limit slavery's spread, and so place it on the "course of ultimate extinction," as Lincoln often put it. These efforts had been the cornerstones of the antislavery movement from the beginning. Acting at the first moment the Constitution gave it the power to do so, Congress banned the slave trade in 1808; the coming of the war created the chance to carry through the other long-standing goals of the antislavery constitutionalists, as Congress exercised its constitutional authority over the District of Columbia, the territories, and the admission of new states to ban slavery where it directly could, and require West Virginia and Nevada to forbid slavery in their constitutions as a condition of statehood.

The Second Confiscation Act, passed in July 1862, was a more muddled matter. Invoking the constitutional crime of treason, it provided for forfeiture of slaves, along with other property, as punishment for slaveholders engaged in rebellion. Lincoln had doubts about its constitutionality, particularly because the Constitution appears to limit forfeiture of property as a penalty for treason to a life interest, meaning in theory that the forfeited slaves of traitors would have to be returned to their heirs. But his more serious objection went back to his core legal understanding of the constitutional compromise over slavery: "It is startling to say that Congress can free a slave within a state." It was for that same reason that he continued, in parallel to all his other incremental efforts to tighten the noose on slavery, to induce the border states to voluntarily act to eliminate slavery within their borders, since the states were where the ultimate legal authority over slavery rested.

But, as a military measure, emancipation might rest on an entirely different legal basis, one that depended on the fundamental fact which lay at the core of his own moral beliefs, that slaves were men, not property. Lincoln had often called attention to a point all the antislavery constitutionalists stressed: that everywhere in the Constitution where slavery is alluded to, slaves are described as *persons*, not property. Even the so-called Fugitive Slave Clause avoids the words slave or slavery in the actual text, referring instead to a "person held to service or labour." The constitutional convention had in fact explicitly rejected attempts by Southern slaveholders to have slaves recognized as property within the document. Other foundational clauses of the Constitution, notably the Fifth Amendment, made clear that all "persons," not just citizens, are entitled to due process and the protection of the laws.

The very necessity of the Fugitive Slave Clause pointed to an even more momentous legal consideration that Lincoln would build upon in issuing the Emancipation Proclamation. Shortly before the Revolution, in a case decided by Lord Mansfield, the Lord Chief Justice, an English court held that a slave purchased in Virginia and carried to England was released from bondage. *Somerset v. Steuart* enunciated a fundamental principle of the common law: the state of slavery was "so odious" that it exists only where supported by "positive law," and such laws do not reach across borders. Once outside the jurisdiction in which he was legally held to bondage, any slave could in theory apply to a local court for a writ of habeas corpus, freeing him from the physical control of his owner.

As Southern slaveholders perfectly well understood, that clearly articulated precedent of English common law—freedom was the rule, slavery the exception—meant that any slave who set foot in a Northern state where slavery was not explicitly sanctioned by local law would likewise be instantly freed. The constitutional provision requiring that "No Person held to Service or Labour in one State, under the Laws thereof, escaping into another, shall, in Consequence of any Law or Regulation therein, be discharged from such Service or Labour, but shall be delivered up on Claim of the Party to whom such Service or Labour may be due" was a direct response to *Somerset,* intended to cut short its effect.

It was self-evident to Lincoln that the war had made the Fugitive Slave Clause inoperative as far as it extended to the seceded states. "The rebels could not at the same time throw off the Constitution and invoke its aid," Gideon Welles quoted the President as telling the cabinet. But it had done something else of even more monumental importance. The law of nations had always held that local ordinances are suspended when armies occupy enemy territory and military law temporarily takes their place. Francis Lieber, a renowned American legal scholar who had been tasked by General Halleck to revise the Articles of War, concluded that that in itself meant an end to slavery wherever the U.S. Army went in time of war. Halleck himself was an authority on the laws of war and international law, and the key point, which he would repeat in a treatise on the subject published right after the war, was embodied in Articles 42 and 43 of the "Lieber Code," as the revised military laws were known.

Art. 42. Slavery . . . exists according to municipal or local law only. The law of nature and nations has never acknowledged it. The digest of the Roman law enacts the early dictum of the pagan jurist, that "so far as the law of nature is concerned, all men are equal." Fugitives escaping from a country in which they were slaves, villains, or serfs, into another country, have, for centuries past, been held free and acknowledged free by judicial decisions of European countries, even though the municipal law of the country in which the slave had taken refuge acknowledged slavery within its own dominions.

Art. 43. Therefore, in a war between the United States and a belligerent which admits of slavery, if a person held in bondage by that belligerent be captured by or come as a fugitive under the protection of the military forces of the United States, such person is immediately entitled to the rights and privileges of a freeman. To return such person into slavery would amount to enslaving a free person, and neither the United States nor any officer under their authority can enslave any human being. Moreover, a person so made free by the law of war is under the shield of the law of nations, and the former owner or State can have, by the law of postliminy, no belligerent lien or claim of service.

The British had invoked that very principle in freeing slaves who reached their lines during the Revolutionary War and the War of 1812, even though slavery still existed in the British Empire at the time, and declined even to return those carried off by British navy vessels after the end of hostilities, in violation of the terms of the treaties ending both wars. Among those successfully reaching British protection in the Revolution were an estimated one-quarter of the slaves in South Carolina and 30,000 from Virginia, including some of George Washington's own slaves who had made their way to British ships in New York harbor. In offering "freedom and protection" to escaping slaves, the decrees issued by British commanders plainly drew on the legal principles enunciated in *Somerset* and reinforced in published authorities on the law of nations.

"The Emancipation Proclamation," noted Oakes, "was an extension of well-established legal and historical precedents." That, as both Lincoln's supporters and his critics did not always perceive, then or later, was exactly Lincoln's point. The absence of any soaring words about the wrongs of slavery or the moral triumph of its abolition or the historic momentousness of his action puzzled many, as it had Marx. The irascible diarist Count Adam Gurowski, a Polish nobleman who worked as a translator for the State Department in Washington, complained that it was "written in the meanest and the most dry routine style," not a word to evoke the lofty feelings of the people.

But Marx conceded there might be something great, after all, in the fact that "an ordinary man of good will" could "accomplish feats which only heroes could accomplish in the old world." Though Lincoln "does not possess the grandiloquence of historical action," Marx wrote, he had done "such as to transform the world." It was Hegel, he added, who observed that as comedy is superior to tragedy, so humorous reasoning is superior to grandiloquent reasoning. Lincoln, "as a man of the people, has its humor."

IF WE NEVER TRY WE SHALL NEVER SUCCEED

Oliver Wendell Holmes recalled talking during the war with a fellow Massachusetts officer, Charles Russell Lowell, about who from the war would be remembered as a great man. "He mentioned Lincoln," Holmes said, "but I think we both smiled." Holmes's own assessment of Lincoln changed only many years later. "Until I reached middle age I believed that I was watching the growth of a myth about Lincoln," he told his friend the American diplomat Lewis Einstein in 1924. "In the war time like other Bostonians I believed him a second rate politician. But later I saw and read things that convinced me that I was wrong."

Even among the officers of the 20th Massachusetts—the "Harvard Regiment"—Holmes's antislavery views were in the minority. To officers throughout the Army of the Potomac who, like McClellan, bridled at fighting for "the accursed doctrine" of abolition, the proclamation provoked much less temperate assessments of Lincoln's abilities than Holmes's. "The absurd proclamation of a political coward," Fitz John Porter privately termed it, noting the "disgust and expressions of disloyalty" it had triggered in the army. Holmes's close friend in the 20th Henry Abbott wrote home that everyone was demoralized by the turn of events. "The president's proclamation is of course received with universal disgust, particularly the part which enjoins officers to see that it is carried out. You may be sure that we shan't see to any thing of the kind, having decidedly too much reverence for the constitution." Ezra Carman reckoned that two-thirds of the division and brigade commanders, along with every one of McClellan's corps commanders, were of the same view, and "were opposed to the administration."

Lincoln, in deciding to act, characteristically put behind him the political worries that had been at the forefront of his mind during his months of deliberation. The border states, he told the cabinet, "would acquiesce, if not immediately, soon": they could not now avoid the reality that slavery had received its "death blow" and "could not survive the rebellion." Nor was he terribly concerned about the predictable attacks by Democrats featuring lurid denunciations of the proclamation as "a proposal for the butchery of women and children, for scenes of lust and rapine," which would set loose "two or three million semi-savages" to overrun the North and steal jobs from the white laboring masses. "Their clubs would be used against us take what course we might," Lincoln calmly observed of his political foes.

The army was another matter. There was no barometer of public opinion more accurate than military success. During the days of despair in the summer following the failures on the Peninsula and Bull Run, both parties fully expected the Democrats to take a solid majority of the House of Representatives in the coming elections. The success at Antietam, equivocal though it was, had swung the pendulum the other direction. But now the army's idleness again brought a return of frustration and unease about the conduct of the war. The states at that time cast their votes for Congress on separate schedules in October and November, and Democrats made significant gains in Pennsylvania's election on October 13. The *New York Tribune* put its finger on the political crux of the situation when it complained of the irony "that Republicans should lose because Democratic Generals won't fight."

It was not just Democratic generals who represented a potentially serious source of opposition within the army to the administration's policy. The immigrants who were now making up a significant source of new recruits included many who bitterly opposed emancipation. Although German Protestants mostly held strong antislavery views, German and especially Irish Catholics, along with lower-income nativist whites in the coalfields of Pennsylvania and in the southern Midwest, rioted against the draft, bearing banners that read, "We won't fight to free the n——er"; on September 24 Lincoln issued an order subjecting all persons interfering with enlistments or the draft to military arrest and punishment.

A visitor to the White House during the weeks of the elections and McClellan's continued inactivity that fall thought Lincoln seemed to be "literally bending under the weight of his burdens," like "a man walking in his sleep." He was passing sleepless nights at the cottage on the grounds of the Soldiers Home in northwest Washington that was his family's summertime retreat, returning each morning to his White House office for a long day's work.

The one immediate bright spot was the wholly favorable effect Antietam and the Emancipation Proclamation had in England. Prime Minister Palmerston had been edging perilously close to British intervention in the war and de facto recognition of the Confederacy, discussing with Emperor Napoleon III of France a serious proposal for the two European powers to call for a six-month armistice and mediation of the conflict, during which time Southern cotton exports would resume. But following Lee's retreat from Maryland, Palmerston told his foreign secretary that the moment had passed: "We must continue merely to be lookers-on till the war shall have taken a more decided turn."

And despite the hostility of the conservative British press and ruling class, the Emancipation Proclamation galvanized tremendous support among the working and middle classes across England, even among the Lancashire millworkers out of work from the blockade of Southern cotton, support Lincoln skillfully encouraged with messages of appreciation to the dozens of tumultuous mass meetings in English cities heralding the proclamation and the antislavery cause. Since at least the Slavery Abolition Act of 1833, official British government policy had long opposed slavery. And just in April 1862, the United States and Britain had agreed to a bilateral treaty allowing their navies to stop and search merchant ships of either nation and seize and condemn any that appeared to be engaged in the transatlantic slave trade. The only recourse of British conservatives in siding with the South and avoiding the charge of hypocrisy lay in the supposed insincerity of Northern intentions regarding slavery. Lincoln's action more than called their bluff.

Meanwhile Lincoln was urging McClellan to move against Lee, a final repetition of a now overfamiliar script. "Cross the Potomac and give battle to the enemy," he had Halleck wire McClellan. "Your army must move now while the roads are good." When Stuart repeated his earlier feat on the Peninsula and rode a circle completely around McClellan's army, his 1,800 troopers raiding deep into Maryland on October 10–12 and recrossing the Potomac unscathed, McClellan used the opportunity to complain again about his lack of horses. Lincoln exasperatedly ordered Halleck to reply, "The President has read your telegrams, and directs me to suggest that, if the enemy had more occupation south of the river, his cavalry would not be so likely to make raids north of it." Halleck for his part confessed himself "sick, tired and disgusted" of dealing with the immovable general. "There is an immobility here that exceeds all that any man can conceive of. It requires the lever of Archimedes to move this inert mass."

Lincoln, his secretary John Nicolay recalled, was reduced to "poking sharp sticks under little Mac's ribs," sending short, pointed messages hoping to stir him into action. When McClellan complained yet again of his tired, sore-backed, sore-tongued horses, Lincoln replied, "Will you pardon me for asking what the horses of your army have done since the battle of Antietam that fatigue anything?" McClellan fumed to his wife that this was "one of those dirty little flings" from "the Gorilla" he could not abide.

On October 13 Lincoln sent McClellan a long, thoughtful letter trying calmer persuasion. Jacob Cox, reading it after the war, thought that "as a mere matter of military comprehension and judgment of the strategic situation, the letter puts Mr. Lincoln head and shoulders above" both McClellan and Halleck. Fully grasping the principles of lines of communication and interior lines, he urged McClellan to move down east of the Blue Ridge to place himself between Lee's army, now around Winchester, and both Richmond and Washington. Lee's lines of supply were twice as long as McClellan's, and he had half as many wagons; moreover, the route Lee would have to take to get ahead of McClellan was the arc of a circle, while McClellan would be moving directly across the shorter chord of the arc. Waiting for the construction of new railroads before advancing, Lincoln pointed out, was to "ignore the question of *time*," McClellan's perennial blind spot. "Are you not being over-cautious when you assume that you can not do what the enemy is constantly doing?" Lincoln asked. "At least try to beat him to Richmond on the inside track. I say 'try'; if we never try, we shall never succeed."

On October 26 the Army of the Potomac crossed the river at last and began to move south. Lincoln had already vowed to himself that if Lee crossed the Blue Ridge ahead of McClellan, he would relieve him of his command. On the same day that the last state, New York, held its elections, word reached Washington that the rebels were across McClellan's line of advance. The next day, November 5, Lincoln directed Halleck to order Burnside to assume the command of the Army of the Potomac. Lincoln remarked to his advisor Francis P. Blair Sr. that he had "tried long enough to bore with an auger too dull to take hold."

The Republicans suffered the expected setback in the elections, losing more than two dozen seats in the House. But it was far from the rout that had been anticipated before Antietam. With the support of border-state members from the Unconditional Union Party, Republicans retained control of the House and reelected a Republican Speaker, while in the Senate they actually added several seats to their existing solid majority. McClellan took his dismissal with dignity, already contemplating an avenging bid for the presidency in 1864 as a leader of the Democratic Party's conservative wing. But the pace of events the war itself had unleashed would again be ahead of McClellan. The overwhelming majority of Union soldiers who would cast their vote for Lincoln that year were no longer in any mood to listen to McClellan's call for restoration of the Union through "conciliation and compromise."

The greater irony was in how wrong McClellan's consoling thought had been that his failure on the Peninsula had been God's way to prevent an early victory that would have strengthened the hands of the radical abolitionists and made reunion with slavery intact impossible. The exact opposite had been the result. Nothing had so ensured that the policy of emancipation would become a paramount aim of the war than McClellan's military failures in the long summer of 1862, and his small but undeniable success at Antietam on that long single day in September.

Epilogue

MISTS OF
MEMORY

REMEMBRANCE

Every year on the anniversary of the Battle of Antietam, Oliver Wendell Holmes solemnly drank a glass of wine, "to the living and the dead." He was intensely aware how the war had changed him and shaped a generation of Americans. But he studiously avoided dwelling on the details. "I hate to read about those days," he told friends, "the blunders and worse" of the battles and the "squalid preliminaries" to the war itself.

His reaction was no different from most veterans in the first two decades after the war. The first inclination was to forget. Fewer than 2 percent of Union soldiers initially joined the Grand Army of the Republic, the major Northern veterans' group. Three years after the war's end, a third of its posts were inactive; as of 1878 it had only 30,000 members. When Mary Livermore was approached at the close of the war to publish her experiences, she refused. People were still in the throes of bereavement and anguish, she said, and wanted to put the war's "horrors" behind them, and "forget." Major periodicals like *Harper's Monthly* that had written about almost nothing but the war while it was being fought scarcely mentioned the war in the decade following its conclusion.

The 1880s brought a stunning reversal as veterans approached middle age. Membership in the GAR jumped to 233,000 in 1884, 428,000 in 1890. When *The Century* magazine in 1884 launched a series of articles on "Battles and Leaders of the Civil War," circulation doubled. It was the right "psychological moment," *Century*'s editor Robert Underwood Johnson calculated, the war twenty years distant, many of its key participants still alive but passions cooled enough to allow commanders of both sides to write side-by-side accounts of its major battles. "Battles and Leaders" was a harbinger of a wave of publishing on the Civil War that would remain unabated a century and a half later. "The Civil War has spilt more ink than blood," one wit remarked on the occasion of the war's centennial; it was probably already a correct observation by its twenty-fifth anniversary.

Yet it was a highly selective, or at least reordered, kind of memory of the war that these publications brought forward. With an emphasis on grand tactics explicitly and sectional reconciliation implicitly, they ignored both gore and larger significance in recounting the war's events. *Century* asked its contributors to adhere to a "nonpolitical point of view." What was left was the kind of celebration of mutual valor, in which brave men on both sides fought for a cause—details unstated—that they believed in, that would characterize nearly all writing on the Civil War to follow. Ezra Carman's meticulous work in seeking out veterans' recollections of the Battle of Antietam was not explicitly an effort to advance the same sort of both-sides-were-right narration but inescapably had that effect: his questionnaires focused entirely on pinning down the location and lines of advance of individual regiments, and while he produced a superb military analysis at the level of grand tactics and strategy, he inescapably fell into the language of neutrality and conventional euphemism in describing the events of the battle. "The vast majority of veterans writing to Carman," noted a historian who has examined his correspondence, "chose to tailor their memories to the scaffolding created for them. They talked about tactics, bravery, heroism, and the glory of battle," in ways that "came together to dominate the narrative and memory of Antietam."

Politics and prejudice abetted postwar forgetfulness. Jacob Cox, running for governor of Ohio on the Republican ticket in 1867, astonished his prewar radical friends by taking a conservative line on Reconstruction and opposing Negro suffrage in the South, fearing that giving Blacks the vote would provoke a furious backlash among Southern whites, fracture the national Republican Party, and ruin its political fortunes forever. It was a straw in the wind, and Cox accurately read the sentiment of many returning Union soldiers to win his election. The dwindling number of Northern veterans who kept working for the cause of the freedmen soon found themselves in a minority in even mentioning what the war had been fought for. Reading the popular accounts of battles, said one, it was as if the leaders and generals of both sides "were merely players in a great game of chess," the writers seeming to have forgotten altogether "that a war could not be waged for the preservation of the Union unless some one was responsible for the attempt to destroy it."

Reconciliationist sentiment rose with the nostalgic gloss that settled over the war. A plan pressed by the strong contingent of ex-Confederates in Maryland's postwar legislature for both Union and Confederate dead from the battlefield to be reburied in Antietam National Cemetery, created in 1867, was a bridge too early and too far, and the idea was abandoned in the face of angry protests by Union veterans over "making Antietam a burial place for traitors." (The Confederate dead were ultimately relocated to a cemetery in Hagerstown, which had had a more Confederate-leaning populace.) But by 1885, when McClellan returned for his first visit to Antietam since the war to deliver the Decoration Day oration at the cemetery, the reconciliationist mood was in the ascendant. McClellan in his speech blamed the war upon "fanatics" on both sides, and for the first time Confederate veterans joined the procession to the cemetery.

For the first time, too, veterans began returning regularly to the Antietam battlefield for tours and reunions, where nostalgia predominated. At the twenty-fifth anniversary of the battle in 1887, the old soldiers slept in tents on the field and, a local newspaper reported, "were regaled besides with regulation hard tack, bacon and bean

Antietam's first tour guide,
Oliver T. "Pop" Reilly

soup." Locals in Sharpsburg did a regular business providing tours and selling relics, with one Oliver T. "Pop" Reilly taking the lead in turning his "wagon load" of items scavenged from the battlefield into the standard souvenir kitsch that touring Americans picked up on their visits everywhere, including such "unique and useful articles" as defused artillery shells refashioned into table lamps.

The tendency to subsume the horrors of the war into anodyne generalizations was of course part of the way the mind deals with trauma. Holmes even in the moment noted with a certain amazement the way the facts of battle "so rapidly escape the memory in the mist which settles over a fought field."

"Time heals all wounds" was a catchphrase of veterans of the war and embodied a truth for many. There remained, too, the stigma of unmanliness in dwelling on the suffering of their experiences, and the very real fear that to speak honestly of its horrors would make them all too real. In his classic novel of the First World War, *All Quiet on the Western Front*, Erich Remarque's narrator parries his father's questions of what it was like on the front. "I realize he does not know that a man cannot talk of such things; I would do it willingly, but it is too dangerous for me to put these things into words. I am afraid they might then become gigantic and I be no longer able to master them. What would become of us if everything that happens out there were quite clear to us?"

Others more subtly saw that to preserve what still remained ennobling in the heroism and sacrifice of men who go to war could not survive the squalor of too much truth. Those who quote Walt Whitman's famous words written in the Civil War's aftermath, "The real war will never get in the books," seldom quote the other words that followed: "I say, will never be written—perhaps must not and should not be." In part he was saying that the "interior history of the war," what it did to men, is not reducible to words; in part he was saying that to do so would devalue its meaning. Holmes, in an address to the Harvard graduating class on Memorial Day of 1895, which he titled "The Soldier's Faith," saw this as part of what bound together those who shared the "incommunicable experience of war": "Having known great things, to be content with silence."

Holmes was irked afterward to be accused of advising "young men to wade in gore" in that speech for having extolled the soldier's faith that leads him to throw away his life willingly in a cause he may not even comprehend and for having said of his fellow soldiers, "You know that man has in him that unspeakable somewhat which makes him capable of miracle, able to lift himself by the might of his own soul, unaided. . . . Out of heroism grows faith in the worth of heroism." But more perceptive than most, he recognized that to draw that lesson from war and keep it alive in our "snug oversafe corner of the world" required both memory and forgetfulness. "War, when you are at it," he acknowledged, "is horrible and dull." But it is better, he insisted, for soldiers not to think about wounds. In war or in life, "if it is our business to fight, the book for the army is a war-song, not a hospital-sketch."

MADNESS

The hidden side of suppressed trauma and disillusionment from the war was an epidemic of mental illness among veterans that went mostly undiagnosed, and frequently denied outright. The capital city was already "notorious" for the number of "lunatics strolling about the streets of Washington and Georgetown," but the war swelled their numbers by the hundreds and thousands. Dorothea Dix had earned renown before the war for her crusade to reform the treatment of the insane, in asylums dedicated to the purpose, and applying the principles of "moral therapy" she had observed on a tour of progressive European institutions. St. Elizabeth's Hospital had opened in Washington in 1855 as a government hospital dedicated to the purpose, and by the end of the war at least 1,500 soldiers had been sent there, with another 1,300 in the following decade and a half.

But while the problem of insane soldiers had been recognized early in the war, the procedure for handling such cases was haphazard, and many regimental commanders and surgeons simply took the easy route and discharged obviously insane men. "Insane soldiers have been found wandering about the country, in railroad depots and about the streets of cities, with ordinary and sick furloughs, so insane as to be incompetent to provide for their wants, or find their way home," three physicians from the New York State Lunatic Asylum complained to the army's surgeon general. More than a few army doctors took the opposite tack and were sure that soldiers complaining of nervous symptoms were shamming. Infuriated at what one physician termed this "fraud on the Government," they devised medical torments to expose shirkers they were convinced were simply pretending to have lost their voices or suffered paralysis: patients were put under with ether to get them talking, jabbed with needles or electric shocks to prove they could feel pain, or more simply subjected to "treatments" like castor oil purgatives and painful applications of blisters to their shaven heads until they pleaded to be returned to their regiments.

Even those physicians who recognized the existence of mental illness generally denied that the ordeals of the war were the cause. The prevailing theory was that "insanity" was the product of a dissipation of vital energy; it might, to be sure, be brought on by some of the physical hardships soldiers endured—sunstroke, exposure to cold, malaria, fevers—but physicians and authorities evaluating claims for disability pensions were always quicker to attribute it to some preexisting moral dissipation that had nothing to do with the war at all. Alcoholism was regarded not as a symptom but rather as a prime cause of mental illness; it was the most frequent diagnosis of veterans treated at St. Elizabeth's. Other cases were attributed to uncontrolled immoral habits such as excessive jealousy or ambition, overwork, religious fanaticism, or masturbation. (The files of pension applicants are full of earnest investigations in which family members and acquaintances are asked about the masturbatory habits of the individual, in the apparent hopes of finding evidence for denying any government compensation on the grounds of mental insanity. "There was a rumor, then, that he was a masturbator, but I never saw anything of the kind," reads a typical affidavit.)

What small evidence is available suggests that African American soldiers suffered fewer lasting traumas. Fighting to secure their own freedom was a powerfully redemptive act, and the trauma of combat was after all not necessarily worse than the trauma of slavery, while offering the considerable consolation of action, and revenge, not to mention the simple practical respect of receiving pay, decent food, good clothing, and footwear. Prince Rivers, a sergeant in the first-formed regiment of U.S. Colored Troops, who had escaped on his master's horse riding 100 miles through the Confederate lines to join the Union army at Port Royal Island on the South Carolina coast, spoke at a freedmen's meeting in Beaufort in 1863. "Now we soldiers are men—men the first time in our lives. Now we can look our old masters in the face. They used to sell and whip us, and we did not dare say a word. Now we an't afraid, if they meet us, to run the bayonet through them." Confederate soldiers, lacking any such consolation, were by contrast more likely than Northerners to suffer postwar traumas of suicide, alcoholism, and opium addiction.

The letters and diaries of distressed wives and family members contain scattered hints of a more widespread but equally hidden toll, describing men withdrawn, bitter, emotionally numb, silent for days at a time only to give way to unpredictable and embarrassing emotional displays in public; and many more who simply could never settle down after the war, wandering from place to place, unable to hold down any job for long. The restlessness of postwar America is usually seen as a product of the opening of the West, and the opening of the eyes of soldiers to new opportunity that the war had shown them, as they traveled far and wide from small hometowns for the first time during its campaigns. But for thousands of veterans of the war, continual relocation was an escape from traumas that pursued them. Ambrose Bierce, who had the unusual ability to remember the war in all its manifest terrors and the obsessive drive to try to put them into words, had the consolation of the true cynic who expects nothing of his fellow man and thus is rarely disappointed. But he had a furious temper and a preoccupation with suicide and death, drank ferociously, and bounced around as a writer, from San Francisco to England to Washington, interrupted by a disastrous stint as manager of a South Dakota gold mining venture. In the fall of 1913, after revisiting five of his old Civil War battlefields, he sent a letter from Mexico to his family saying he was leaving "tomorrow for an unknown destination," and was never seen again, one of tens of thousands for whom the war had never left, and for whom time had evidently failed to heal all wounds.

PRACTICALITY

The Dunkers, one of the historical "peace churches" that believe all war is sin, hoped that their plain small church on the Antietam battlefield would be a lasting reminder to visitors of the evils of war and "an eternal symbol of peace." History had other plans. A strong streak of pacifism had been part of the civic culture of antebellum America, part of the exceptionalism that Americans felt set them apart from benighted Europe and its perpetual wars of kings. But few of the hundreds of thousands of veterans who had fought America's longest and bloodiest war had much patience with the message that war was wickedness. Many of the members of the postwar peace movement had come from the peace churches, and theirs was now a diminishing voice. When a peace congress wired the GAR during one of its reunion encampments urging it to join their protest against war, "that there may never more be another war encampment," the veterans wired back, "The Grand Army of the Republic is determined to have peace, even if it has to fight for it."

Justice Holmes once erupted when, at the start of the First World War, his young secretary fresh from Harvard Law School tried to explain that he was a pacifist because war was irrational. "I find myself very fond of him," Holmes said, but the remark brought "blood in my eye." The justice fired back that "war is the ultimate rationality," since when two nations irreconcilably disagree, the only logical recourse is for each to try to impose its will through force. Yet such realism was also to Holmes the greatest cautionary lesson of the war. He had seen, he said, the power that prejudice gives a man to hate and kill, and that profoundly informed his legal and political skepticism. "Every law means I will kill sooner than not have my way," he said—which means men should be careful about what principles they seek to inflict upon the world.

The war had marked a definable turning point from revelation to experience as a guide to truth. Lincoln's practicality—"we must use the tools we have"—was an avatar of the coming change. His law partner William Herndon recalled that Lincoln had always distrusted general principles, grounding his conclusions in the more prosaic but durable earth of the practical. It was not coincidental that the first president of Harvard after the war was the first in its history not an ordained minister; a chemist, Charles Eliot promptly threw the classics overboard, revitalized the teaching of science and modern languages, and introduced electives and majors to permit students to acquire focused professional competence in place of a smattering of gentlemanly erudition. Dr. Oliver Wendell Holmes Sr. wisecracked that Eliot "turned the whole university over like a flapjack"; but as another observer said of Harvard's new practical-minded president, "He loved skill."

The newfound recognition that war itself could be viewed as a body of expert knowledge which "could be codified, imparted, and regulated," in J. P. Clark's words, was an equally striking break from centuries of tradition. What systemization of military procedures and officer training that existed before the Civil War was limited to areas "most susceptible to standardization"—administration, equipment, small-unit drill—while leaving the essence of command, that small matter of how to fight and win a war, entirely to the discretion of individual commanders whose "guild-like conception" of professional autonomy resented any suggestion to the contrary. "Conventional wisdom held that military competence was a product of character, common sense, and natural aptitude; these innate qualities might be refined through experience or study but were largely beyond the ability of the institution to manufacture," Clark wrote.

A half century later, standardized doctrine, professional officer education, and umpired field exercises that brought national guard and regulars together in grand maneuvers that could replicate at least some elements of a real war, "as much for benefit of generals and their staffs as for the common private," had become the norm throughout the U.S. Army. In the late 1880s the War Department began preserving Civil War battlefields chiefly for the purpose of officer education, and Antietam became one of the first battlefield classrooms for the nearby Army War College in Carlisle, Pennsylvania. By 1903 metal tablets had been installed indicating all principal lines and positions at Antietam, and a stone observation tower was erected at the end of Bloody Lane to command a view of the surrounding terrain.

The needs of professional officer training were the impetus not only behind preserving the battlefield but for the first serious studies of Civil War military history, and the objective lessons to be drawn from it. As the commandant of the War College on the eve of the First World War observed in irritation, "How grossly have the historians who have attempted to describe the events of our Civil War been deceived and deceived their readers. The quarrels of generals, the distribution of the blame or the credit for the outcome, the bravery of troops—these are the sputterings which fill the pages of our histories; foolish camp-fire fables of the veterans' later days usurp the place of the reliable contemporaneous data." Young officers of the new century, trained in modern staff procedures and drilled in the paramount need for clear written orders, would find themselves astounded at McClellan's failings in such basic matters of organization and command ("My God what a poor general McClellan was," one captain wrote his wife in 1908 after a day touring Antietam with his class of officer students), and at Lee's strategic miscalculations. Antietam would be an enduring link in the transformation of war from an art to a science, and generalship from the realm of individual inspiration to rigorous study and procedure.

Dr. Holmes's veteran son often remarked that the war had taught him a more human lesson about the meaning of skill: he had learned, he said, to respect men whom he would have looked down on had not experience taught him to look up, and to recognize that knowing how to do something and keeping a cool head was worth more than any amount of lofty idealism or spiritual zeal. Returning from the funeral of one old friend from the 20th Massachusetts, Holmes recalled how his comrade had had "the coldest head on the spot and reasoned as serenely among a lot of half crazy men as if he were discussing it now" during one chaotic moment of terror during the Battle of the Wilderness. "He had no complex views of the cosmos," wrote Holmes, "but I learned to take off my hat to many a simple minded man like him." He was not meaning "simple minded" as an insult; simplicity was part of the practical virtues now admired.

Holmes never abandoned his idealism, his belief in man's ability to strive for great things. But it was a practical idealism that met the age and reflected the truth the veterans had so painfully learned. His ideal do-gooder society agitating for a cause, he liked to say, was an imaginary "Society of Jobbists," who were free to be "altruists or egoists" on the weekends provided they were neither while on the job: their contribution to the general welfare consists in putting all their energy into whatever problem at hand they have to solve, leaving the unsolvable cosmic questions to fate.

There was a practical courage that matched the practical idealism of those who like Holmes had fought through the bloody day of Antietam and "somehow survived." When the post office intercepted a bomb mailed to him following his decision upholding the conviction of the labor leader Eugene V. Debs, Holmes shrugged it off. "If I worried over all the bullets that have missed me I should have a job," he remarked. And that was not bravura, simply the conviction of a man to whom war had taught a lesson in the "irony of life." The only solution to the puzzle of life, he often told young friends, was "to file in and do your damndest," and not worry about all of its ironic twists that were beyond one's control anyway. The great Civil War historian Bruce Catton, growing up in the Midwest in the early years of the twentieth century, remembered the assurance and certainty of the old Civil War veterans, the way they seemed to represent "the continuity of human experience."

Fatalism and detachment, nostalgia and reconciliation, may have dimmed the gore and meaning of the battles of their youth, but never entirely. Ezra Carman, dedicating a monument on the Antietam battlefield on a beautiful blue-skied September day exactly forty years after the battle, spoke in one sentence of what that "greatest and most momentous" battle of the Civil War had done. "Here was made history, here was rolled back the first Confederate invasion of the North; on this field was arrested the recognition of the Southern Confederacy and foreign intervention; on this field died human slavery."

APPENDIX
The Opposing Forces

Army of the Potomac, George B. McClellan

First Corps, Joseph Hooker

First Division, Abner Doubleday

Second Division, James B. Ricketts

Third Division, George G. Meade

Second Corps, Edwin V. Sumner

First Division, Israel B. Richardson

Second Division, John Sedgwick

Third Division, William H. French

Sixth Corps, William B. Franklin

First Division, Henry W. Slocum

Second Division, William F. "Baldy" Smith

Ninth Corps, Ambrose E. Burnside, Jesse L. Reno, Jacob D. Cox

First Division, Orlando B. Willcox

Second Division, Samuel D. Sturgis

Third Division, Isaac P. Rodman

Kanawha Division, Jacob D. Cox, E. P. Scammon

Twelfth Corps, Joseph K. F. Mansfield

First Division, Alpheus S. Williams

Second Division, George S. Greene

Couch's Division, Darius N. Couch

Fifth Corps (reserve), Fitz John Porter

First Division, George W. Morrell

Second Division, George Sykes

Cavalry Division, Alfred Pleasonton

Army of Northern Virginia, Robert E. Lee

Longstreet's Command, James Longstreet

    Anderson's Division, Richard H. Anderson

    Jones's Division, David R. Jones

    Hood's Division, John Bell Hood

    Evans's Brigade, Nathan G. Evans

    McLaws's Division, Lafayette McLaws

    Walker's Division, John G. Walker

Jackson's Command, Thomas J. "Stonewall" Jackson

    Ewell's Division, Alexander R. Lawton

    A. P. Hill's Light Division, Ambrose P. Hill

    Jackson's Division, John R. Jones

    D. H. Hill's Division, Daniel H. Hill

Cavalry, James E. B. Stuart

NOTES ON SOURCES

An extraordinary quantity of primary and secondary source material related to the Civil War is now available online: the complete official records of both armies, Lincoln's every written word and utterance, most of Robert E. Lee's correspondence, tens of thousands of published histories and memoirs, and thousands more contemporary newspaper reports and soldiers' letters and diaries, among much else. An internet search of a key phrase can, with few exceptions, bring up the source in question.

In the confidence I am not doing a serious disservice to readers seeking to track down a particular quotation or fact, I have accordingly provided in the notes below a general description of the sources I used in each chapter, mentioning specific citations only where it would not be obvious where they came from by context or by consulting the Bibliography. (Full citations are found in the Bibliography to all the works cited below in abbreviated form with author's last name and short title.) Published editions and archival collections of soldiers' letters and diaries are listed in the Bibliography under the author's name, rather than the editor or institutional location, to facilitate identification of these sources.

I feel justified, too, in dispensing with the usual endless acknowledgments that seem to be de rigueur these days, in which the author mentions every person he ever exchanged an email with (the more famous the better), and ends by thanking his spouse and cat for their patience while he valiantly struggled through the labors of authorship. I would, however, definitely be remiss were I fail to acknowledge Terry Reimer, director of research at the Museum of Civil War Medicine in Frederick, Maryland, for her kind and knowledgeable assistance.

Prologue

Dr. Holmes's account of his search for his wounded son was published (much to the annoyance of the latter) in an *Atlantic Monthly* article, "My Hunt after 'The Captain.'" Justice Holmes's oft-quoted epigrams about the experience of war come from two speeches, "The Soldier's Faith" in 1895 and his Remarks Before the Second Army Corps Association in 1903, which can be found in his *Occasional Speeches*. The recollections of the unnamed hired man on the Nicodemus farm appear in Johnson, *Battleground Adventures* (p. 103).

For the role of religious thought in mid-nineteenth-century views about American democracy, I drew on Howe, *Unitarian Conscience;* Wood, *Empire of Liberty;* Miller, Stout, and Wilson, eds., *Religion and the American Civil War;* Haven, *National Sermons*; and the brief but very insightful discussions in McPherson, *For Cause & Comrades* (especially p. 67 on soldiers as "practical Arminians").

The attacks on West Point are quoted in Ambrose, *Duty, Honor* (p. 115). Statistics on population and labor at mid-century are from the 1850 and 1860 Censuses; Lebergott, "Labor Force and Employment"; and Laurie, *Artisans into Workers*.

1. Who Would Be a Soldier

My account of Lee's early life and family comes primarily from Guelzo, *Robert E. Lee*, which in its thoroughness and tough-minded fairness stands alone among the many Lee biographies. Lee's views on slavery and loyalty are from the letter to his wife dated December 27, 1856, and to James A. Seddon, January 10, 1863, Lee Family Archive. Gallagher, "Question of Loyalty," offers a subtle examination of the nature of loyalty and Lee's conception of it.

The role of the Corps of Engineers and West Point in civil engineering and engineering education are covered in Ambrose, *Duty, Honor;* Shallat, "Engineering Policy"; and Clark, *Preparing for War.* For Jeffersonian and Jacksonian criticism of the military academy, see also Williams, "Attack upon West Point." The stultification of army life in the years before the Civil War is vividly recounted in Coffman, *The Old Army*, and Newell, *Regular Army.*

There is a large literature on the development (or lack thereof) of strategic thought in the pre–Civil War U.S. Army, and the influence of Dennis Hart Mahan. I found especially useful Coffman, *The Old Army;* Clark, *Preparing for War;* Hope, "Scientific Way of War"; Phipps, "Mahan at West Point"; McWhiney and Jamieson, *Attack and Die*; and Hagerman, *Civil War and Modern Warfare,* all of which also contain valuable discussions of the lessons, right and wrong, which American officers drew from the Mexican War. The primary sources by Duane, O'Connor, Mahan, and Halleck provide a snapshot of American military thought in the early and mid-nineteenth century. Czarnecki, "Lincoln's Secret Visit to West Point," recounts this interesting historical footnote; the letter from Colonel A. H. Bowman to Lincoln, May 6, 1863, National Archives, confirms the delivery to the White House of the requested copy of the map of Napoleon's campaigns. Erath, "Union Success," makes the important point about the straightforward strategy of a war against a dictator.

The quoted observations about Lee's aggressiveness are from Guelzo, *Lee*; Mosby, *Memoirs*; and McPherson, *Battle Cry of Freedom*. Lee's strategic thinking is well discussed in Gallagher, "Lee as General."

2. A Problem of Engineering

Sears, *George B. McClellan*, is a comprehensive account and analysis of the man which allows McClellan to damn himself very effectively with his own words and vanity. Sears's essay "Lincoln and McClellan" presents a more detailed study of McClellan's personal relations with the President. The observations concerning McClellan's lack of character are from the letters of Halleck to his wife, July 5, 1862, reprinted in Wilson, "Halleck Memoir"; and Mahan to Gouverneur Kemble, September 26, 1864, in Mahan, Papers. Many of McClellan's revealing personal letters, in which "his vanity and his ill-will toward rivals and superiors are shockingly naked," as Jacob Cox put it, appear in McClellan's posthumously published memoirs, *McClellan's Own Story*; some of his equally revealing private letters to Burnside, including his boasts of being the "chosen instrument" of God and of his empty victories at Manassas and Yorktown being "my brightest chaplets in history," were included in the official record (*The War of Rebellion*, vol. IX), perhaps through Burnside's carelessness.

Hagerman, *Civil War and Modern Warfare*, has an excellent discussion of the modern staff system and its slow development in the Army of the Potomac; Henderson, *Science of War*, and Hattaway and Jones, *How the North Won*, also offer valuable perspective and background on this extremely important, and often neglected, factor in the performance of Civil War armies.

Fishel, *Secret War for the Union*, examines McClellan's intelligence failures in unrivaled depth, based on a thorough examination of a wealth of material in the archival records of the Army of the Potomac that does not appear in the published official record. He also offers a meticulously worked-out timeline relating McClellan's delay in exploiting Lee's Special Orders No. 191 to the disposition of forces on September 13 and 14 that, to my mind, shows the untenability of recent efforts by a few brave historians to rehabilitate McClellan with the questionable assertion that he did act boldly and decisively.

Hagerman offers an illuminating discussion of logistics requirements and organization; Moore, "Mobility and Strategy," has some useful numerical comparisons of Napoleonic and Civil War armies on this point.

My account of the reactions of citizens of Frederick during its brief occupation by Lee's army is drawn mainly from Steiner, *Diary*; Ernst, *Too Afraid to Cry*; and McPherson, *Antietam*.

Ezra Carman's remarkable history of the Maryland campaign was published in 2008, more than a century after its completion, in a magnificent edition by Joseph Pierro. The two standard histories of the Battle of Antietam, Sears, *Landscape*

Turned Red, and Murfin, *Gleam of Bayonets*, have proved their enduring power, and both cover the initial stages of the Maryland Campaign and the events leading up to the Battle of South Mountain well; Hartwig, *To Antietam Creek*, a more recent and exhaustive (795-page) treatment of the campaign up to the eve of the Battle of Antietam, contains some newly discovered details that correct errors in the accepted accounts. While not exactly light reading, it is an invaluable reference.

I discuss George Sharpe in my article, "America's Unknown Intelligence Czar," as (in much more depth) does Fishel.

3.　The Assault Heroic

Cox's memoir is a notably well-written and objective account of his military career, the Maryland Campaign, and his candid and well-substantiated criticisms of McClellan's failings as a commander.

The main sources for the Battle of South Mountain I drew on were Carman, *Maryland Campaign*; Hartwig, *To Antietam Creek*; Priest, *Before Antietam*; Hoptak, *Battle of South Mountain*; and vol. XIX of *The War of Rebellion*.

The detailed studies by Earl J. Hess, *The Rifle Musket in Civil War Combat*; *Civil War Infantry Tactics*; and *Field Armies & Fortifications in the Civil War* have done much to revise long-accepted ideas about the impact of the rifle on Civil War combat. Although like most who set out to slay false premises he is too categorical in places, his basic conclusions are impossible to ignore and are backed by an extraordinarily impressive array of data and research. Lockhart, *Firepower*, is a useful survey of the history of weapons with good coverage of the development of the rifle and artillery. Stanage, "Rifle vs. Smoothbore," reproduces the targets used in the prewar accuracy tests of these weapons. The statistics on wounds caused by various weapons are from the *Medical and Surgical History*, part 3, vol. II (pp. 696 and 685).

The vivid examples of difficulties in training Americans are quoted in Castleman, *Army of the Potomac*; Linderman, *Embattled Courage*; and Hess, *Infantry Tactics*. Criticisms of the use of fortifications are from Williams, "Attack Upon West Point"; Linderman; McWhiney and Jamieson, *Attack and Die*; and Edwin Stanton's letter to the *New York Tribune*, reprinted in Dana, *Recollections*.

Armstrong, "United States Tactical Doctrine"; Clark, *Preparing for War*; Hess, *Infantry Tactics*; and Hagerman, *Civil War and Modern Warfare*, have good discussions and analysis of U.S. Army tactical manuals; Orr, "Sharpshooters," adds useful detail on the role of skirmishers and their effectiveness, in particular at Gettysburg. Upton's innovative ideas are well covered in McWhiney and Jamieson and in Ambrose, *Upton*; his detailed report of September 1, 1864, describing the assault at Spotsylvania is reprinted in Michie, *Life and Letters*.

The evolution of signals organization and its difficulties putting technology to effective use are thoroughly covered by Hagerman.

"We use these to fight with" is from Walcott, *Twenty-first Regiment* (p. 194) and "What the hell you fellows cheering for" from Murfin, *Gleam of Bayonets* (p. 203).

Luff, "Cavalry from Harper's Ferry"; Blackwell, "Cavalry Escape"; Carman, *Maryland* Campaign, and Hartwig, *Antietam Creek* vividly recount this daring enterprise; Freiheit, *Boots and Saddles,* provides a truly exhaustive account for those who wish to know what every individual cavalry company did, and when.

4. Organizing for Carnage

The observation that the Civil War took place at the "end of the medical Middle Ages" has repeatedly been attributed to Surgeon General William Hammond, but I can find no evidence that he ever said that; the first occurrence of the phrase I find is in Adams, *Doctors in Blue,* in 1952 (where it appears in the author's own words), and it was only in the 1990s that it began being (mis)attributed to Hammond.

Letterman's reports can be found in the *Medical and Surgical History,* part 1, appendix (pp. 92–104), and in *The War of Rebellion,* vol. XI, part 1 (pp. 106–17) and vol. XIX, part 1 (pp. 210–20). His memoir, *Medical Recollections of the Army of the Potomac,* is largely a recapitulation of these official reports with few personal details, but it offers some additional insight into his organizational innovations. The memorial recollections by Bennett Clements provide a few additional details as well, as does (to a very limited degree) the perfunctory biography of Letterman by McGaugh, *Surgeon in Blue.*

Adams's *Doctors in Blue* is a thorough history of the medical corps of the Union army, with coverage of the political infighting and bureaucratic intrigue that so notably shaped its development. The chapter "Evolution of the Ambulance Corps and Field Hospital" in Duncan, *Medical Department in the Civil War,* is another valuable source; Freemon, "Hammond," covers the background of the army's effective surgeon general.

Contemporary theories of disease transmission and gangrene are discussed in Devine, *Learning from the Wounded;* the classic memoir of Civil War soldier life, Billings, *Hardtack and Coffee,* offers colorful examples of army cuisine; the soldier's request for potatoes and onions to be sent from home is from the letter of Albert A. Manley to his wife, October 18, 1862, in Manley, Letters; and the complaint of surgeons amputating limbs for "practice" is from Allen, *Rhode Island Volunteers* (pp. 172–73).

Statistics on disease, fatalities, anesthetic use, and outcomes are from the *Medical and Surgical History,* part 3, vol. II, especially the tables on pp. 877 and 878 (amputations and excisions), and from the exhibits at the Museum of Civil War Medicine; other useful summaries are found in Sartin, "Infectious Diseases in the Civil War," and Reilly, "Medical and Surgical Care." The vivid quoted description of rapidly advancing gangrene is from surgeon Silas Weir Mitchell, quoted in Devine.

Keen's observations are from his papers "Military Surgery in 1861 and 1918" and "Surgical Reminiscences"; his report connecting gangrene to poor air circulation in hospitals is in the *Medical and Surgical History*, part 3, vol. II (pp. 826–29). Goldsmith's work on bromine to treat and prevent the spread of gangrene is covered by Devine, *Learning from the Wounded*, and Trombold, "Gangrene Therapy."

The chapter in Duncan's *Medical Department in the Civil War*, "The Bloodiest Day in American History—Antietam"; Dyer, *Journal of a Surgeon*; and Breeden, "Field Medicine at Antietam," provide a picture of care for the wounded on the field of Antietam.

5. Passion and Irony

Holmes's recollections of the eve of the Battle of Antietam are from his letter to John Wu, June 16, 1923, in Holmes, "Some Unpublished Letters." His contemporaneous observations in his letters and diaries are collected in Holmes, *Touched with Fire*. His comments about the lessons the army taught him, and life in the army as "an organized bore," are from his letters of December 15, 1926, in Holmes, *Holmes-Laski Letters*; and February 1, 1920, in Holmes, *Holmes-Pollock Letters*. I discuss Holmes's attitudes and experiences further in my biography, *Oliver Wendell Holmes: A Life in War, Law, and Ideas*.

The memoirs by Wightman and Wilkeson are striking for their unvarnished views of their army experiences, their introspection, and vivid detail. The soldier who wrote "if the Union be lost, it will be missed by many" was George I. Fenno of the 107th New York, whose letter appears in Post, ed., *Soldiers' Letters* (p. 161). The Irish-born Peter Welsh's assertions of his stake in the fight are from his letters of February 3, 1863, to his wife and June 1, 1863, to his father-in-law, Patrick Prendergast, in Welsh, *Irish Green and Union Blue*.

Linderman, *Embattled Courage*, offers a deeply documented argument about soldiers' attitudes toward courage and battle. Although I agree with James McPherson that he takes his case too far and overstates the disillusionment of soldiers as the war progressed, Linderman has assembled an impressive and invaluable body of evidence on the subject. McPherson's two short books on the motivations of Civil War soldiers, *What They Fought For* and *For Cause and Comrades*, are based on a careful reading and statistical analysis of thousands of diaries and letters, and add additional crucial perspective here. The evening chorus of officers' defalcations ("Who got behind the tree?") is from Carmichael, *War for the Common Soldier* (p. 60); the rumors about Grant's death are from Phillips, "Rumors and Confederate Persistence."

Bierce's ironic observation "An army's bravest men are its cowards" is from his short story "What I Saw of Shiloh"; his "business of the soldier to kill" from "One of the Missing." The "good coward" anecdote is related in Burdette, *Drums of the*

47th (pp. 101–3); "mechanical, dull, dogged, machine-work" is from Kirkland, *Captain of Company K* (p. 83).

Holmes's comments about the lack of animosity toward the enemy are from his "Memorial Day" speech and his letter of April 9, 1918, to Charlotte Moncheur, quoted in Budiansky, *Holmes* (p. 364); his hating to hear "what heroes they were" from his Remarks at a Meeting of the 20th Regimental Association, 1897, reprinted in Holmes, *Essential Holmes* (p. 73); "a real horror" from his secretary Mark Howe's diary, quoted in Budiansky, *Holmes* (p. 107); and "file in and do your damndest" and not worrying the "cosmos would collapse" from his letter to Lucy Clifford, January 21, 1928, quoted in ibid. (p. 4).

Again, I have drawn upon the admirable works of Sears, Murfin, and Carman, and the official record, for my account of the battle. Alpheus Williams's letters to his brother-in-law and daughters are some of the most vivid eyewitness accounts. Francis Palfrey's history, *Antietam and Fredericksburg*, provides useful perspectives. The first-hand account of the 15th Massachusetts being flanked is from the letters reprinted in Bowen, *Ball's Bluff to Gettysburg*.

6. War at the Operational Level

The major sources of Longstreet's life, military experiences, and opinions are his memoir, *From Manassas to Appomattox*, and the biographies by Wert and Piston. Knudsen, *James Longstreet and the American Civil War: The Confederate General Who Fought the Next War*, is a quirky but fascinating examination of Longstreet's development of important operational concepts, viewed from the perspective of an artillery officer who served in Europe and Iraq in the modern U.S. Army.

Jackson's ruthlessness is well described in Robertson, *Stonewall Jackson*.

The strategic alternatives proposed by McLaws and Longstreet are well covered in Carman's history of the Maryland Campaign, as are McClellan's shifting explanations of what his plan was; Cox's memoir is particularly lucid in his criticisms on this point and in exposing McClellan's craven attempts to blame Burnside.

The fighting at Bloody Lane is described in regiment-by-regiment detail in Priest, *Antietam*. The anecdote of the Ohio soldier mistaking bullets for crickets is from the memoir by Thomas Galwey, *Valiant Hours* (p. 42). D. H. Strother's recollections, published in *Harper's Monthly* in February 1868, are quoted in Murfin, *Gleam of Bayonets* (p. 262).

The travails of the 16th Connecticut are chronicled in Gordon, *A Broken Regiment*.

McPherson, *Antietam* (p. 177 n. 56) offers a succinct summary and analysis of casualty statistics at Antietam. The fate of the 20th Massachusetts's Colonel Lee is described in a letter of November 20, 1862, in the collected letters of Henry L. Abbot, *Fallen Leaves*. Abbott is also the source of the "Give them Fredericksburg" quote, which appears in his letter of July 6, 1863.

7. Laid in Our Dooryards

Starr, *Bohemian Brigade*, and Andrews, *North Reports the Civil War* and *South Reports the Civil War*, offer comprehensive and colorful accounts of news reporting of the war. Smalley recounted his experiences in a *Harper's Monthly* article published in 1894 and in his 1911 memoir. Dr. Holmes's contemporaneous observations about news reporting and about Gardner's photographs appear in his *Atlantic* pieces "Bread and the Newspaper" and "Doings of the Sunbeam."

Cobb, "Alexander Gardner," and Katz, *Witness to an Era*, cover Gardner's life and work and provide useful background on the commercial and technical evolution of photography before and during the war, as does Zeller, *Blue and Gray in Black and White*; William Frassanito in his book focusing on the photography of Antietam identifies, to the extent possible, the precise location where each of Gardner's famous images was shot. All of these photographs, now in the Library of Congress, have been digitized and are available on the library's website; several accompanying articles on the site relate Frassanito's unsettling discoveries concerning Gardner's staging of his photographs.

The Confederate soldiers' letters mentioning ghoulish relics fashioned from dead Yankees are quoted in McPherson, *Cause and Comrades* (p. 151).

De Forest's correspondence with William Dean Howells is quoted in *Harper's Monthly*, May 1887 (p. 987).

Mark Schantz had the misfortune to come out with his book on death and the Civil War at almost the exact moment Drew Gilpin Faust came out with her book on death and the Civil War, and the attention generated by Faust's book (not hurt by her having just been named president of Harvard) overshadowed Schantz's important and almost precisely opposite conclusions. Faust sensitively explores the way the Civil War challenged traditional ways of dealing with death, but Schantz more convincingly emphasizes how nineteenth-century Americans' traditional acceptance of death in many ways abetted the appalling casualty rates of the war. Marshall, "The Great Exaggeration," sets forth the demographic and social evidence for the terrible ordinariness of death and suffering in antebellum American culture.

The effect of the battle on civilians in and around Sharpsburg is ably covered in Ernst, *Too Afraid to Cry*.

8. Woman's Work

Pryor, *Clara Barton*, is a thorough, meticulous, and balanced biography that does not shy away from the less admirable aspects of its subject's character. The author's extended essay in the National Park Service booklet on Barton offers a concise summary, with some additional information. For further details, including Barton's diary entries, lecture notes, scrapbooks, and correspondence, I consulted the

Library of Congress Clara Barton Papers (which have been digitized and are available online at the library's website). Barton's *Story of My Childhood* casts some revealing light on her early life. Stephen Oates's largely pandering biography, *A Woman of Valor*, contains some useful historiographic information not available elsewhere.

Among the considerable literature on women in the nineteenth century, I found particularly useful Winthrop, "Tocqueville's Women"; Zagarri, "Rights of Man and Woman in Post-revolutionary America"; Clinton, *The Other Civil War*; and the relevant sections of Furnas, *The Americans,* and Wood, *Empire of Liberty.*

Wood, "Women Nurses," has an excellent discussion of the traditional role of women and how this shaped their service in the Union army. Mary Livermore's *My Story of the War* is an exceptional memoir that stands out for its moments of reflectiveness, insight, and humor; other notable firsthand accounts of nurses' experiences include Hannah Ropes's diary and Louisa May Alcott's *Hospital Sketches.* Adams, *Doctors in Blue*, offers additional overview and detail on the role of women nurses, and doctors' reactions to them. McNeil, "Daughters of Charity," summarizes the work of Catholic nurses. An analysis of statistical data available on nurses in the Civil War is contained in Schultz, *Women at the Front*; notably, her new research corrects the previous significant underestimate of the number of women employed in Union army hospitals during the war.

The work of the Sanitary Commission and the discomfort it gave to more traditional do-gooding charities is ably covered in the chapter "The Sanitary Elite" in Fredrickson, *Northern Intellectuals;* Bremner, "Impact of Civil War on Philanthropy"; and the somewhat breezy treatment in Maxwell, *Lincoln's Fifth Wheel* (which nonetheless has some valuable overview, statistics, and anecdotes).

The case in the Maryland Court of Appeals in which Hubbell won back the Glen Echo property is *Hirons v. Hubbell*, 149 Md. 593 (Md. 1926).

9. Emancipation

There are probably almost as many books about Lincoln as there are about the Civil War; I found especially useful David Herbert Donald's classic volume. Carpenter's reminiscences of his six months painting Lincoln's portrait offers some surprisingly acute insights.

Welles, "History of Emancipation," and Whiting, *War Powers of the President*, provide a contemporary background to the Emancipation Proclamation and Lincoln's understanding of the war powers he relied upon; Oakes's article "Was Emancipation Constitutional?" and his book *Crooked Path to Abolition* carefully analyze the legal and historical basis of emancipation in the laws of war, and the long tradition of antislavery constitutionalism in America. Lindsay, "Return of Negro Slaves," documents in detail Britain's refusal to return or pay compensation for American slaves emancipated by them during the belligerent periods of the Revolution and

War of 1812, and the postwar negotiations that underscored this important precedent. The Lieber Code was promulgated as General Orders No. 100 by President Lincoln, April 24, 1863.

Holmes's views on Lincoln appear in his letter to Lewis Einstein, March 8, 1924. The reaction in the army to the Emancipation Proclamation is covered in McPherson, *Antietam* (p. 140), and the quoted views of Henry Abbott are from his letter of January 10, 1863. Lincoln's diplomatic and public-relations efforts to encourage British popular support for the Emancipation Proclamation are discussed in Peraino, *Lincoln in the World*.

The denouement of the Maryland Campaign is well documented in McPherson, *Antietam;* Carman, *Maryland Campaign;* Sears, *McClellan;* and vol. XIX of *The War of Rebellion.*

Epilogue

I discuss Holmes's intertwined beliefs about war, skepticism, tolerance, and pragmatism in my biography *Oliver Wendell Holmes.*

Blight, *Race and Reunion*, and Linderman, *Embattled Courage*, are both invaluable for their treatment of postwar memory. The history of battlefield commemoration at Antietam is ably discussed in Trail, "Remembering Antietam," and Hulver, "Ezra Carman," the latter also based on a thorough and revealing examination of Carman's correspondence with veterans; Hulver is the source of the quoted observation about how Carman's questionnaires to veterans shaped the dominant narrative of the battle. The author of the line about postwar histories treating the two sides of the conflict as "merely players in a great game of chess" was Albion Tourgée, a courageous fighter for Black rights during Reconstruction, in Tourgée, "Renaissance of Nationalism."

Carroll, *Invisible Wounds*, is I believe the only major study to date devoted to mental illness among Civil War soldiers, and I found it an invaluable resource on this complex subject. Prince Rivers's speech in Beaufort is quoted in Pennsylvanian Freedmen's Relief Association, *Report.*

Schmidt and Barkley, *September Mourn*, is a local-history-focused treatment of the Dunker church with some useful background on the Dunkers and their history. An excellent discussion of postwar professional training of officers is found in Clark, *Preparing for War.* Smith, "Five Paragraph Order," is a useful history of procedures developed to systematize written orders. Reardon, "Antietam to Argonne," provides an in-depth look at the history of the U.S. Army's use of Antietam as an outdoor classroom for professional military education.

BIBLIOGRAPHY

Abbott, Henry L. *Fallen Leaves: The Civil War Letters of Major Henry Livermore Abbott.* Edited by Robert Garth Scott. Kent, Ohio: Kent State University Press, 1991.

Adams, George Worthington. *Doctors in Blue: The Medical History of the Union Army in the Civil War.* New York: H. Schuman, 1952.

Alcott, Louisa M. *Hospital Sketches.* Boston: Redpath, 1863.

Allen, George H. *Forty-Seven Months with the R.I. Volunteers.* Providence: J. A. & R. A. Reid, 1887.

Ambrose, Stephen R. *Upton and the Army.* Baton Rouge: Louisiana State University Press, 1964.

———. *Duty, Honor, Country: A History of West Point.* Baltimore, Md.: Johns Hopkins University Press, 1966.

Andrews, J. Cutler. *The North Reports the Civil War.* 1955. Reprint. Princeton: Princeton University Press, 1970.

———. *The South Reports the Civil War.* 1970. Reprint. Princeton: Princeton University Press, 2015.

Armstrong, Marion Vincent, Jr. "United States Tactical Doctrine, 1855 to 1861: The Mismeasure of Technology." Master's thesis, Old Dominion University, Norfolk, Va., 1991.

Ballard, Ted. *Battle of Antietam. Staff Ride Guide.* Washington, D.C.: Center of Military History, United States Army, 2008.

Barton, Clara. *The Story of My Childhood.* New York: Baker & Taylor, 1907.

———. Papers. Library of Congress, Manuscript Division, Washington, D.C.

Bierce, Ambrose. *Tales of Soldiers and Civilians.* San Francisco: E. L. G. Steele, 1891.

———. *Collected Works.* Vol. 1. New York: Neale, 1909.

Billings, John D. *Hardtack and Coffee.* Boston: George M. Smith, 1887.

Blackwell, Samuel J., Jr. "Cavalry Escape from Harper's Ferry." *Journal of the Illinois State Historical Society* 105, no. 2–3 (Summer–Fall 2012): 183–201.

Blight, David W. *Race and Reunion: The Civil War in American Memory.* Cambridge: Harvard University Press, 2001.

Bowen, Ronald E. *From Ball's Bluff to Gettysburg . . . and Beyond: The Civil War Letters of Private Roland E. Bowen, 15th Massachusetts Infantry, 1861–1864.* Edited by Gregory A. Coco. Gettysburg, Pa.: Thomas, 1994.

Breeden, James O. "Field Medicine at Antietam." *Caduceus* 10, no. 1 (Spring 1994): 9–22.

Bremner, Robert H. "The Impact of the Civil War on Philanthropy and Social Welfare." *Civil War History* 12, no. 4 (December 1966): 292–303.

Budiansky, Stephen. "America's Unknown Intelligence Czar." *American Heritage* 55, no. 5 (October 2004).

———. *Oliver Wendell Holmes: A Life in War, Law, and Ideas.* New York: Norton, 2019.

Burdette, Robert J. *The Drums of the 47th.* Indianapolis: Bobbs-Merrill, 1914.

Carman, Ezra Ayer. *The Maryland Campaign of September 1862: Ezra A. Carman's Definitive Study of the Union and Confederate Armies at Antietam.* Edited by Joseph Pierro. London: Routledge, 2008.

Carmichael, Peter S. *The War for the Common Soldier: How Men Thought, Fought, and Survived in Civil War Armies.* Chapel Hill: University of North Carolina Press, 2018.

Carpenter, F. B. *Six Months at the White House with Abraham Lincoln: The Story of a Picture.* New York: Hurd and Houghton, 1866.

Carroll, Dillon J. *Invisible Wounds: Mental Illness and Civil War Soldiers.* Baton Rouge: Louisiana State University Press, 2021.

Castleman, Alfred L. *The Army of the Potomac behind the Scenes.* Milwaukee, Wis.: Strickland, 1863.

Child, William. *Letters from a Civil War Surgeon: The Letters of Dr. William Child of the Fifth New Hampshire Volunteers.* Solon, Maine: Polar Bear, 2001.

Clark, J. P. *Preparing for War: The Emergence of the Modern U.S. Army, 1815–1917.* Cambridge: Harvard University Press, 2017.

Clarke, Frances. "'Honorable Scars': Northern Amputees and the Meaning of Civil War Injuries." In *Union Soldiers and The Northern Home Front: Wartime Experiences, Postwar Adjustments,* edited by Paul A. Cimbala and Randall M. Miller. New York: Fordham University Press, 2002.

Clements, Bennett A. "Memoir of Jonathan Letterman, M.D." *Journal of the Military Service Institution of the United States* 40 (September 1883): 204–30.

Clinton, Catherine. *The Other Civil War: American Women in the Nineteenth Century.* 1984. Rev. ed. New York: Hill and Wang, 1999.

Cobb, Josephine. "Alexander Gardner." *Image* 7, no. 6 (June 1958): 124–36.

Coffmann, Edward M. *The Old Army: A Portrait of the American Army in Peacetime, 1784–1898.* New York: Oxford University Press, 1986.

Cox, Jacob Dolson. "Stonewall Jackson—II." *The Nation* 67, no. 1744 (December 1, 1898), 412–15.

———. *Military Reminiscences of the Civil War.* New York: Scribner's, 1900.

Czarnecki, Anthony J. "Mr. Lincoln's Secret Visit to West Point: The Sesquicentennial of a Military Mission." *New York History* 93, no. 1 (Winter 2012): 4–51.

Dana, Charles A. *Recollections of the Civil War: With the Leaders in Washington and in the Field in the Sixties.* New York: D. Appleton, 1902.

De Forest, J. W. *Miss Ravenel's Conversion from Secession to Loyalty.* New York: Harper & Brothers, 1867.

Devine, Shauna. *Learning from the Wounded: The Civil War and the Rise of American Medical Science.* Chapel Hill: University of North Carolina Press, 2014.

Donald, David Herbert. *Lincoln.* New York: Simon & Schuster, 1995.

Duane, William. *The American Military Library; or, Compendium of Modern Tactics.* Philadelphia, 1809.

Duncan, Louis C. *The Medical Department of the United States Army in the Civil War.* Washington, D.C.: Surgeon General's Office, U.S. Army, [191-?]. archive.org/details/cu31924030749588.

Dyer, J. Franklin. *The Journal of a Civil War Surgeon.* Edited by Michael B. Chesson. Lincoln: University of Nebraska Press, 2003.

Erath, John. "Union Success in the Civil War and Lessons for Strategic Leaders." *Joint Forces Quarterly* 77, no. 2 (2015): 128–36.

Ernst, Kathleen A. *Too Afraid to Cry: Maryland Civilians and the Antietam Campaign.* Mechanicsburg, Pa.: Stackpole, 1999.

Faust, Drew Gilpin. *This Republic of Suffering: Death and the American Civil War.* New York: Vintage, 2008.

Favill, Josiah Marshall. *Diary of a Young Officer Serving with the Armies of the United States During the War of the Rebellion.* Chicago: Donnelley, 1909.

Fishel, Edwin C. *The Secret War for the Union: The Untold Story of Military Intelligence in the Civil War.* Boston: Houghton Mifflin, 1996.

Forbes, Edwin. *Thirty Years After: An Artist's Story of the Great War.* New York: Fords, Howard & Hulbert, 1890.

Frassanito, William A. *Antietam: The Photographic Legacy of America's Bloodiest Day.* New York: Scribner's, 1978.

Fredrickson, George M. *The Inner Civil War: Northern Intellectuals and the Crisis of the Union.* Champaign: University of Illinois Press, 1965.

Freemon, Frank R. "Lincoln Finds a Surgeon General: William A. Hammond and the Transformation of the Union Army Medical Bureau." *Civil War History* 33, no. 1 (March 1987): 5–21.

Freiheit, Laurence H. *Boots and Saddles: Cavalry During the Maryland Campaign of September 1862.* 2nd ed. Iowa City: Press of the Camp Pope Bookshop, 2013.

Furnas, J. C. *The Americans: A Social History of the United States, 1587–1914.* New York: Putnam, 1969.

Fussell, Paul. *The Great War and Modern Memory.* New York: Oxford University Press, 1975.

Gallagher, Gary W. "An Old-Fashioned Soldier in a Modern War?: Robert E. Lee as Confederate General." *Civil War History* 45, no. 4 (December 1999): 295–321.

————. "A Question of Loyalty." *Civil War Times* 52, no. 5 (October 2013): 30–37.

Galwey, Thomas Francis. *The Valiant Hours: Narrative of 'Captain Brevet,' an Irish-American in the Army of the Potomac*. Harrisburg, Pa.: Stackpole, 1961.

Gordon, Lesley J. "All Who Went into That Battle Were Heroes: Remembering the 16th Regiment Connecticut Volunteers at Antietam." In *The Antietam Campaign*, edited by Gary W. Gallagher. Chapel Hill: University of North Carolina Press, 1999.

————. *A Broken Regiment: The 16th Connecticut's Civil War*. Baton Rouge: Louisiana State University Press, 2014.

Gottfried, Bradley M. *The Maps of Antietam*. New York: Savas Beatie, 2012.

Graham, Mathew J. "Concerning the Battle of Antietam," September 27, 1894. 9th New York Vertical File. Antietam National Battlefield Library, Sharpsburg, Md.

Guelzo, Allen C. *Robert E. Lee: A Life*. New York: Knopf, 2021.

Hagerman, Edward. *The American Civil War and the Origins of Modern Warfare: Ideas, Organization, and Field Command*. Bloomington: Indiana University Press, 1988.

Halleck, H. Wager. *Elements of Military Art and Science: Or, Course of Instruction in Strategy, Fortification, Tactics of Battles, &c, Embracing the Duties of Staff, Infantry, Cavalry, Artillery, and Engineers. Adapted to the Use of Volunteers and Militia*. 2nd ed. New York: Appleton, 1861.

Hartwig, D. Scott. *To Antietam Creek: The Maryland Campaign of 1862*. Baltimore: Johns Hopkins University Press, 2012.

Hattaway, Herman, and Archer Jones. *How the North Won: A Military History of the Civil War*. Urbana: University of Illinois Press, 1983.

Haven, Gilbert. *National Sermons: Sermons, Speeches and Letters on Slavery and Its War*. Boston: Lee and Shepard, 1869.

Henderson, G. F. R. *The Science of War*. London: Longmans, Green, 1912.

Hess, Earl J. "'Tell Me What the Sensations Are': The Northern Home Front Learns about Combat." In *Union Soldiers and The Northern Home Front: Wartime Experiences, Postwar Adjustments*, edited by Paul A. Cimbala and Randall M. Miller. New York: Fordham University Press, 2002.

————. *Field Armies & Fortifications in the Civil War: The Eastern Campaigns, 1861–1864*. Chapel Hill: University of North Carolina Press, 2005.

————. *The Rifle Musket in Civil War Combat: Reality and Myth*. Lawrence: University Press of Kansas, 2008.

————. *Civil War Infantry Tactics: Training, Combat, and Small-Unit Effectiveness*. Baton Rouge: Louisiana State University Press, 2015.

Hitchcock, Frederick L. *War from the Inside*. Philadelphia: Lippincott, 1904.

Holmes, Oliver Wendell, Jr. *The Occasional Speeches of Justice Oliver Wendell Holmes*. 1891. Rev. ed., edited by Mark De Wolfe Howe. Cambridge: Harvard University Press, 1962.

———. "Some Unpublished Letters of Justice Holmes." Edited by John C. H. Wu. *T'ien Hsia Monthly* 1, no. 3 (October 1935): 251–302.

———. *Touched with Fire: Civil War Letters and Diary of Oliver Wendell Holmes, Jr., 1861–1864.* Edited by Mark De Wolfe Howe. Cambridge: Harvard University Press, 1946.

———. *Holmes-Laski Letters: The Correspondence of Mr. Justice Holmes and Harold J. Laski, 1916–1935.* Edited by Mark De Wolfe Howe. 2 vols. Cambridge: Harvard University Press, 1953.

———. *Holmes-Pollock Letters: The Correspondence of Mr. Justice Holmes and Sir Frederick Pollock, 1874–1932.* Edited by Mark De Wolfe Howe. Cambridge: Harvard University Press, 1961.

———. *The Holmes-Einstein Letters: Correspondence of Mr. Justice Holmes and Lewis Einstein, 1903–1935.* Edited by James Bishop Peabody. New York: St. Martin's, 1964.

———. *The Essential Holmes: Selections from the Letters, Speeches, Judicial Opinions, and Other Writings of Oliver Wendell Holmes, Jr.* Edited by Richard A. Posner. Chicago: University of Chicago Press, 1992.

Holmes, Oliver Wendell, Sr. "Bread and the Newspaper." *Atlantic Monthly*, September 1861, 346–48.

———. "My Hunt after 'The Captain.'" *Atlantic Monthly*, December 1862, 738–64.

———. "Doings of the Sunbeam." *Atlantic Monthly*, July 1863, 1–15.

Holt, Daniel M. *A Surgeon's Civil War: The Letters & Diary of Daniel M. Holt, M.D.* Edited by James M. Greiner, Janet L. Coryell, and James R. Smither. Kent, Ohio: Kent State University Press, 1994.

Hope, Ian C. *A Scientific Way of War: Antebellum Military Science, West Point, and the Origins of American Military Thought.* Lincoln: University of Nebraska Press, 2015.

Hoptak, John David. *The Battle of South Mountain.* Charleston, S.C.: History Press, 2011.

Howe, Daniel Walker. *The Unitarian Conscience: Harvard Moral Philosophers, 1805–1861.* Cambridge: Harvard University Press, 1970.

Johnson, Clifton. *Battleground Adventures in the Civil War.* Boston: Houghton Mifflin, 1915.

Johnson, Curt, and Richard C. Anderson, Jr. *Artillery Hell: The Employment of Artillery at Antietam.* College Station: Texas A & M University Press, 1995.

Joinville, Prince de. *The Army of the Potomac: its Organization, its Commander, and its Campaign.* Translated by William Henry Hurlbert. New York: A. D. F. Randolph, 1863.

Katz, D. Mark. *Witness to an Era: The Life and Photographs of Alexander Gardner.* New York: Viking, 1991.

Keen, W. W. "Surgical Reminiscences of the Civil War." *Transactions of the College of Physicians and Surgeons of Philadelphia* 27 (1905): 95–114.

———. "Military Surgery in 1861 and in 1918." *Annals of the American Academy of Political and Social Science* 80 (November 1918): 11–22.

Kirkland, Joseph. *The Captain of Company K.* Chicago: Dibble, 1891.

Knudsen, Harold M. *James Longstreet and the American Civil War: The Confederate General Who Fought the Next War.* El Dorado Hills, Calif.: Savas Beatie, 2022.

Laurie, Bruce. *Artisans into Workers: Labor in Nineteenth Century America.* Champaign: University of Illinois Press, 1997.

Lebergott, Stanley. "Labor Force and Employment, 1800–1960." National Bureau of Economic Research. nber.org/chapters/c1567.

Lee Family Digital Archive. leefamilyarchive.org.

Letterman, Jonathan. *Medical Recollections of the Army of the Potomac.* New York: D. Appleton, 1866.

Linderman, Gerald. *Embattled Courage: The Experience of Combat in the American Civil War.* New York: Free Press, 1987.

Lindsay, Arnett G. "Diplomatic Relations between the United States and Great Britain Bearing on the Return of Negro Slaves, 1783–1828." *Journal of Negro History* 5, no. 4 (October 1920): 391–419.

Livermore, Mary A. *My Story of War: A Woman's Narrative of Four Years Personal Experience as Nurse in the Union Army.* Hartford: A. D. Worthington, 1889.

Lockhart, Paul. *Firepower: How Weapons Shaped Warfare.* New York: Basic Books, 2021.

Longstreet, James. *From Manassas to Appomattox: Memoirs of the Civil War in America.* Philadelphia: Lippincott, 1896.

Luff, William M. "March of the Cavalry from Harper's Ferry, September 14, 1862." *Military Essays and Recollections.* Vol. 2, Papers Read before the Commandery of the State of Illinois, Military Order of the Loyal Legion of the United States. Chicago: A. C. McClurg, 1894.

Luvass, Jay, and Harold W. Nelson, eds. *The U.S. Army War College Guide to the Battle of Antietam: The Maryland Campaign of 1862.* New York: Harper Collins, 1988.

Mahan, D. H. *A Treatise on Field Fortification.* 1836. New York: Wiley, 1856.

———. *An Elementary Treatise on Advanced-Guard, Out-Post, and Detachment Service of Troops, and the Manner of Posting and Handling them in Presence of an Enemy.* 1847. Rev. ed. New York: Wiley, 1862.

———. Papers. United States Military Academy Library, Archives and Special Collections, West Point, N.Y.

Manley, Albert A. Letters. 20th Massachusetts Vertical File. Antietam National Battlefield Library, Sharpsburg, Md.

Marshall, Nicholas. "The Great Exaggeration: Death and the Civil War." *Journal of the Civil War Era* 4, no. 1 (March 2014): 3–27.

Marx, Karl, and Friedrich Engels. *The Civil War in the United States.* Edited by Richard Enmale (pseud.). 1937. Reprint. New York: International Publishers, 2016.

Maxwell, William Quentin. *Lincoln's Fifth Wheel: The Political History of the United States Sanitary Commission.* New York: Longmans, Green, 1956.

McClellan, George B. *The Life, Campaigns and Public Services of General McClellan (George B. McClellan): The Hero of Western Virginia! South Mountain! and Antietam!* Philadelphia: T. B. Peterson, 1864.

———. *McClellan's Own Story: The War for the Union.* New York: Charles L. Webster, 1887.

McGaugh, Scott. *Surgeon in Blue: Jonathan Letterman, the Civil War Doctor Who Pioneered Battlefield Care.* New York: Arcade, 2013.

McNeil, Betty Ann. "Daughters of Charity: Courageous and Compassionate Civil War Nurses." *U.S. Catholic Historian* 31, no. 1 (Winter 2013): 51–72.

McPherson, James M. *Battle Cry of Freedom: The Civil War Era.* New York: Oxford, 1988.

———. *What They Fought For.* 1994. New York: Doubleday, 1995.

———. *For Cause and Comrades: Why Men Fought in the Civil War.* New York: Oxford University Press, 1997.

———. *Crossroads of Freedom: Antietam.* New York: Oxford, 2002.

McWhiney, Grady, and Perry D. Jamieson. *Attack and Die: Civil War Military Tactics and the Southern Heritage.* Tuscaloosa: University of Alabama Press, 1982.

The Medical and Surgical History of the War of Rebellion (1861–65). 6 vols. Washington, D.C.: Government Printing Office, 1870–88.

Michie, Peter S. *The Life and Letters of Emory Upton.* New York: Appleton, 1885.

Miller, Randall M., Harry S. Stout, and Charles Regan Wilson, eds. *Religion and the American Civil War.* New York: Oxford, 1998.

Moore, John G. "Mobility and Strategy in the Civil War." *Military Affairs* 24, no. 2 (Summer 1960): 68–77.

Mosby, John S. *The Memoirs of Colonel John S. Mosby.* Boston: Little, Brown, 1917.

National Archives and Records Administration. Records of the United States Military Academy. Record Group 404, West Point, N.Y.

National Park Service. *Clara Barton.* National Park Handbook No. 110. Washington, D.C.: Government Printing Office, 1981.

Newell, Clayton R. *The Regular Army before the Civil War.* Washington, D.C.: Center of Military History, United States Army, 2014.

Nosworthy, Brent. *Anatomy of Victory: Battle Tactics 1689–1763.* New York: Hippocrene Books, 1990.

Oakes, James. *The Crooked Path to Abolition: Abraham Lincoln and the Antislavery Constitution.* New York: Norton, 2021.

———. "Was Emancipation Constitutional?" Review of *The Broken Constitution* by Noah Feldman. *New York Review of Books,* May 12, 2022.

Oates, Stephen B. *A Woman of Valor: Clara Barton and the Civil War.* New York: Free Press, 1994.

O'Connor, John Michael. *A Treatise on the Science of War and Fortification.* New York: J. Seymour, 1817.

O'Connor, Thomas H. *Civil War Boston: Home Front & Battlefield.* Boston: Northeastern University Press, 1997.

Oliver, James. *Civil War Diary of Dr. James Oliver, Surgeon, 21st Massachusetts Volunteer Infantry, 1862–1864.* Compiled by Mike Bearrow, Trevor Beemon, and Sallie Loy. Kenesaw, Ga.: Southern Museum of Civil War and Locomotive History, 2006.

Orr, Timothy J. " 'Sharpshooters Made a Grand Record This Day.' Combat on the Skirmish Line at Gettysburg on July 3." In *The Third Day: The Fate of a Nation, July 3, 1863.* Papers of the 2008 (12th) Gettysburg Seminar. Gettysburg, Pa.: National Park Service, 2008.

Palfrey, Francis Winthrop. *The Antietam and Fredericksburg.* Vol. 5, *Campaigns of the Civil War.* New York: Scribner's, 1882.

Pennsylvania Freedmen's Relief Association. *Report of the Proceedings of a Meeting Held at Concert Hall, Philadelphia on Tuesday Evening, November 3, 1863, to Take into Consideration the Condition of the Freed People of the South.* Philadelphia: Merrihew & Thompson, 1863.

Peraino, Kevin. *Lincoln in the World: The Making of a Statesman and the Dawn of American Power.* New York: Crown, 2013.

Phillips, Jason. "The Grape Vine Telegraph: Rumors and Confederate Persistence." *Journal of Southern History* 71, no. 4 (November 2006): 753–88.

Phipps, Michael. "Mahan at West Point, 'Gallic Bias,' and the 'Old Army': The Subconscious of Leadership at Gettysburg." In *I Ordered No Man to Go Where I Would Not Go Myself: Leadership in the Campaign and Battle of Gettysburg.* Papers of the Ninth Gettysburg National Military Park Seminar. Gettysburg, Pa.: National Park Service, 2002.

Piston, William Garrett. *Lee's Tarnished Lieutenant: James Longstreet and His Place in Southern History.* Athens: University of Georgia Press, 1990.

Post, Lydia Minturn, ed. *Soldiers' Letters from Camp, Battle-Field and Prison.* New York: Bunce and Huntington, 1865.

Priest, John Michael. *Antietam: The Soldier's Battle.* New York: Oxford University Press, 1989.

———. *Before Antietam: The Battle for South Mountain.* New York: Oxford University Press, 1992.

Pryor, Elizabeth Brown. *Clara Barton: Professional Angel.* Philadelphia: University of Pennsylvania Press, 1987.

Reardon, Carol. "From Antietam to the Argonne: The Maryland Campaign's Lessons for Future Leaders of the American Expeditionary Force." In *The Antietam Campaign*, edited by Gary W. Gallagher. Chapel Hill: University of North Carolina Press, 1999.

Reilly, Robert F. "Medical and Surgical Care during the American Civil War, 1861–1865." *Baylor University Medical Center Proceedings* 29, no. 2 (April 2016): 138–42.

Risley, Ford. *Civil War Journalism.* Santa Barbara, Calif.: Bloomsbury Academic, 2012.

Robertson, James I., Jr. *General A. P. Hill: The Story of a Confederate Warrior.* New York: Random House, 1987.

———. *Stonewall Jackson: The Man, the Soldier, the Legend.* New York: Macmillan, 1997.

Ropes, Hannah Anderson. *Civil War Nurse: The Diary and Letters of Hannah Ropes.* Edited by John R. Brumgardt. Knoxville: University of Tennessee Press, 1980.

Sartin, Jeffrey S. "Infectious Diseases during the Civil War: The Triumph of the 'Third Army.'" *Clinical Infectious Diseases* 16, no. 4 (April 1993): 580–84. Correction in 34, no. 2 (January 2002): 292.

Schantz, Mark S. *Awaiting the Heavenly Country: The Civil War and America's Culture of Death.* Ithaca, N.Y.: Cornell University Press, 2008.

Schmidt, Alann, and Terry Barkley. *September Mourn: The Dunker Church of Antietam Battlefield.* El Dorado Hills, Calif.: Savas Beatie, 2018.

Schultz, Jane. *Women at the Front: Hospital Workers in Civil War America.* Chapel Hill: University of North Carolina Press, 2004.

Sears, Stephen W. *George B. McClellan: The Young Napoleon.* New York: Ticknor & Fields, 1988.

———. "Lincoln and McClellan." In *Lincoln's Generals,* edited by Gabor S. Boritt. 1994. Reprint. Lincoln: University of Nebraska Press, 2010.

Shallat, Todd. "Engineering Policy: The U.S. Army Corps of Engineers and the Historical Foundation of Power." *The Public Historian* 11, no. 3 (Summer 1989): 6–27.

Simpson, Brooks D. "General McClellan's Bodyguard: The Army of the Potomac after Antietam." In *The Antietam Campaign,* edited by Gary W. Gallagher. Chapel Hill: University of North Carolina Press, 1999.

Smalley, George W. "Chapters in Journalism." *Harper's Monthly,* August 1894, 426–35.

———. *Anglo-American Memories.* New York: Putnam, 1911.

Smith, Matthew L. "The Five Paragraph Field Order: Can a Better Format Be Found to Transmit Combat Information to Small Tactical Units?" Fort Leavenworth, Kans.: School of Advanced Military Studies, United States Army Command and General Staff College, 1988.

Starr, Louis M. *Bohemian Brigade: Civil War Newsmen in Action.* New York: Knopf, 1954.

Steiner, Lewis H. *Report of Lewis H. Steiner, M.D., Inspector of the Sanitary Commission.* New York: Randolph, 1862.

Tocqueville, Alexis de. *Democracy in America.* 2 vols. 1840. Translated by George Lawrence. New York: Doubleday, 1969.

Tourgée, Albion W. "The Renaissance of Nationalism." *North American Review* 144 (1887): 1–11.

Trachtenberg, Alan. "Albums of War: On Reading Civil War Photographs." *Representations* 9 (Winter 1985): 1–32.

Trail, Susan W. "Remembering Antietam: Commemoration and Preservation of a Civil War Battlefield." Ph.D. diss. University of Maryland, College Park, 2005.

Trollope, Anthony. *North America*. New York: Harper, 1862.

Trombold, John M. "Gangrene Therapy and Antisepsis Before Lister: The Civil War Contributions of Middleton Goldsmith of Louisville." *The American Surgeon* 77, no. 9 (September 2011): 1138–43.

Walcott, Charles F. *History of the Twenty-first Regiment Massachusetts Volunteers in the War for the Preservation of the Union, 1861–1865*. Boston: Houghton Mifflin, 1882.

The War of Rebellion: A Compilation of the Official Records of the Union and Confederate Armies. 128 vols. Washington, D.C.: Government Printing Office, 1880–1901.

Welles, Gideon. "The History of Emancipation." 1872.

Welsh, Peter. *Irish Green and Union Blue: The Civil War Letters of Peter Welsh, Color Sergeant, 28th Regiment, Massachusetts Volunteers*. Edited by Frederick Kohl with Margaret Cossé Richard. New York: Fordham University Press, 1986.

Welsh, Thomas. Letters. 45th Pennsylvania Vertical File. Antietam National Battlefield Library, Sharpsburg, Md.

Wert, Jeffrey D. *General James Longstreet: The Confederacy's Most Controversial Soldier*. New York: Touchstone, 1994.

Whiting, William. *The War Powers of the President and the Legislative Powers of Congress in Relation to Rebellion, Treason and Slavery*. Boston: Shorey, 1862.

Wightman, Edward King. *From Antietam to Fort Fisher: The Civil War Letters of Edward King Wightman, 1862–1865*. Rutherford, N.J.: Fairleigh Dickinson University Press, 1985.

Wilkeson, Frank. *Recollections of a Private Soldier in the Army of the Potomac*. New York: Putnam's Sons, 1887.

Williams, Alpheus S. *From the Cannon's Mouth: The Civil War Letters of General Alpheus S. Williams*. Edited by Milo M. Quaife. Detroit: Wayne State University Press, 1959.

Williams, Harry. "The Attack Upon West Point During the Civil War." *Mississippi Valley Historical Review* 25, no. 4 (March 1939): 491–504.

Wilson, James Grant. "Types and Traditions of the Old Army. II. General Halleck—A Memoir." *Journal of the Military Service Institution of the United States* 36 (1905): 537–59.

Winthrop, Delba. "Tocqueville's Women and 'The True Conception of Democratic Progress.'" *Political Theory* 14, no. 2 (May 1968): 239–61.

Wood, Ann Douglas. "The War within a War: Women Nurses in the Union Army." *Civil War History* 18, no. 3 (September 1972): 197–212.

Wood, Gordon S. *Empire of Liberty: A History of the Early Republic, 1789–1815*. New York: Oxford, 2009.

Zagarri, Rosemarie. "The Rights of Man and Woman in Post-Revolutionary America." *William and Mary Quarterly* 55, no. 2 (April 1998): 203–30.

Zeller, Bob. *The Blue and Gray in Black and White: A History of Civil War Photography*. Westport, Conn.: Praeger, 2005.

INDEX